QUICK ESCAPES

in
Southern California
21 Weekend Trips from
Los Angeles and San Diego

by

Eleanor Harris

A Voyager Book

The Globe Pequot press

Old Saybrook, Connecticut

Photo Credits
P. 40: San Diego Convention and Visitors Bureau; p. 63: Knott's Berry Farm; p. 82: San Diego Wild Animal Park; p. 100: Santa Catalina Island Company; p. 109: Hearst Monument/Ken Raveill; p. 111: J. Paul Getty Museum; pp. 194, 204: Las Vegas News Bureau. All others by the author.

Library of Congress Cataloging-in-Publication Data

Harris, Eleanor.
    Quick escapes in southern California: 21 weekend trips from Los Angeles and San Diego / by Eleanor Harris. — 1st ed.
    p. cm.
  "A Voyager book."
  ISBN 1-56440-139-1
  1. California, Southern—Guidebooks. I. Title.
F867.H3 1993
917.94'90453—dc20   93-20232
                                                     CIP

Manufactured in the United States of America
First Edition/Third Printing

To Ben, the very best person in the world to escape with

Contents

Introduction

This is a Southern California guide to select destinations of particular scenic beauty and year-round outdoor recreational attractions for overnight, weekend, or longer getaways. Each has something special to recommend it. Some places are deservedly well known and others—small towns and villages—may be new discoveries you can claim for your own.

Each "escape" is presented as a detailed itinerary for the best of sightseeing, dining, and overnight accommodation in the featured area. Easy-to-follow, road-tested directions, including driving time and distance, get you there and back with the easiest, most direct route.

In all areas of its spectacular countryside, Southern California is an enchanting, carefree, warm, and sunny vacationland. The mild Mediterranean climate and weather are unfailingly wonderful. Usually there's no rain from mid-April to mid-October, so you can pretty much depend on blue skies for perfect vacations almost year-round.

Few places in the world are as beautiful and abundantly rich in natural scenic and geographical diversity. This book escorts you to its mile-high snowcapped mountains, sun-kissed deserts, romantic, secluded beaches, sleepy rural villages, peaceful farmlands, and quiet harbors—all ideal change-of-pace getaways where you can have fun, unwind, and relax.

You'll visit parks, boat-filled marinas, zoos, a popular offshore island in the Pacific, avocado and orange groves, museums, a sunny all-Danish city, world-famous theme parks, art colonies, a gold camp town, missions, a legendary private castle, and gaming casinos. An extra bonus is the region's proximity to Mexico, a foreign country just a few hours' drive from Los Angeles. One escape takes you to the world's most popular and exciting border city (a duty-free zone), and another continues farther south into the "real" Mexico to a lively bayside resort town along the seductive Mexican Riviera. U.S. and Canadian citizens do not need a passport or tourist card for a stay of less than seventy-two hours.

Hotels and resorts range from upscale world-class and glamorous with unlimited amenities to cozy, quiet hideaways, all first-rate and nontouristy. Sports and fitness enthusiasts will find plenty of golf, tennis, bicycling, horseback riding, watersports, skiing, and hiking. The gourmet and the wine maven will be delighted as will the sun-worshipper, the nature lover, and the culture-vulture. Shoppers will find Nirvana, and children will find warm welcomes and much to keep them busy.

Since Southern California is the heart of the world's entertainment industry, film stars, celebrities, movies, and TV have long been an important part of its glamour and life-style. Many picturesque locales showcased throughout the years in films are highlighted in passing. Besides serendipitous spotting of celebrities at any time, anywhere, you're also apt to come upon film crews at work on location throughout the area shooting a TV episode or a movie.

Additionally, Southern California has a wealth of romance associated with its past and with its Spanish and Mexican heritage: the great rancheros, pioneer settlers, the Wild West, cowboys, missions, stagecoaches, gold strikes, and gold camp towns. History is kept alive and celebrated in many of the small cities with museum exhibits, living-history events, and other special presentations.

The region has the finest freeway system in the world, enabling motorists to drive long distances in the shortest of times. Get to know the freeways and their routes as well as their traffic patterns. Odd number freeways travel north and south, even numbers east and west. Read maps and plot out your routes beforehand.

Take advantage of the seasons and what they offer. Contrary to what most people believe, Southern California has four distinct seasons. There's spring, when the air is soft and fragrant with lilacs and apple blossoms and the deserts are ablaze with wildflowers as far as one can see. In summer's long, lazy afternoons of daylight hours you can travel farther distances or linger indefinitely at the beaches and lakesides to watch the sunsets. In fall the days become shorter, the air is brisk, and the landscape turns russet as the golden leaves flutter to the ground and aromatic wisps of smoke curl from chimneys during apple harvests and merry Oktoberfests. Mild winter months bring a blustery nip to the breeze, crisp clear air, and endless vistas. The brief rainy season begins, and snowy mountain winter sports beckon, while the sunbaked desert with warmer temperatures and less rain, is a brilliant colorwheel of lavender mountains, green golf courses, and blue swimming pools. Energetic vacationers can spend a morning skiing in a mountain resort and then bask in the warm desert sun or swim in the ocean a few hours later.

Throughout the year these getaways offer a happy grab-bag full of colorful regional, seasonal, historical, and holiday festivals, carnivals, fiestas, cookouts, sports tournaments, ethnic and cultural celebrations, pageants, and other long-running events and activities of every kind to attend and enjoy.

There are actually forty-one escapes in these twenty-one chapters, since many chapters include more than one destination. I have pointed out many places of interest and other cities along the way you may wish to visit as a side trip or mark for future exploration. Further, the destination cities follow in logical geographical and freeway sequence, so they're easy to revisit en route or returning from another getaway in the same general direction.

All the time-consuming and pesky details have been researched in each custom itinerary to offer the maximum freedom from stress on your getaways. Look for the special headings at the end of each chapter. *There's More* points out additional attractions to investigate this time or next visit. *Special Events* highlights local happenings and festivities that may be of interest. *Other Recommended Restaurants and Lodgings* offers fine alternative dining and accommodations not listed in the itinerary. Lastly, *For More Information* tells sources to contact for brochures, city maps, and further visitor attractions in each destination.

Fees and fares are mentioned but not quoted, as they are subject to change. Prices are reasonable unless otherwise indicated. While missions and museums usually charge admission, special "free" days are noted. Hotel reservations are definitely recommended (mid-week anywhere is less crowded than weekends). Be sure to make your plans as early as possible for holidays and busy seasons.

A great deal of time and effort has gone into ensuring accuracy of information and honest appraisal of places mentioned in this guide. There may, however, be a change of ownership, a renumbered highway, or a place gone out of business altogether, and admission fees may be added where none existed at press time. It's always advisable to call establishments you plan to visit before embarking on your escapes.

Have a great time!

Maps provided at the beginning of each section are for reference only and should be used in conjunction with a road map. Distances are approximate.

All directions given in this book originate from downtown Los Angeles.

Southern Escapes

Newport Beach/Balboa

Car ferry crosses Newport Harbor in three minutes.

Living on the Water

_____ 1 NIGHT _____

Beach · Piers · Boating · Harbor cruise
Decorative gardens · Shopping · Amusement park

This two-day getaway to a nearby exclusive resort city is short on mileage but long on diversion and year-round appeal. Catering to an elite life-style, about 9,000 sumptuous yachts preen in sparkling bays surrounded by miles of white sandy beaches. The friendly coastal city

is a collection of several small villages offering watersports, world-
class hotels, gourmet dining in some 300 restaurants, and fanciful
shopping. Exploring individual islands and piers, you'll go on harbor
cruises, lunch on a Mississippi-style paddlewheeler, relax at a waterfront amusement park, eat chocolate-dipped frozen bananas, and dine
in bayside bistros.

Day 1

Morning

Take San Diego Freeway 405 south past the small beach cities—
Manhattan Beach, Huntington Beach, and others—to Corona del Mar
Freeway 55, which becomes Newport Boulevard. Continue on Newport Boulevard, cross the Pacific Coast Highway to Via Lido, and turn
left to Lido Marina Village at the entrance to Balboa Peninsula, about
55 miles.

In **Lido Marina Village,** an attractive, curving, red-brick-paved
street of flowers, fountains, and flower baskets hanging from decorative streetlamps, the shops back up to the boardwalk cafes facing the
water, with pleasant outdoor dining on little tables overlooking the
luxe yachts bobbing in their slips. Among them are the Coffee Peddler
for sandwiches, George's Cameo for beer-batter fish-and-chips, and
the Newport Marina Waterfront deli where they know how to make a
hearty sandwich.

Lunch: **The Warehouse,** 3450 Via Oporto, Newport Beach. (714)
673-4700. Rustic wood siding and tin roof provide atmosphere. All tables enjoy a view of Newport Bay—or go for patio dining. Generous,
inviting salad bar takes top billing, but sandwiches, hamburgers, and
seafood cocktails are further good choices. Sunday champagne buffet
brunch. Monday through Friday Happy Hour features complimentary
hors d'oeuvres. Free validated parking.

Afternoon

After lunch, drive around the posh Lido Isle residential section.
Then take Newport Boulevard to the **Newport Pier** area, passing the
landmark 1952 Crab Cooker restaurant in its red building with a tall
sidewalk clock out front, and continue past The Old Spaghetti Factory
and popular Woody's Wharf, where some hungry guests arrive for
lunch by boat. At Newport Pier and McFadden Square, a small tram
takes you to the end of the pier and back for 25 cents per person.
Newport Pier is where the historic Dory Fleet fishermen, the last on
the West Coast, have arrived each morning since 1891 with their catch.
Early risers can watch the dories roll in from the ocean and onto the
beach, then watch the Dorymen prepare the fish for public sale in a

small, enclosed, open-air fish market on the sand behind their boats, where large gray pelicans patrol the rooftops waiting for handouts and gulls hover even closer. Lively McFadden Square has many snack places, and Fishermen's Restaurant at the end of the pier is a congenial spot for cocktails and lunch and dinner. In this area along Oceanfront, you'll also find Portofino Beach Hotel and Doryman's Inn.

As you drive along the 2.5-mile-long stretch of Balboa Peninsula from Newport Pier, Newport Boulevard changes to Balboa Boulevard. You'll notice that it becomes more crowded as you approach Balboa Village and the distinctive dome-shaped cupola silhouette of the famous **Balboa Pavilion,** where all the big bands played in the 1930s and 1940s. It was the focal hub of the peninsula, built in 1906 as a Victorian bath house and Pacific Electric Red Car Terminal, where the big red cars delivered visitors from Los Angeles to spend the day. It now houses Tale of the Whale restaurant. The adjacent old-fashioned General Store, with its worn wooden flooring and large barrels of candy, is worth browsing for mementos.

Appealing **Balboa Village,** a compact area at the tip of the peninsula, with the pavilion on one side and the Balboa Inn on the other, has small-town flavor, with tall ficus trees, wooden benches, cafes, kids, people, rollerskaters, shops, and a bakery. Residents recommend Britta's Cafe for breakfast, but it seems busy all day. Across the street at Blue Sails, you'll find postcards, above-average souvenirs, windchimes, and books. Buy a postcard, sit down on a bench to write it, and drop it off at the post office a few doors away.

Next to Balboa Pavilion is where you board for your forty-five-minute narrated **harbor cruise** on the Mississippi-style riverboats, the *Pavilion Queen* or the *Pavilion Paddy,* which depart every half-hour from 10:00 A.M. to 7:00 P.M. (in winter, from 11:00 A.M. to 3:00 P.M.; fare). You can take better photos and probably see a bit more up on the sundeck. During the cruise, which focuses on famous past or present movie stars and celebrities' homes and luxury yachts berthed here, you see where John Wayne, Newport Beach's most famous resident, lived and anchored his boat, *The Wild Goose;* pass James Cagney's house and Joan Crawford's boat, *The Queen of Sheba;* and cruise past unpretentious, million-dollar bayfront mansions with swimming pools, twenty-five-car garages, bowling alleys, and the like built beneath the homes due to shortage of land. At Edgar Bergen's house you see daughter Candice's ("Murphy Brown") playhouse, a dollhouse-size sailboat.

You pass Charley Brown's restaurant in the bay, see the sailboarder school with students in the water, note where Jack Benny, George Burns, and Roy Rogers and Dale Evans lived. It's a lovely cruise, with the sun dancing on the water and kayaks and boats of all sizes crisscrossing your path. The longer, ninety-minute cruise goes out of the harbor, where the seals cavort offshore and where "Gilligan's Island" and *Treasure Island* were filmed. This is one of the country's largest marinas and the launching site of the spectacular annual Newport-Ensenada race of more than 500 yachts of all sizes.

After your harbor cruise turn right and stroll down the oceanfront boardwalk to the **Balboa Fun Zone,** a miniature waterfront amusement park built in 1956 as an old-fashioned California seaside attraction. Watch the arcade games, ride the bumper cars, or take a turn on the Ferris wheel and small merry-go-round with its unmistakable calliope music. You'll find snackbars for ice cream and frozen yogurt, as well as benches to sit on and watch the ocean or the Fun Zone action. Stop for a slice of pizza or the whole pie at Ginna's Pizza, or, if they're crowded, walk back a few steps to Pizza Pete's or Mrs. Field's Cookies. It's a happy scene, with boats in the water, people licking ice cream cones, pigeons fluttering about, skateboarders, rollerskaters, children, and strollers.

At Palm Avenue you can watch the car ferry arrive at the pier and unload its three cars, passengers, and bicyclists and pick up more of the same to sail back across the harbor for the four-minute ride to **Balboa Island** for a modest fee. This is a nostalgic way to get to the island. The privately-owned car ferries date back to 1916, and probably the line of cars waiting to board began then too.

Following Main Street back toward Balboa Beach, **Kites, Etc.,** at 711 East Bay, is a marvel of kites of all sizes, shapes, and colors. Across the boulevard at Balboa Pier's end, Ruby's Diner has been a popular eatery since 1982. The broad beach is uncrowded, and the water is tempting. Time to stretch out on the sand around the pier and watch the waves, or go for a swim. This beautiful, clean beach can be yours for the afternoon.

Along Main Street at beachside you'll find more restaurants and shops. Albatross general store is well stocked with clothing and beach supplies. The Balboa Inn, at 105 Main Street, built in 1929 on the beach, with Spanish-style architecture, was belle of the coast, a place where Errol Flynn, Howard Hughes, and other bons vivants overnighted. It's been remodeled and modernized many times and is still a popular hostelry.

Dinner: **Villa Nova,** 3131 West Coast Highway, Newport Beach. (714) 642–7880. This warm, friendly restaurant, set back from the highway, resembles an exotic movie set of an Italian castle, with balconies, arches, and murals on its ochre facade. The intimate, candlelit dining rooms at water's edge, offering constant views of boats in the water, feature fine service and good Italian cuisine. Start with Caesar salad, followed by a savory fettucine with roasted chicken and red

peppers. Nightly music at the piano bar. Dinner only, from 5:00 P.M.
Lodging: **Newport Beach Marriott Hotel and Tennis Club,** 900
Newport Center Drive, Newport Beach, CA 92660. (800) 228–9290
(reservations only); (714) 640–4000. Excellent central location near
Fashion Island, with 585 large, nicely furnished guestrooms and 15
suites with sitting areas, private patios, or balconies with views. TV
with free in-room movies, clock, hair dryer, iron and ironing board,
two heated swimming pools with spas, sauna, exercise room, eight
tennis courts, three restaurants, and lounges.

Day 2

Morning

Breakfast: In **JW's** at Newport Beach Marriott Hotel or **Coco's** in
Fashion Island, 151 Newport Center Drive. Reasonably priced breakfast fare, with friendly but slow service—better bring a book or your
knitting to keep you awake until your order arrives. Besides eggs and
pancakes, there are many interesting breakfast specialties; lower-
priced senior specials.

Fashion Island, in sleek Newport Center marked by Mediterranean-
style architecture, fountains, courtyards, and tree-lined walkways, features four major upscale department stores, cinemas, boutiques, and
many restaurants.

The soaring, dramatic Farmer's Market Atrium Court, rimmed with
fast-fooderies, sweet shops, a deli, and a bakery, is a convenient and
popular meeting place. Shop Fashion Island Monday through Friday
from 10:00 A.M. to 9:00 P.M., Saturday from 10:00 am. to 6:00 P.M., and
Sunday from noon to 5:00 P.M. (714) 721–2000.

Take Newport Center Drive to the Coast Highway, turn right to
Jamboree Road, and then turn left. Go over the short bridge to the
small, lighthearted world of **Balboa Island,** which has seventy shops
and restaurants along its one main street, Marine Avenue—a funky,
crowded, youth-oriented, upbeat area where car traffic barely moves
and parking spaces are hard to come by. Along Marine Avenue, with
its tall, thick eucalyptus trees, munch on the island treat, frozen bananas dipped in chocolate, as you browse the small, trendy shops and
cafes. Amelia's with fancy grillwork is a longtime local dinner favorite
with fine Italian cuisine. Peek in Rybo's window and watch them making fudge. Also here are Hershey's market on the corner of Park, a
post office, Marcelle's Boutique, a bookstore, and jewelry, souvenir,
and clothing shops. Strollers stand in line for the house specialty at
Dad's Old Fashioned Ice Cream, watch the car ferries land, or stroll
around the whole island, with its small beach cottages.

Lunch: **Charley Brown's** (formerly Reuben E. Lee), 151 East Coast Highway, Newport Beach. (714) 675–5910. Walk up the gangway to dine aboard the showboat paddlewheeler restaurant in the harbor, offering Victorian decor and unlimited views of the water from the large dining room. Noted for fresh fish selections, steak, and prime rib; lunch options also include salads, sandwiches, hamburgers, and the nicely grilled herb chicken. The food is good and the service friendly, but the wait for your order is unreasonably long when all of Newport Beach is waiting to be explored.

Afternoon

A special place to visit any time of year is **Roger's Gardens,** 2301 San Joaquin Hills Road, Corona del Mar (714–640–5800). Take Pacific Coast Highway south to MacArthur Boulevard, and turn left to San Joaquin Hills Road; it's on the corner—turn right, into the entrance. Even nongardeners appreciate the spectacular beauty of the hundreds of colorful hanging flower baskets for which the nursery is famous. Its seasonal holiday decor in the large, well-stocked giftshop is inspiring. Pick up a brochure and garden map for self-guided tours of this botanical showplace.

From here go back on MacArthur to Pacific Coast Highway and turn left (south) for a few blocks to the small beach town of **Corona del Mar,** with its warm sands and parks that provide fine places to lounge around, catch some sun, and watch technicolor sunsets. East Coast Highway, the main street of this little city, is a long, browsable strip of boutiques, galleries, and restaurants, including noted silversmith Allan Adler's shop and the landmark dinner house Five Crowns restaurant.

Next is **Sherman Library and Gardens,** 2647 East Pacific Coast Highway, Corona del Mar (714–673–2261), which covers an entire block in low-rise, California residential–style tan buildings. The library is a research center focusing on the development of the region. The gardens are stunning, in attractive settings of hanging baskets, fountains, a lathhouse, a serene tea garden, reflecting pools, and tall trees: a lovely escape from the city. The giftshop has cards, baskets, and books. Admission. Open daily, 10:30 A.M. to 4:00 P.M. (tea garden, 11:00 A.M. to 3:00 P.M.).

Retrace your way back to Los Angeles.

There's More

Golf. Two courses open to the public:
Newport Beach Golf Course, 3100 Irvine Avenue, Newport

Beach. (714) 852–8681. Near the airport; eighteen holes, lighted for night play, driving range, pro golf shop, restaurant, lounge.

Pelican Hill Golf Club, 22653 Pelican Hill Road South, Newport Beach. (714) 760–0707. Between Corona del Mar and Laguna Beach; two 18-hole golf courses with coastal hillsides and ocean bluff fairways; large clubhouse.

Harbor cruises, whale-watching, Catalina Island cruise, sportfishing. Balboa Pavilion Ticket Office, Balboa. (714) 673–5245.

Newport Harbor Art Museum, 850 San Clemente Drive, Newport Beach. (714) 759–1122. Modern and contemporary art featured in changing exhibitions. Permanent collection focuses on post–World War II California art, including works by Richard Diebenkorn, Joe Goode, Billy Al Bengtsen. Bookstore offers art books, artisan showcase puppets. Museum open Tuesday through Sunday, 10:00 A.M. to 5:00 P.M.; free admission on Tuesday. Sculpture Garden Cafe open Monday through Friday, 11:30 A.M. to 2:30 P.M.

Newport Harbor Nautical Museum, 1714 West Balboa Boulevard, on the peninsula, Newport Beach. (714) 673–3377. History of the harbor and region is shown in photographs, artifacts, ship models, navigational and nautical instruments, boat models, ships in bottles, and more in this small museum. Open .Wednesday through Sunday, 10:00 A.M. to 3:00 P.M. Donations accepted.

Parasailing. Davey's Locker, Balboa Pavilion. (714) 673–1434.

Tennis (all in Newport Beach): John Wayne Tennis Club. (714) 644–1700.

Marriott Tennis Club. (714) 640–4000.

Newport Beach Tennis Club. (714) 644–0050.

Upper Newport Bay Ecological Reserve, Jamboree Road and Back Bay Drive. Surrounded by bluffs and cliffs that encircle Newport Back Bay, this 752-acre wetland has been a designated wildlife preserve since 1975. Bird-watchers can spot nearly 200 bird species; additionally, from August to April up to 30,000 birds are present, including many endangered species. Information: Friends of Newport Bay, (714) 646–8009.

Special Events

Late February. Annual 5K/10K Spirit Run.
Late April. Annual new and used boat shows. (714) 660–6150.
Early May. Newport-Ensenada Race.
Early June. Wooden Boat Parade.
July–August. Newport Dukes Professional Team Tennis. Jazz Concert Series (Hyatt Newporter and Fashion Island).

Mid-July. Orange County Fair.
Second and third weekend in September. Annual Newport Seafest. Includes Sandcastle Contest, Taste of Newport, and many other activities.
Early December. Christmas Walk, Corona del Mar.
Mid-December. Annual Christmas Boat Parade.

Other Recommended Restaurants and Lodgings

Newport Beach

The Cannery Restaurant, 3010 Lafayette Avenue. (714) 675-5777. The old cannery was razed and reopened as an architectural-award-winning restaurant using recycled machinery, catwalks, and other equipment as authentic decor. Dine at water level on the bay as boats drift dreamily past your Oriental chicken salad or shrimp Louis. Sunday champagne brunch; champagne brunch harbor cruises.

The Arches, 3334 West Coast Highway. (714) 645-7077. Handsome, comfortable restaurant—a local tradition since 1922 for good food, though a bit pricey. New York steak sandwich, Caesar salad prepared tableside.

Chili's Grill and Bar, 3300 West Coast Highway. (714) 631-7515. Easy atmosphere for southwestern specialties like grilled chicken, BBQ, baby back ribs, salads, burgers, and sandwiches.

Yankee Tavern, around the corner from Charley Brown's, 333 Bayside Drive. (714) 675-5333. Dinners highlight fresh seafood, salads, traditional Yankee pot roast with crisp potato pancakes, and steaks. Sunday brunch.

Hyatt Newporter Inn, 1107 Jamboree Road. (800) 233-1234; (714) 729-1234. Lush tropical landscaping and relaxed feeling in rambling low-rise buildings built in 1961 on twenty-six acres overlooking Newport's Back Bay. Offers 410 nicely furnished rooms, 20 suites with minibar and refrigerator, TV, free in-room movies, three swimming pools, three whirlpools, sauna, nine-hole executive golf course, sixteen lighted tennis courts, fitness room, jogging paths, three restaurants, lounge. Golf and getaway packages.

The Balboa Bay Club, 1221 West Coast Highway. (714) 645-5000. Exclusive bayfront beach resort, with private beach, 127 rooms, 15 suites, heated swimming pool, sauna, exercise room, tennis courts, private golf course, restaurant, lounge. Outstanding Sunday champagne buffet brunch.

Newport Dunes Resort, 1131 Back Bay Drive. (800) 288-0770; (714) 729-3863. Upscale RV park on one hundred acres, with full hookups, individual picnic area, cafe, swimming pool and spa, clubhouse, showers, laundry facilities, restrooms. Launch area; bring your own boat or rent one here.

For More Information

Newport Beach Conference and Visitors Bureau, 366 San Miguel, Suite 200, Newport Beach, CA 92660. (800) 94–COAST; (714) 644–1190.

Laguna Beach/Dana Point/ San Juan Capistrano

Replica of 1835 brig *Pilgrim* in Dana Point harbor

Swallows and Sunshine

_____ 1 NIGHT _____

Beaches • Art galleries • Museum • Watersports
Historic port • Marinas • Mission

This two-day seaside jaunt takes you to Southern California's most popular artists' enclave. In this small, friendly oceanside village, you'll visit galleries and a museum, enjoy superb watersports and wide beaches, go shopping, and relax in a coffee pub. You'll also wander through a romantic, historic port and continue on to the famous mission where the swallows return every year.

Day 1

Morning

Drive south on I–5, Santa Ana Freeway, passing the **Citadel Outlet Stores,** where you can pick up some designer bargains. You pass Anaheim and Disneyland. After Tustin, exit Highway 133 south, which becomes Laguna Canyon Road and winds down to Pacific Coast Highway and Laguna Beach.

Laguna Beach has been called the quintessential casual Southern California beach town, a small, unfettered, happy and sunny place where houses roost atop steep ocean cliffs and where curving, narrow streets are graced with tall eucalyptus trees planted by pioneer homesteaders.

Busy Pacific Coast Highway, the main thoroughfare cutting through the city alongside the ocean, is flanked by a multitude of shops, restaurants, hotels, and businesses. Laguna Beach is as well known for its beautiful beaches and nonpareil surfing and other watersports as it is for its art galleries.

With its mild climate and windblown landscape of ocean and bluffs, Laguna Beach has been a successful artists' enclave since the early 1900s, when thirty or so artists began straggling in by horse-and-buggy or stagecoach. They came to paint the spectacularly scenic hills and untamed surf, and they tried to capture the clear and changing light in the manner of the French impressionists. But one doesn't have to be a Gauguin to appreciate the considerable natural beauty of Laguna Beach's 7-mile rocky canyon and craggy cliffs, which plunge dramatically some 40 feet down to the restless ocean. Though lively throughout the year, the little city fairly overflows with throngs of visitors during its annual eight-week summer art festivals, which attract about three million people (see Special Events at the end of this chapter).

Lunch: **The Terrace,** Hotel Laguna, 425 South Coast Highway, Laguna Beach. (714) 494–1151. In the middle of the village, the sunfilled Terrace, mere yards from the bounding surf, is unbeatable for a midday break. Menu selections range from hamburgers, pizza, and salads to seafood and sautéed chicken.

Afternoon

One of Laguna Beach's most pleasant small-town aspects is its intimate size. You can walk to everywhere (a good thing, since parking spaces are hard to find), from restaurants and beaches to shops along Pacific Coast Highway in the village. Stroll **Forest Avenue,** Laguna Beach's tree-shaded main street and gallery row, which expresses the city's friendly atmosphere in its bustle of people, flowers, sidewalk cafes, architecturally attractive multistory plazas, art galleries, restaurants, and boutiques. The window of McCall's Pharmacy is jammed with straw hats; Three Foxes Trot, at 264, features handcrafted home and personal accessories. Scandia Bakery and Deli, which sells bulk coffees, buzzes with hungry patrons.

Hollywood discovered Laguna Beach's photogenic attributes during the silent-film era, when moviemakers D. W. Griffith, Mack Sennett, and other legendary innovators substituted its craggy coastline for such foreign locales as the French Riviera, Hawaii, and Italian and Greek coastal villages. Errol Flynn's *Captain Blood* was shot near Three Arch Bay; *Robinson Crusoe* was filmed here in 1922; and many scenes in Harold Lloyd's movies took place on Forest Avenue. Between 1913 and 1930 more than fifty silent movies were filmed in Laguna Beach.

Through the years many Hollywood stars, authors, and other creative people have found the city to be a perfect escape. Among former residents are Mary Pickford, Bette Davis, Judy Garland, Rudolph Valentino, Charlie Chaplin, and Mickey Rooney. John Steinbeck wrote *Tortilla Flat* while hunkered down at 540 Park Avenue. Many prominent celebrities still call Laguna home.

In the heart of downtown, at Bay and Coast Highway, **Main Beach Park** resembles a sunlit, nostalgic Norman Rockwell painting of young, happy, sun-bronzed people enjoying themselves on the beach. This is the most "fun" beach for all ages, a place where everyone meets and mingles and plays basketball and volleyball, the bikini bunch swims and sunbathes, and towheaded kids soar on the swings.

Drive a few blocks north on Pacific Coast Highway, turning left on Cliff Drive to number 307, the **Laguna Art Museum** (714-494-6531), on a hilltop corner overlooking the ocean and beach. Site of the first gallery built in Laguna Beach, in 1929 for the Laguna Beach Art Association, the museum was extensively expanded and renovated in 1986. Its permanent collection focuses on the 1890–1920 period of California impressionist painters; changing exhibits are offered as well. The Museum Store sells art books, stationery, and jewelry. (Open Tuesday through Sunday, 11:00 A.M. to 5:00 P.M.; admission; kids free.)

Drive around to the right past the museum to **Heisler Park,** overlooking the ocean. Its long, narrow, grassy terrace edges the oceanside cliff above two of the city's most popular diving beaches—Rockpile and Diver's Cove—and luminous turquoise bays. There's no finer spot for picnics, barbecues, sunset-watching, or sitting on a bench looking out at little boats on the horizon. The small, rustic gazebo, frequently used for weddings, offers closer viewing of the ocean and surfers below.

Dinner: **Dizz's As Is,** 2794 South Coast Highway, Laguna Beach. (714) 494-5250. Tucked in a small wooden cottage, typical Laguna style, this cozy, informal dinner hangout serves first-rate cuisine amid an eclectic 1930s and 1940s decor, photos of Marilyn Monroe, antique radios, and the like. International menu spotlights filet mignon with béarnaise sauce, rack of lamb, fresh seafood.

Lodging: **Surf and Sand Hotel,** 1555 South Coast Highway, Laguna Beach, CA 92651. (800) 524-8621 (nationwide); (714) 497-4477. At the southerly edge of town away from the hubbub, this hotel, which recently underwent a $20-million-plus renovation, offers 157 luxurious rooms, apartments, and penthouses on the ocean and sandy beach. Elegant rooms face ocean views from private balconies; minibar, refrigerator, in-room safe, marble bath, whirlpool tub, and hair dryer. Heated swimming pool, two restaurants, complimentary daily newspaper. Seasonal rates. Overnight parking fee.

Day 2

Morning

Breakfast: Surf and Sands Hotel in **Splashes Restaurant,** a sophisticated room with glass-topped tables, cedar-beamed ceiling, and doors opening to the languid surf. Start your day with a power breakfast—order Swedish pancakes, oat bran waffles, *huevos rancheros,* or grilled salmon with poached eggs and spinach.

Drive south about 5 miles along Pacific Coast Highway to historic **Dana Point,** with its boats dancing in the harbor, awesome cliffs, and dreamy beaches. Turn right at Golden Lantern to **Mariner's Village,** where dozens of smart specialty shops and restaurants are connected by dining terraces and dockside walkways.

With 2,500 yachts and a sportfishing and charter fleet residing in the sunny marina, a slender white forest of masts swaying in the soft briny breeze invites you to linger awhile in this delightful, romantic setting. Listen to the ships' bells and the water slapping against the docks as trim pleasure-boats glide in and out of the harbor.

Lunch: **Delaney's Inc.,** 25001 Dana Drive, Dana Point. (714) 496-6195. Lunch is refreshing beneath a patio umbrella at the water's edge, with choice of sandwiches, seafood, salads, and a winner of a tostada shell filled with Caesar salad and topped with strips of blackened salmon.

Afternoon

The area is named for author Richard Harding Dana, a young Harvard law student who went to sea to improve his delicate health and wrote a successful book, *Two Years before the Mast,* exposing the severe hardships of life at sea during the 1800s and also describing the ports he visited. When his two-masted brigantine *Pilgrim* sailed into San Juan Port in 1835, Dana called the sheltered cove and promontory surrounded by tall protective bluffs, "the only romantic spot in California." The book was made into a movie starring Alan Ladd.

The community was renamed after the writer. In 1971 the old anchorage was transformed into a popular, recreation-oriented marina with a New England seacoast theme in honor of Dana's birthplace. At **Dana Wharf** watch the sportfishing boats set out mornings and afternoons for adventures at sea, or join a narrated harbor cruise. Or just relax on a bench along cobbled walkways, where anglers throw a line over the railing and fish, while you settle back to daydream about tallships drifting into the peaceful harbor.

Follow along Dana Point Harbor Drive past the small park and go over the bridge to **Dana Island** to see the large bronze statue of the author-seaman on a tall pedestal facing the cliffs. Then continue on Dana Point Harbor Drive around the bend of the water where the 121-foot gleaming replica of Dana's brig *Pilgrim* stands tall in the calm water beneath the 100-foot, wind-eroded tawny cliffs mentioned in his book.

Alongside, the **Marine Institute,** at 24200 Dana Point Harbor Drive (714–496–2274), offers tours of the ship and is an oceanographic educational facility with many exhibits (open daily, 10:00 A.M. to 3:30 P.M.). **Doheny State Beach,** adjacent to the harbor, is California's most popular reserved camping park, with a long, wide beach.

For the 3-mile run to **San Juan Capistrano,** head out Dana Point Harbor Drive to the Pacific Highway, turn right, and follow it to I–5; turn left (north) and stay on I–5 until the Ortega Highway/California 74 exit. Turn left, proceeding for a few blocks to the mission and downtown San Juan Capistrano.

This quiet, small, sun-filled city was founded when the mission was built, in 1776, and their history runs together. San Juan Capistrano was a drowsy little farming pueblo growing oranges and walnuts. But during the 1930s townspeople began noticing the yearly March 19 return of flocks of tiny swallows that nested in the eaves of the old mission, stayed until October, then flew away.

It didn't take long before crowds of visitors began arriving every spring to witness this yearly phenomenon. The popular song "When the Swallows Come Back to Capistrano" aroused national interest in the small town.

Mission San Juan Capistrano, on Ortega Highway at Camino Capistrano (714–493–1111), is called the "Mission of the Swallows." It was founded by Father Junípero Serra and is the seventh in the chain of California missions. Ask for a map as you enter, and try to allow sufficient time to explore the spacious, ten-acre grounds. The mission survived the 1812 earthquake, though its Great Stone Church was destroyed. During California's Mexican rule, when all missions and their lands were confiscated, San Juan Capistrano became part of a large rancho. The mission was auctioned off to a family, who lived there for twenty years, until the U.S. government returned it to the Catholic church. Though the town grew, the mission was completely abandoned until 1895, when restoration was begun.

Beyond the entry plaza gravel paths lead to the broad courtyards and statue of Father Serra and a young Indian boy. Look for swallows' nests up under the eaves. Two nests are visible at the north corridor at the western end of the building. But you'll see many other historic sights and treasures in the old mission: the ancient, graceful arches with the smooth, worn stones beneath your feet; the rose garden and fountain; the strutting white pigeons; the gnarled, one-hundred-year-old pepper tree beside the padre's quarters; the huge millstone, used for grinding wheat and corn into flour and crushing olives for cooking oil and fuel for lanterns; and the sacred garden with its historic bells.

Three museum rooms and a bookstore contain archaeological finds and ancient artifacts. In Serra Chapel, built in 1777 and restored in the early 1920s, you can feel a strong tug of the past. It is the oldest building still in use in California and the only remaining chapel of the missions where Father Serra said mass. In the long, narrow chapel, with its 22-foot-high ceiling, paintings depict the Stations of the Cross. The shining reed organ dates from 1892, and the gilded cherrywood altar from Spain is more than 300 years old. The mission is open daily from 8:30 A.M. to 6:00 P.M. and later in the summer (admission).

When the swallows return every March 19 to build their nests, the sacred garden bells are rung and a week-long fiesta begins. Weekends are very crowded year-round, but far more visitors arrive during spring. The birds remain to care for their young until October 23, when they begin their 6,000-mile journey back to Argentina.

Have a snack or dessert at **The Depot,** 26701 Verdugo Street (714–496–8181), either on the large patio or inside the old Capistrano Depot built by the Atchison Topeka and Santa Fe Railroad in 1895, now a busy Amtrak station. Dining rooms, converted from the baggage room, waiting room, and ticket office, feature sandwiches, salads, and Mexican food. If The Depot is closed between lunch and dinner hours and you're hungry or thirsty, go past the entrance about halfway along the building and up a short wooden stairway. Turn left and you're in the Main Bar of the old Freight House. You're also in the railroad station, with tracks on one side of the platform and unused passenger cars on the other. The Main Bar's menu offers good sandwiches and cheeseburgers with great fries.

You've still time to browse and shop along San Juan Capistrano's small main street, **Camino Capistrano.** Ortega's Capistrano Trading Post, at number 31741, is a large, barn red corner store selling Indian jewelry, souvenirs, and gifts. Moonrose, at number 31766, has interesting windchimes, candles, antiques, jewelry, books, and music.

Every Sunday at 1:00 P.M., the Historical Society provides guided walking tours of the historic Los Rios district's adobes, built in the late 1700s and early 1800s. Tours begin at El Peon Plaza, across from the mission (fee).

Return to Los Angeles via I–5 North.

There's More

Shopping. The Pottery Shack, 1212 South Coast Highway, Laguna Beach. (714) 494–1141. With huge, lifelike deer on its roof, the place has been a local landmark since 1936. Catch the pottery and glass-blowing demonstrations.

Village Faire Shoppes, 1100 South Coast Highway, Laguna Beach. Ethnic restaurants, antiques, galleries, trendy fashions, and more in this large, open-air shopping-dining complex.

Surfing. Rockpile, below Heisler Park, Cliff Drive in Laguna Beach. Has the biggest waves.

Bodysurfing. Victoria Beach, West Street Beach, and Crescent Bay, all in Laguna Beach.

Diving. Glen E. Vedder Preserve, at Rockpile, below Heisler Park in Laguna Beach. Good for reef diving.

Wood's Cove, just north of Heisler Park in Laguna Beach. Tree-kelp dives; made for scuba divers.

For other locations and diving and surfing conditions, call (714) 494–4573.

Golf. Aliso Creek Golf Course, 31105 South Coast Highway, Laguna Beach. (714) 499–1919. Nine-hole public course, clubhouse, Ben Brown's restaurant.

Monarch Beach Golf Course, 33080 Niguel Road, Dana Point. (714) 240–0247. Eighteen-hole public course overlooking the ocean.

Tennis. Laguna Beach High School, 625 Park Avenue, Laguna Beach. Eight lighted courts.

Irvine Bowl, next to Festival of Arts, Laguna Canyon, Laguna Beach. Two lighted courts.

Bicycle rentals. Dana Point Bicycle, 34155 Pacific Coast Highway, Dana Point. (714) 661–8356.

Boat cruises: Adventure Sailing Association, Dana Point Harbor. (714) 493–9493.
Harbor Tours. Dana Island Yachts, Dana Point Harbor. (714) 248–7400.
Boat rentals. Dana Harbor Yachts, Dana Point. (714) 493–2011.
Sportfishing, whale-watching, parasailing. Dana Wharf Sportfishing, Dana Point Harbor. (714) 496–5794.
O'Neill Museum, 31831 Los Rios Street, San Juan Capistrano. (714) 493–8444. This wooden, Victorian-era residence, built in the 1880s, has been restored and refurnished as San Juan Capistrano's Historical Society Office. On view are old photographs and Indian artifacts. Closed Monday.

Special Events

Mid-February, early March, late April, mid-May, and mid-June. Laguna Craft Guild Street Festival, Laguna Beach.
February and March. Festival of Whales, Dana Point.
First week in March. Heritage Festival, San Juan Capistrano.
Early March. Annual Winterfest celebration, Arts and Crafts Fair, Patriot's Day Parade, and Irish Festival of Art—all at Laguna Beach.
March 19. Return of the Swallows and Heritage Fair Fiesta, San Juan Capistrano.
May 5. Cinco de Mayo, San Juan Capistrano.
Mid-May. Laguna Charm House Tour, Laguna Beach.
July–September. Eight-week art celebration, from Fourth of July weekend through Labor Day, at Laguna Beach; admission varies. Events include the Festival of Arts, a juried art show featuring the area's finest artists and craftspeople; the Pageant of the Masters, a nightly event wherein live models re-create great works of art in paintings, sculpture, tapestries, and porcelain; the Sawdust Festival, an unjuried show of local artists and craftspeople (714–494–3030); and Art a Fair, a juried show open to artists from everywhere, free workshops, demonstrations, and entertainment (714–494–4514).
Mid-July, mid-August, and mid-September. San Juan Capistrano Symphony Orchestra concert, Dana Point Resort, Dana Point.
Early October. Oktoberfest, Laguna Beach.
October 23. Farewell to the Swallows, San Juan Capistrano.
Late October. Harvest Festival, San Juan Capistrano.
Thanksgiving Day. Turkey Trot, Dana Point.
Early December. Santa's Arrival and Hospitality Night, Laguna Beach. For specific dates, call the Laguna Beach Chamber of Commerce at (714) 494–1018.

Other Recommended
Restaurants and Lodgings

Laguna Beach

Las Brisas, 361 Cliff Drive. (714) 497–4955. The blue-umbrella'd dining terrace above Main Beach is the popular luncheon and late-after-
noon rendezvous, bubbly with that chic French Riviera look. Mexican
cuisine emphasizes fresh seafood but also grilled New York steak with
borracho beans. Stay for the sunsets. More formal dining inside. Sunday Brunch.

Cedar Creek Inn, 384 Forest Avenue. (714) 497–8696. Old
English–style, great-looking place, with fireplace and busy bar. From
lunch salads, sandwiches, and pastas to steak, prime rib, chicken, and
pasta dinner entrees. Two hours of free parking.

Hotel Laguna, 425 Coast Highway. (800) 524–2927 (in California);
(714) 494–1151. Ideally located in the center of town on its private
beach, adjacent to Main Beach Park; sixty-five rooms, most of which
have been upgraded in this turn-of-the-century hotel. Two restaurants;
continental breakfast is included in the room rate and served in a hospitality room on your floor. Seasonal rates.

Inn at Laguna Beach, 211 North Pacific Coast Highway; (800)
544–4479 (reservations); (714) 497–9722. Opened in 1990 on the hillside just below the museum, overlooking Main Beach. Seventy deluxe
rooms, private balconies, TV, VCR, honor bar, minirefrigerator, hair
dryer, bathrobes; most include microwave ovens. Heated swimming
pool and spa. Complimentary continental breakfast served in your
room with daily *Los Angeles Times*. Seasonal rates.

Dana Point

Cannon's, 34344 Green Lantern. (714) 496–6146. That romantic
view over the harbor just doesn't quit. The lunch bunch goes for
chicken Cajun sandwiches, excellent Cobb salad; the dinner bunch,
for the grilled salmon with lobster tails. Sunday brunch.

Dana Point Resort, 25135 Park Lantern. (800) 533–9748 (United
States and Canada); (714) 661–5000. Rambling, Cape Cod–style resort
on forty-two acres of lawn and flowers; 350 rooms; 17 suites with TV,
hospitality bar/minirefrigerator; two heated swimming pools, spas,
health club; three lighted tennis courts; restaurant. Two- and three-
night packages offer various complimentary amenities.

The Ritz Carlton, Laguna Niguel, 33533 Ritz Carlton Drive, (800)
241–3333 (reservations); (714) 240–2000. Luxurious pricey resort atop
a 152-foot ocean bluff; 362 rooms; 31 suites with private balconies,
two bathrooms, hair dryer, bathrobes, TV, honor bar, minirefrigerator;

two heated swimming pools, two Jaccuzis, seven lighted tennis courts, fitness center, salon; three restaurants, lounge, library; golf nearby; overnight parking fee. Special midweek rates and perks.

San Juan Capistrano

Sarducci's Cafe, 31751 Camino Capistrano. (714) 493–9593. Besides sandwiches and pastas in the attractive cafe, special selections include veal *piccatta,* blackened halibut with Cajun spices. Large dining patio.

El Adobe de Capistrano, 31891 Camino Capistrano. (714) 493–1163. Noted for good Mexican food; formerly a stagecoach stop.

BJ's Chicago Pizzeria, 31781 Camino Capistrano. *The* place for thick-crust pizza.

Best Western Capistrano Inn, 27174 Ortega Highway. (800) 441–9438; (714) 493–5661. Has 108 units, in-room coffee, some kitchenettes; heated swimming pool, spa. Monday through Friday, complimentary full breakfast in poolside Cafe Capistrano, plus two complimentary drinks during 5:30 to 7:30 P.M. Happy Hour. Daily and seasonal rates.

Mission Inn (motel), 26891 Ortega Highway. (714) 493–1151. Across from the mission; twenty-one rooms, all with microwave oven, refrigerator, in-room coffeemaker, VCR; heated swimming pool, Jacuzzi. On four acres with sixty-five orange trees; picking encouraged.

For More Information

Laguna Beach Chamber of Commerce, 357 Glenneyre, Laguna Beach, CA 92651. (714) 494–1018.

Dana Point Chamber of Commerce, P.O. Box 12, Dana Point, CA 92629. (714) 496–1555.

Dana Point Harbor Association, P.O. Box 548, Dana Point, CA 92629. (714) 496–6040.

San Juan Capistrano Chamber of Commerce, 31682 El Camino Real, San Juan Capistrano, CA 92675. (714) 493–4700.

Mission Visitor Center, 31882 Camino Capistrano, San Juan Capistrano, CA 92675. (714) 493–1424.

Carlsbad/Encinitas/Del Mar

Del Mar is noted for gentle surf and warm sandy beaches.

Flower-Filled Seaside

_____ 1 NIGHT _____
Uncrowded beaches · Surfing · Fine dining · Antiques
Flowers · Fairs · Horse racing/horse shows · Hot air ballooning

One of Southern California's greatest assets is its beautiful and inviting coastline, bordered by wide, secluded beaches with gentle surf and small, slower-paced villages with fine restaurants and world-class accommodations. This two-day itinerary covers just over 100 miles as it takes you south to a charming, small, European-style seaside village; through the "Flower Capital of the World," where in spring and fall hillsides are ablaze with millions of poinsettias, ranunculas, and gladioli; and to a quiet but posh coastal community noted for its celebrity racetrack and county fair.

Day 1

Morning

Drive south on I–5, past Anaheim and Santa Ana, and then follow the coastline, continuing through San Clemente, which was Richard Nixon's Western White House, and passing the San Onofre Nuclear Generating Station on the beach. It is then a 20-mile drive alongside **Camp Pendleton,** the largest U.S. amphibious Marine Corps training base in the world. For a self-guided tour of the camp, exit at the main gate on I–5 and ask for the "Windshield Tour," or phone (619) 725–4111. As you continue your coastal drive you'll see drowsy lagoons and farms reaching to the sea. Following Oceanside, take the Carlsbad Village Drive/Elm Drive exit, turn right toward the ocean, and turn left on Pacific Coast Highway. Continue about .5 mile and you're at the ocean. The heart of Carlsbad Village is just up the road.

Carlsbad, known as "The Village by the Sea," has an Old European style—a friendly small town with the ocean at its front door, clear soft air and blue skies, a place where visitors come for a day and stay for weeks or months.

You'll want to stroll Carlsbad's uncrowded beaches, swim and surf in its calm water, unwind watching fiery sunsets over the horizon, and discover restaurants and fine lodgings. The small, attractive downtown village area, with sidewalk cafes, fountains, benches, and flowers, was named for a health spa in Karlsbad, Bohemia. In 1883 a farmer's well tapped both artesian and mineral water, which he then sold to parched railroad passengers, who found it palliative. A hotel was built near the well, and guests indulged in mineral baths. Later, when the water was analyzed and found to contain properties similar to those of the European spa, the spelling was Americanized and the city became Carlsbad.

Among other delights, Carlsbad's twice yearly Village Faires, held in May and November, are California's largest street fairs. Although the railroad doesn't stop here any longer, the old-fashioned 1887 depot is now home of the Carlsbad Convention & Visitor Bureau. The city is also the home of the plush, internationally known celebrity favorite La Costa Hotel and Spa, about 3 miles inland.

A historic reminder of the town's beginning is the site of Frazier's

Well, in front of the **Alte Karlsbad Hanse House,** 2802 Carlsbad Boulevard. The three-story, half-timbered, medieval-style building, which resembles part of a foreign-movie set, contains a museum and giftshop. Its basement leads to the old well location.

Lunch: **Neiman's Restaurant,** 2978 Carlsbad Boulevard, Carlsbad. (714) 729–4131. The town's centerpiece is this 1802, refurbished, three-story gray-and-white landmark mansion, complete with turrets, cupolas, and flags waving from towers. It was formerly the home of a city cofounder and a popular overnight inn during the 1920s. Lunch in the bright American Bar Cafe and Brasserie lends itself to sandwiches, pastas, and chicken. The Neimanburger is a charbroiled top sirloin served on sourdough. Sunday brunch is outstanding.

Afternoon

Browse through Victorian-style **Village Faire shops** behind the restaurant.

Carlsbad's **State Street** is noted for its antiques and is a magnet for treasure hunters and decorators. The three blocks between Oak Avenue and Laguna Drive have about thirty antiques shops along both sides of the street, with some outdoor galleries as well. Among those starting north from Oak Avenue are The Wooden Indian, at number 3019, with Native American jewelry and art; The World's Fare; Lion & Lamb Cottage Shops, at number 3060; Vermont Country Gifts; In Days of Olde, at number 2946; International Imports, at number 2084; and Carlsbad House of Antiques and Dolls, in Antique Art Plaza, at number 2752.

Take time to stroll around this sparkling, compact village area packed with a variety of restaurants, some shops, and its streets named for presidents. Then drive or walk back to the ocean just across Carlsbad Boulevard. Its paved seawall or sidewalk above the low ocean bluffs is where you can join joggers, walkers, runners, and those pushing baby strollers. Or find a bench, sit, and watch people on the beach, surfers riding the waves, pelicans doing their daredevil dives, and the magical sunsets. The beautiful beaches are uncrowded, clean, and irresistible. Follow the broad staircase leading down to the warm sand, and relax as you watch the slow, easy surf rolling in.

Dinner: **Fidel's Norte,** 3003 Carlsbad Boulevard, Carlsbad. (714) 729–0903. A local favorite for good Mexican food and service. The large dining room has a wide terrace, and the moderately priced dinner menu features hefty burritos with spicy *chile verde* or Colorado sauce; classic tostadas are rich in beans and meat.

Lodging: **Tamarack Beach Resort,** 3200 Carlsbad Boulevard, Carlsbad, CA 92008; (800) 324–2199 (United States and Canada); (619) 729–3500. Opened in 1986; just across from the ocean. Sprawling,

Spanish-style architecture; the seventy-seven rooms include twenty-three large hotel rooms and fifty-four one- and two-bedroom condominium suites rentable nightly or weekly. Spacious guestrooms, most with ocean views, have private balconies, honor bar/minirefrigerator, TV, and VCR; complimentary VCR library in Recreation Room. Gym, heated pool, two spas; barbecues, restaurant. Seasonal rates. Hotel/guest activities include daytrips to nearby attractions—Tijuana, Catalina, and so on—plus complimentary wine-and-cheese parties and reduced dining rates to select village restaurants.

Day 2

Morning

Breakfast: **Mariah's Westwind Restaurant and Bakery,** 377 Elm Avenue, Carlsbad. (619) 729–8040. Breakfast is served all day at this busy neighborhood place. Pancake specialties, breakfast combinations, and 150 omelet suggestions. Patio dining if you prefer.

With its mild climate, Carlsbad has been a major flower-growing center since the 1920s, when its flower and bulb industry of gladioli, ranunculas, and irises began and was commercially successful. From mid-March through April about a hundred acres on the hillsides behind Pea Soup Andersen's are an explosion of multicolored ranunculas. The city became a prime avocado-growing center after a nurseryman planted the first avocado groves in 1916 and developed different varieties. Other avocado growers followed and prospered through 1948. But when water shortages arose, growers began selling their land to developers for better profit than farming offered. The first bird of paradise flowers were grown here after seeds planted in greenhouses were transferred to an old avocado grove; the bird of paradise is now Carlsbad's official city flower, appearing in colorful sidewalk and building murals.

The drive south on Carlsbad Boulevard to Encinitas and Del Mar is more pleasant along the ocean than on the freeway, despite the San Diego Gas and Electric Power station that intrudes on the lovely coastal vistas. At times it seems that everyone is on holiday. The bikepath has plenty of pedalers, men fish at the water's edge, and other people swim and wade in the calm frothy surf or relax on the uncrowded beach and watch large brown pelicans dive-bomb like arrows into the water. **South Carlsbad State Beach,** where colorful umbrellas dot the beach, is popular with campers.

Seasonally, this coastal highway (State Highway 21) explodes with dazzling yellow, orange, and purple ranunculas and other flowers grown in the area. A roadside grove of tall, noble eucalyptus trees ushers you into **Leucadia, Encinitas, Cardiff by-the-Sea,** and **Olivenhain.** These four small cities were consolidated in 1986 as the city of Encinitas, though each retains its individual attractions and life-style.

In the 1870s Leucadia's early settlers were English spiritualists seeking freedom of worship, and they named their community after a Greek island meaning "paradise." Many streets have names of Greek gods. The 1881 founder of Encinitas gave his town a Spanish name meaning "little live oaks." When Cardiff was homesteaded in 1875, its developer named it after a large city in Wales. Olivenhain was settled in 1884 by a small group of Germans; their old meeting hall is one of its attractions.

With Encinitas's millions of commercially grown gladioli, ranunculas, and poinsettias, the area has been dubbed "Flower Capital of the World." In spring and fall the Chamber of Commerce conducts tours of those greenhouses or nurseries open to the public. Call (619) 763–6041 in February or September for information.

Along this lively road are cafes, lodgings, many antiques stores (D Street), and the Self Realization Fellowship Retreat and Hermitage. First Street has a strip of Italian restaurants and the good-looking Lumberyard Center's restaurants and shops.

The fine beaches along here are known for great surfing and provide scenic views from the bluffs. The train whistles right through Encinitas, where Moonlight Beach is a favorite family picnic area. These are all wonderful little beach towns you will want to revisit to explore.

Continue south on I–5 past acres of greenhouses, and in ten minutes you'll have arrived in **Del Mar.** Take the Via de la Valle exit to Jimmy Durante Drive (the "Schnozz" was a former resident and mayor). Turn left past the Del Mar Race Track and Fairgrounds, then drive along the town's broad main street, Camino del Mar, to 15th Street and the heart of this small, low-key, genteel town, with its Old World atmosphere and architecture.

Lunch: **Bully's,** 1404 Camino Del Mar in Del Mar. (619) 755–1660. Small, dimly lighted with roomy red leather booths and a congenial bar, Bully's is an old-fashioned steakhouse and the local watering hole, a place known for consistently good food. The succulent Barbecue Beef Bones with fiery barbecue sauce and the excellent french fries are worth the trip. Other options include burgers, sandwiches, prime rib, and fresh fish. There's patio dining in the rear.

Afternoon

Del Mar began in 1885 as a beach resort town and evolved as a vacation getaway for Los Angeles's elite. It's still easy to relax in this amiable, well-heeled residential beach city, which follows a scenic 2.5

miles of curving coastline studded with top-notch restaurants, specialty shops, and noteworthy accommodations. Del Marians also invite you to enjoy their broad beaches for great swimming, fine scuba diving, and matchless surfing atop those long tubular waves that keep rolling in from Hawaii. From sea to the sky is a thrilling transition for hot-air balloon enthusiasts who can enjoy the panoramic overhead views as they drift quietly over the glittering coastline in sunrise and sunset flights.

To see more of the city, begin your stroll along Camino del Mar at 15th Street, where you'll find **Stratford Square,** a mock-Tudor building encompassing shops and restaurants. Carlos and Annie's corner sidewalk cafe is a busy hangout for Mexican food and burgers beneath its umbrellas. Earth Song Bookstore favors best-sellers with book-signing parties, in addition to stocking a selection of architecture, art, and children's books. Through an archway, Ocean Song Gallery, a wonderful, offbeat boutique, has tables piled with fine import pieces, rugs, ethnic records, and cards.

Across the boulevard is the popular new **Del Mar Plaza,** an open-air, multilevel, upscale dining and shopping center. Among its dozens of shops are the Laura Larkin Gallery, Peaches en Regalia luxe apparel, Esmeralda's Bookstore/Cafe, and Daniel's gourmet market. Its fashionable Italian-style indoor/outdoor restaurants boast smashing oceanview terraces and chic, epicurean variety. There's underground parking; an elevator is in the rear.

The city is famous as home of the **Del Mar Race Track** ("where the turf meets the surf") and Fairgrounds. Launched in 1937 by actors Bing Crosby and Pat O'Brien, who lived in the area and began its Hollywood glamour and celebrity status, Del Mar was established as a new playground of the stars, notably Lucille Ball and Desi Arnaz, Harry James, Betty Grable, Jimmy Durante, and Bob Hope. Del Mar buzzes in summer with the annual big Fair and Thoroughbred Racing and, since September 1991, year-round satellite wagering.

Walk or drive downhill on 15th Street the few short blocks to the ocean, where **Seagrove Park,** with stately palm trees, overlooks the beach just a few steps down the bluff. Side-by-side at the beach on Coast Boulevard, two of Del Mar's waterfront dining institutions, Jake's and the Poseidon, offer beachfront terrace dining, and are generally packed with seafood aficionados.

Across the narrow road is Amtrak's small station, which has many daily stops. The relaxing, two-hour trip from Los Angeles is still as popular with visitors as it was long ago, when Mary Pickford, Charlie Chaplin, Douglas Fairbanks, Rudolph Valentino, and other film stars and vacationers arrived by train for a refreshing holiday.

The wide beach with gentle waves spilling onto the sand is too hard to resist. To better savor beautiful Del Mar, you need to spend some time strolling barefoot in the sand . . . sit and relax for a while and watch the bathers, listen for the train whistle, and let the sun work its magic.

Return to Los Angeles by heading back inland on Via de la Valle to connect with I–5 north.

There's More

Smith-Shipley-Magee House, 258 Beech Avenue, Carlsbad. The 1887 home of Samuel Church Smith is now headquarters for the Carlsbad Historical Society.

Shipley-Magee Barn, Magee Park, Carlsbad. Collection of old farming implements and a cistern.

St. Michael's Episcopal Church, 2775 Carlsbad Boulevard, Carlsbad. Small redwood chapel, built in 1896.

Carlsbad Raceway, at the city's eastern edge, is the site of weekend world-class motocross racing; elaborate skateboard area. Year-round. For information, call (619) 727–1171 (recording).

Watersports. Snug Harbor Marina, in Agua Hedionda Lagoon, 4215 Harrison Street, Carlsbad. Water-ski, jet-ski, waverunner rentals.

Golf. Rancho Carlsbad Golf Course, 5200 El Camino Real, Carlsbad. (619) 438–1772. Executive, 18-hole public course.

Tennis. Carlsbad High School, 3557 Monroe Street, Carlsbad. Nine courts; open after school and evenings.

Tennis and Golf. Del Mar Recreation Center, 15555 Turf Road, Del Mar. (619) 481–0363. Eight lighted courts and lighted golf driving range.

Stage Coach Park, 3420 Camino de los Coches, Carlsbad. (619) 434–2895. Four courts; open evenings.

Hadley Fruit Orchards, 6115 Paseo Del Norte/I–5 at Palomar Airport Road, Carlsbad. (619) 438–1260 or (800) 854–5655. Free catalog. Large selection of California dried fruits and nuts, giftpacks, wine cellar/tasting room.

Hot-Air Ballooning: Skysurfer Balloon Company, 1221 Camino del Mar, Del Mar. (619) 481–6800. Sunrise and sunset flights over the scenic canyons and coastline, followed by champagne party. Reservations required.

Farmer's Market, City Hall parking lot, 1050 Camino del Mar, Del Mar. Every Saturday, 1:00 to 4:00 P.M. Fresh produce, beautiful fresh flowers, plants, honey, avocados, and eggs.

Del Mar Trolley. Helps you sightsee in comfort; runs regularly to and from the racetrack to Del Mar Plaza and the train depot. Fare. For information, call (619) 755–7300.

Special Events

Early January. Five-day Infiniti Tournament of Champions, La Costa Resort, Carlsbad.
Late January. San Diego Marathon, Carlsbad.
Late March. Carlsbad 5000 (5K race). Attracts the world's fastest distance runners, Carlsbad.
Late April. North San Diego Rockhoppers Volksmarch (10K walk), Carlsbad.
Early May. Strawberry Festival. St. Michael's by the Sea, Carlsbad.
First two weeks in May. National Horse Show, Del Mar Fairgrounds, Del Mar. (619) 296–1441.
First Sunday in May. Carlsbad Village Faire, largest one-day street fair in California, Carlsbad.
Early June through August. Evening jazz concerts in the park, Carlsbad.
Mid-June to early July. Del Mar Fair, Del Mar Fairgrounds.
Mid-July. Summer Village Art Festival, Carlsbad.
Second Sunday in July. Carlsbad Triathlon, Carlsbad.
End of July through September. Thoroughbred racing. Closed Tuesday, Del Mar.
Late August. Mazda Tennis Classic, Carlsbad.
Early October. Oktoberfest, Carlsbad.
Mid-October. Two day Southern California Grand Prix, Del Mar.
First Sunday in November. Carlsbad Village Faire. Largest single-day street fair in California, Carlsbad.
Early December. Christmas tree lighting, Carlsbad.

Other Recommended Restaurants and Lodgings

Carlsbad

Armenian Cafe, 3126 Carlsbad Boulevard. (619) 720–2233. Small cottage features Belgian and other waffles for breakfast, plus Armenian specialties—pita bread, lamb, and so on. Closed Monday and Tuesday.

Daily News Cafe, 3001 Carlsbad Boulevard. (619) 729–1023. At the Carlsbad Inn. Place your order at the counter, and food is brought to your table inside or on the busy patio. Cute menu. Omelets, buttermilk pancakes, salads, sandwiches, freshly made croissants, cinnamon rolls, Belly Bombers (burgers). Breakfast and lunch only.

Jay's Gourmet Restaurant, 2975 Carlsbad Boulevard. (619)

720–9668. Opposite Neiman's. Prepare to stand in line at this small, checkered-tablecloth beehive for its seafood, pizza, calzone, pastas, and veal dishes, with homemade sauces.

Carlsbad Inn, 3075 Carlsbad Boulevard. (800) 235–3939 (United States and Canada); (619) 434–7020. Across from the beach in the center of town; 58 hotel rooms, many with kitchenettes; 132 condominiums. In-room coffeemakers, TV, video players, satellite TV; heated swimming pool, Jacuzzi, health club gym-sauna. Picnic cabana on the beach.

La Costa Resort and Spa, Costa del Mar Road. (800) 854–5000 (national); (619) 438–9111. Internationally known luxury celebrity resort of 478 rooms, suites, and private residences on 400 acres. Five restaurants, Tournament of Champions lounge; two championship golf courses, twenty-one tennis courts, beauty/health spa; shopping gallery, salon, movie theater. Golf, tennis, and spa packages.

Encinitas

Raddison Hotel, 85 Encinitas Boulevard. (800) 333–3333 (worldwide); (619) 942–7455. Dramatically situated atop a bluff overlooking the ocean. Ninety-one rooms and suites, some with kitchenettes, all with balconies, cable TV. Heated swimming pool, whirlpool; coffeeshop and restaurant. Complimentary continental breakfast in coffeeshop or lobby, plus daily newspaper.

Del Mar

Baja Grill and Fish Market, 1342 Camino del Mar. (619) 792–6551. Patio diners prefer the great chicken salad and fish tacos.

Del Mar Inn, 720 Camino del Mar (at 9th Street). (619) 755–9765; (800) 453–4411 (in California); (800) 451–4515 (elsewhere). Warm, English-style architecture and decor; eighty good-size rooms, half with kitchenettes, overlook ocean or garden. Satellite TV and free movie channel; heated swimming pool, spa; complimentary continental breakfast served in your room; complimentary afternoon English Tea and Cakes in the cozy library.

The Inn L'Auberge, 1540 Camino del Mar. (800) 555–1336; (619) 259–1515. Opened in 1989, on the site of the landmark old Hotel Del Mar. Luxurious amenities in French country decor in 128 rooms and suites, many with coastal views, large balconies, minibar and refrigerator, marble baths. Two heated swimming pools, fitness center, beauty spa; two tennis courts; restaurant. Sunday brunch. Special getaway packages.

For More Information

Carlsbad Convention and Visitors Bureau, P.O. Box 1246, Carlsbad, CA 92008. (800) 227–5722; (619) 434–6093.

Encinitas Chamber of Commerce, 345H First Street, Encinitas, CA 92024. (619) 753–6041.

Self-Realization Fellowship Retreat and Hermitage, 215 K Street, Encinitas, CA 92024. (619) 753–1181.

Greater Del Mar Chamber of Commerce, 1104 Camino del Mar, Del Mar, CA 92014. (619) 755–4244.

La Jolla

The sheltered La Jolla Cove

Coves and Caves

_____ 1 NIGHT _____

Beaches • Watersports • Dining • Shopping
Museums • Parks • Galleries • Hang gliding • Aquarium

Here's a two-day itinerary south to an energetic little seaside resort perched atop the edge of the Pacific Ocean. In addition to all manner of watersports, golf, tennis, and hang gliding, you'll have a tantalizing choice of good dining, visit an ocean-view museum and a delightful, aquarium, picnic in the park, prowl upscale galleries, poke around chic boutiques, relax, sun and swim in a protected cove, and pedal a bike on a scenic path along the ever-present ocean.

Day 1

Morning

Drive south on I–5 about 115 miles to **La Jolla.** Exit at La Jolla Shores Drive, continue to Torrey Pines Road, turn left, and stay on it to Girard Avenue, in the heart of downtown.

Though La Jolla (pronounced "La Hoya") is probably best known for its variety of summer activities, any season is perfect for a visit. In an exuberance of natural beauty, its 7 miles of sandy beaches are wrapped around a spectacular coastline of towering cliffs, scraggy coves, and hilly terrain. Often referred to as a quaint little village, La Jolla is about as quaint as Burt Reynolds.

Creative people have long been attracted to the scenic locale. The first group of artists and actors seduced by the windswept coast and long, lonely stretches of beach settled here in the 1890s. They created the legendary **Green Dragon Colony** on Prospect Street, with homes and studios overlooking the peaceful cove. Art is still a major part of village life, with dozens of galleries tucked throughout the city.

Additionally, La Jolla is a renowned think-tank hub, framed by the prestigious Salk Institute for Biological Studies, with its Nobel laureates; the University of California at San Diego campus; and Scripps Institution of Oceanography, whose enchanting aquarium attracts some 300,000 yearly visitors.

With its rolling hills, lush tropical planting, palms and tall aromatic eucalyptus trees, winding streets, posh hotels, dazzling ocean vistas, world-class shopping, and cheery sidewalk cafes, the effervescent little city just 15 miles north of San Diego has a decidedly Mediterranean flavor and is frequently compared with the French Riviera.

Lunch: **Putnam's,** 910 Prospect Street, La Jolla. (619) 454–2181. In the Colonial Inn. A classy, popular pub with marble floors and a warm setting. You'll find friendly service and good, hearty food, continental-American style, in pastas, sandwiches, and fresh seafood. Moderately priced; free valet parking.

Afternoon

The best thing about La Jolla is that its small downtown area is so compact you can explore the city by foot, thus avoiding the busy traffic and hard-to-find parking spaces. Even the beaches are an easy stroll from downtown.

Begin with stately **Girard Avenue,** the city's main thoroughfare. This lovely, broad street, lined with tall palms and eucalyptus trees, is vaguely reminiscent of Santa Barbara, with its landscaped areas and wrought-iron benches. Anchored by Saks Fifth Avenue in a rambling one-story building, the shops here include Laura Ashley; Polo Ralph Lauren; Gallery Alexander, with ever-creative exhibits and collections; a preponderance of fine jewelry shops; and Banana Republic.

Girard leads into lively, attractive **Prospect Street,** a sweeping terrace atop the cliffs overlooking the ocean that offers a complete change of ambience. You won't find many streets quite like this one, where shops and restaurants facing the water offer spectacular views of the cove and the famous La Jolla Caves. It's a bustling, pedestrian-oriented street for shopping, dining, and browsing, filled with sleek boutiques, galleries, sidewalk cafes and posh restaurants, people, cars, and traffic.

On the ocean side the pink-domed landmark La Valencia Hotel is flanked by cafes and shops. The Chart House Restaurant, 1270 Prospect Street, leads into **Coast Walk,** where boutiques and galleries housed in small cottages set far back from the sidewalk on wide expanses of lawn and brick-paved courtyards, pretty gazebos, and wide shade trees are the legacies of the famed Green Dragon Art Colony. The Collector is a fine source for pink tourmalines mined in San Diego, tanzanite from Africa, and decorative mineral specimens. The Gallery of Two Sisters shows a pleasing selection of oil paintings, watercolors, stoneware, and ironwood sculpture by California artists at good prices.

Shoppers and adventurers won't want to miss La Jolla Cave & Shell Shop, 1325 Coast Walk, (619–454–6080), one of the city's oldest shops. Ensconced atop the cliffs since 1903, the shop features decorative and specimen shells, jewelry, and the like from all over the world. From the shop you can descend the 133 steps built into a man-made, lighted tunnel to **Sunny Jim Cave,** the largest of La Jolla's original seven sea-level smugglers' caves and the only one that can be entered (fee charged for the adventure).

At the end of Coast Walk, follow bikers, joggers, and strollers along the curving and scenic Cliff Walk atop the bluffs overlooking **La Jolla Cove,** the center of attraction for residents and visitors alike. The small, protected beach, with its calm and crystalline water, is the favorite area for swimming, scuba diving, snorkeling, sunbathing, and socializing. Cliff Walk also overlooks La Jolla's notorious smugglers' caves in the shallow water below, and from here you can watch people clambering all over them. Especially Sunny Jim Cave.

Wander farther down to the **Ellen Browning Scripps Park** at the foot of Coast Walk bordering the cove. Here you're apt to find an old-fashioned tableau of people picnicking or lazily sprawled on the warm grass in the dappled shade of slender palms and the lofty Torrey pines, evoking a feeling of having stumbled into an impressionist painting. La Jolla's balmy climate nurtures the rare, prehistoric, sea-loving Torrey pines, which exist in only one other place on earth: Santa Rosa Island off Santa Barbara. Bring your own picnic lunch or snack, stake out a bench or patch of grass, and enjoy the superb ocean view or watch the surfers. Many picnickers arrive as late as 5:00 P.M. with food hampers and blankets to enjoy the blazing sunsets over the ocean.

Dinner: **Sammy's California Woodfired Pizza Kitchen,** 702 Pearl (corner of Draper), La Jolla. (619) 456–5222. One of the most popular places in town. They don't take reservations, so feel lucky to find a seat at the counter, where you can watch the chefs make designer pizzas and generous salads; both can be shared.

Lodging: **The Empress Hotel,** 7766 Fay Avenue, La Jolla, CA 92037. (800) 525–6552 (nationwide); (619) 454–3001. In the heart of the village, sixty-eight oversize ocean-view rooms and four suites offer complimentary continental breakfast in a hospitality room. In-room coffeemaker, refrigerator, cable TV with in-room movies, daily newspaper; restaurant; sauna, Jacuzzi, exercise room; sundeck. The suites feature glamorous marble Jacuzzi tubs in the bedrooms.

Day 2

Morning

Breakfast: Enjoy the complimentary continental breakfast in your hotel.

Walk or drive to the **San Diego Museum of Contemporary Art,** 700 Prospect Street (619–454–3541). The long, low structure and sculpture garden overlooking the ocean are the former home of heiress Ellen B. Scripps, the city's benefactress, and were remodeled as a museum by noted architect Irving Gill, who designed many buildings in La Jolla. The museum showcases major paintings, sculpture, photography, drawings, and graphic art produced since 1950. The well-stocked Book Shop has a fine selection of books about artists for children, in addition to adult material. (Open daily, except Monday and occasionally the second week of August, from 10:00 A.M. to 5:00 P.M. and on Wednesday until 9:00 P.M.; admission.)

Two doors away, John Cole's Book Shop, 7800 Prospect Street, tucked in a historic wisteria-covered cottage, is a bookworm's haven, offering a wide selection of titles, in addition to folk art, imported toys, ocean views, and a cozy fire.

Lunch: **The Spot,** 1005 Prospect Street, La Jolla. (619) 349–0800. A local favorite, friendly and casual for sandwiches, good Chicago-style pizza, salad, barbecued baby back ribs, and daily gourmet chef special.

Afternoon

Drive north on Torrey Pines Road to Expedition Way, off La Jolla Shores Drive; turn left toward the ocean and south to the **Stephen Birch Aquarium Museum** (619–534–FISH) on the campus of the University of California San Diego in **Scripps Institution of Oceanography,** one of the oldest, largest, and most important centers for marine science research. This new, $14-million facility, which opened in September 1992, is larger and more impressive than the Scripps Aquarium it replaces.

The large, boulder-decked outdoor tide pool that overlooks the sparkling coastline captivates children looking for starfish, mussels, and other small local sea animals. Inside, the aquarium features thirty-three large tanks displaying more than 3,000 colorful fish from tropical waters as well as from the chill waters of the Pacific Northwest.

Among the stunning, shimmering variety of rainbow-colored fish and plants are a giant octopus, elegant vertical seahorses, fast-moving sharks, which always draw considerable interest, spooky moray eels, and venomous yellow-and-brown lionfish. A dramatic 16-foot-deep kelp forest in a 50,000-gallon tank is viewed through a 21-by-13-foot acrylic wall.

The museum features the largest oceanographic exhibit in the United States. The bookshop offers more than 1,500 gifts, as well as extensive science and oceanographic literature. Open daily except Christmas Day, from 9:00 A.M. to 5:00 P.M. Admission.

Salk Institute for Biological Studies, 10010 North Torrey Pines Road, (619) 453–4100, on a promontory adjacent to University of California San Diego, is renowned for medical research, and foremost biologists come here to study. The powerful building was designed by the late architect Louis Kahn specifically for Dr. Jonas Salk, its founding director. The sprawling complex is a dramatic masterwork of poured concrete, glass, and travertine and is visited by many architects. Public tours are available weekdays at 10:00 A.M., 11;00 A.M., and noon.

For those interested in **hang gliding,** Torrey Pines Gliderport, La Jolla Village Farms Road (619–457–9093)—a popular, expert-rated launching site for hang gliders—is just up the road from the Salk Institute. Drive up the coastal hilltop and park on the towering bluff 300 feet above the ocean (overlooking Black's Nude Beach). Walk up to the knoll and watch the hang gliders assemble their craft, which they bring rolled up like tall masts in long zippered cases. Then watch them take flight in their fragile, multicolored craft like giant butterflies, as the wind off the sea lifts them from cliff's edge and they ride the updrafts to altitudes up to 1,500 feet, soaring over the cliffs and sand out to sea. Weekends are the best time to watch. In spring, when winds are strong, many hang gliders are in the air at once. Whatever the season, the best hours are between noon and 5:00 P.M., when the updrafts are strongest. For rentals, sales, and instruction, contact the Hang Gliding Center, 4206 Sorrento Valley Center, Del Mar (619–450–9008).

From here, retrace your way back to Los Angeles on I–5 north.

There's More

Golf. Try the 9-hole Pitch & Putt course at Spindrift Golf Course, 2000 Spindrift Drive (619–454–7126). Torrey Pines Municipal Course, 11480 Torrey Pines Road (619–453–0381), will remind you of Pebble Beach, where cliffside fairways on two 18-hole championship courses overlook the blue Pacific.

Bike riding. Follow the marked scenic route along the coast or through town. Bike rentals at La Jolla Cyclery, 7443 Girard Avenue.

Skin and scuba diving. The craggy coves of Bird Rock, La Jolla Underwater Park, and underwater Scripps Canyon are the best areas for skin and scuba diving.

Surfing. Windansea Beach, considered one of the best surfing beaches along the West Coast, is at the end of Nautilus Street, between the village and Bird Rock to the south. For gear, contact Mitch's Surf Shop, 631 Pearl Street (619–454–5933).

Snorkeling/swimming. Can't beat La Jolla Cove.

Tennis. La Jolla Recreation Center, 615 Prospect Street (619–454–2071); La Jolla YMCA, 8355 Cliffridge Drive (619–453–3483); La Jolla High School, 750 Nautilus Street (619–454–2071).

Hanson Art Galleries, 1227 Prospect Street (619–454–9799), is filled with the works of such twentieth-century masters as Erte, Picasso, Hockney, and Peter Max. Original paintings, sculptures, limited editions, and contemporary art exhibits.

Special Events

First week in June. La Jolla Festival of the Arts & Food Faire.

June through September. Concerts by the Sea, in Scripps Park series.

Last Sunday in August. Off the Wall Street Party.

Second Sunday in September. Annual Rough Waterswim, at La Jolla Cove.

First Sunday in December. Holiday Festival Arts & Crafts Fair.

Other Recommended
Restaurants and Lodgings

La Jolla

Alphonso's of La Jolla, 1251 Prospect Street. (619) 454–2232. A lively, crowded hangout for Mexican specialties but hard to get in the door or find a seat at a patio table.

Avanti Ristorante, 875 Prospect Street. (619) 454–4288. Locals recommend the fine cuisine of this elegant, black-and-white art deco room with pink tablecloths and dim lighting. Tuxedoed waiters are familiar with its northern Italian menu.

George's at the Cove, 1250 Prospect Street. (619) 454–4244. A longtime, convivial favorite for creative regional cuisine amid romantic candlelit tables overlooking the cove. Dressy and expensive. Sunday brunch. Free valet parking.

Harry's Coffee Shop, 7545 Girard Avenue. (619) 454–7381. Where late risers go for breakfast. Sometimes everyone in town shows up when you do. Admire the wall paintings while waiting for your eggs or hamburgers. Park in the rear; open Monday through Saturday, 6:00 A.M. to 3:00 P.M., and Sunday until 2:00 P.M.

John's Waffle Shop, 7906 Girard Avenue. (619) 454–7371. A busy breakfast landmark for waffles, pancakes, and omelets. If you sit at the counter in this small cafe, you can watch your order sizzling. Breakfast served, with luncheon specialties included; open Monday through Saturday, 7:00 A.M. to 3:00 P.M.

Top O' the Cove, 1216 Prospect Street. (619) 454–7779. Set high on the bluffs in an ocean-view bungalow with candlelit tables; expensive but a consistent winner for fine continental cuisine and sublime desserts.

El Crab Catcher, 1298 Prospect Street. (619) 454–9587. Overlooking the coastline, with a variety of fresh crab and seafood entrees. Pleasant service. Sunday brunch.

Manhattan of La Jolla, 7766 Fay Avenue. (619) 454–1182. In the Empress Hotel. Sleekly sophisticated northern Italian cuisine in a New York setting. Sink into an upholstered booth and watch the tropical fish drift by. Pasta, seafood, steaks, and chicken in generous portions; attentive waiters.

La Valencia Hotel, 1132 Prospect Street. (800) 451–0772 or (619) 454–0771. Eighty-nine rooms and eleven suites, heart-shaped swimming pool—the choice of distinguished visitors since Garbo and other stars used to hide out in the 1930s. TV, clock radio, hair dryer, coffeemaker, minibar, refrigerator, daily newspaper, nightly turndown service; twenty-four-hour room service; three restaurants, lounge.

Overnight parking fee. The Mediterranean Room's tropical, palm-fringed patio is a lively rendezvous for breakfast, lunch, dinner, and Sunday brunch. (619) 454–1199.

Colonial Inn, 910 Prospect Street. (619) 454–2181; (800) 826–1278 (California); (800) 832–5525 (nationwide). Fully restored, historic 1913 landmark in Victorian-style hotel, 1 block from the beach. Sixty-seven elegantly appointed rooms and eight suites; TV, clock radio, refrigerator on request (no charge), daily newspaper, complimentary continental breakfast in Putnam's; turndown service. Heated swimming pool. Complimentary valet and self-parking.

Inn by the Sea (Best Western), 7830 Fay Avenue. (800) 526–4545; (619) 459–4461. In the heart of the village. Private balconies for 132 rooms and 2 suites; TV with movie channels, clock radio, minirefrigerator available on request (no charge), hair dryer, room service, complimentary continental breakfast in lobby. Heated swimming pool, spa, fitness room; restaurant; conference facilities; complimentary valet and self-parking.

For More Information

Official Visitor's Bureau, La Jolla Town Council, 1055 Wall Street (corner of Herschel Street), La Jolla, CA 92037. (691) 454–1444.

La Jolla Historical Society, 7846 Eads Avenue, La Jolla, CA 92037. (619) 459–5335. Open Tuesday and Thursday, 2:00 to 4:00 P.M., or write to Box 2085, La Jolla, CA 92038.

San Diego/Coronado

Balboa Park is the cultural hub of San Diego.

Lively Seafront Holiday

_____ 2 NIGHTS _____

Zoo • Parks • Old Town • Trolley Tours • History
Historic hotels • Museums • Harbor cruise • Marine park

In this two-night, three-day excursion, you'll barely get to sample all the highlights of this versatile seaport city where California was born in 1769. Cheer a performing killer whale; ride a ferry across the sparkling bay to a tony Victorian resort enclave. Historic San Diego has been host to Franciscan Father Junípero Serra, Wyatt Earp, Charles Lindbergh, the Prince of Wales, Clint Eastwood, and Marilyn Monroe.

Day 1

Morning

Drive south on I–5, the Santa Ana Freeway, for this 120-mile excursion, which should take about two and a half to three hours, depending on freeway traffic. The scenic drive passes through orange groves, farms, little beach cities, and rolling countryside of low, cinnamon-colored foothills and sweet, soft air.

At the northern edge of San Diego, adjacent to I–5, that gleaming, elaborate, white, Gothic-style structure with 190-foot-tall twin spires is the new landmark San Diego Mormon Temple. As you near San Diego, you can see the skyline high-rise beyond the water-skiers and sailboats. Your first stop is the world-famous **zoo** in Balboa Park.

Take the Civic Center/10th Avenue exit to A Street, turn left, and turn left again at 12th/Park. Follow signs to the zoo and parking area along President's Way. The zoo, spread over one-hundred well-landscaped acres, is the city's most popular attraction, noted for its exotic and rare wildlife. Cuddly teddy-bear koalas and playful pigmy chimpanzees are among its collection of 3,200 animals of 800 species. Most are in barless, moated enclosures resembling their natural habitat.

You can wander about on your own or pay a bit more for admission that includes the forty-minute, narrated, 3-mile double-deck bus tour (better view from the upper deck) that roams through 60 percent of the zoo.

Besides the galaxy of graceful flamingos poised for photos near the entrance, among animals you'll see on the bus tour are the 500-pound pygmy hippos, California sea lions working on their suntans, the elusive Chinese leopard, Alaskan brown bears, zebras, 17-foot-tall giraffes, and the slinky jaguar. Roosters and chickens strut and fly freely throughout.

Though the bus tour covers a lot, by taking it you'll miss the world's largest collection of monkeys and apes, the children's petting zoo, the birds, and the Skyfari Aerial Tram. The bus tour also makes it difficult to see many animals that aren't out front and center, or to see above or through groups of people along the paths. Though walking may become tiring, you can stop, watch animals of interest, and take photos. (Open daily from 9:00 A.M. to 5:00 P.M. Admission; free parking; public information, 619–234–3153.)

To see more of the park's attractions, drive out Park Boulevard, turn right on President's Way, and turn right again at the first boulevard; park behind the Spreckels Organ Pavilion.

Lunch: **Cafe Del Rey Moro,** 1549 El Prado, in the House of Hospitality building (between the Fine Arts Gallery and the statue of El Cid). (619) 234–8511. A popular midday gathering place in a romantic, fourteenth-century-style Moorish palace. Pleasing terrace or indoor dining on moderately priced southwestern regional cuisine, of salads, grilled fish, shrimp, or chicken. Sunday champagne brunch.

Afternoon

Balboa Park is a lush, 1,400-acre visual and cultural treasure one can happily spend several days exploring, with its hub of museums, theaters, and cafes. The ornate Spreckels Organ Pavilion, with curving, colonnaded walks and large outdoor organ, offers free concerts, Sundays at 2:00 P.M. and Monday evenings in summer.

The park's rich, sixteenth-century Spanish-Moorish baroque architecture is enhanced with ornamental gardens and fountains, arched walkways, and a 200-foot bell tower. Ride the free red tram shuttling from one plaza to another, with frequent stops.

The Prado, across the center of the park, is embroidered with a cluster of ten museums and two art galleries winding through plazas, rose gardens, and a lily pond. **The San Diego Museum of Art**'s extensive collection ranges from pre-Columbian to twentieth-century art; it also has a Sculpture Court and Garden and a charming cafe (closed Mondays). The Reuben H. Fleet Space Theater and Science Center envelops you in a giant domed screen showing 3-D Omnimax films.

Some museums charge admission; hours vary, but most are open daily from 10:00 A.M. to 4:30 P.M. You can buy a map and guide for 60 cents at the **Balboa Park Visitors Center,** 1549 El Prado (619–239–0512). The renowned **Old Globe Theater,** designed in round, sixteenth-century style, is part of a three-theater complex presenting Shakespeare and musicals. Purchase same-day tickets at the box office if they are available (information, 619–239–2255), or buy half-price, day-of-performance tickets at Tim's Art Tix downtown at the Horton Plaza ticket booth (619–238–3810). With Balboa Park's evening theater performances, plus many cafes and snackbars, you can spend a pleasurable, stimulating day and evening here.

Dinner: **Fifth and Hawthorn,** 515 Hawthorn (corner of Fifth Avenue), San Diego. (619) 544–0940. Convenient uptown location close to the park; smart-looking, with white napery on candlelit tables. The menu favors California cuisine of fresh seafood, innovative salads, and light summer or smaller-portion entrees (also lower-priced) like filet mignon and pasta.

After dinner, head south to Coronado on I-5 to Highway 75, which comes up very soon; take 75 over the Coronado Bay Bridge. Stay to the right as you approach the toll gates at the exit to avoid paying the toll. (There's no toll returning to San Diego)

Lodging: **Le Meridien San Diego at Coronado,** 2000 Second Street, Coronado, CA 92118. (800) 543–4300; (619) 435–3000. French elegance throughout this sixteen-acre, world-class hotel. Features 300 deluxe spacious rooms with sitting area, 7 suites, and 28 villas in country French decor; terraces, TV, minibar/refrigerator, hair dryer, terry robes, marble bathroom with tub and stall shower, excellent lighting, concierge service. Three heated swimming pools, two whirlpools, six lighted tennis courts, beauty spa, health club. Two restaurants and a cocktail lounge. Overnight parking fee.

Day 2

Morning

Breakfast: At the hotel. Or, if it's Sunday, investigate the buffet brunch at the noted **Hotel Del Coronado,** 1500 Orange Avenue, Coronado (619–522–8000). Each Sunday buffet brunch features a different international theme menu, served in the famed, enormous (156-by-66-foot) Crown Room. Brunch is a lavish array of hot and cold dishes, including salad bar, omelet station, hand-carved prime rib, sizzling pasta station, and incomparable desserts. Purchase your brunch tickets in the lobby. (Brunch served Sunday 9:00 A.M. to 2:00 P.M.; reservations suggested; free validated parking.)

Following brunch, explore this rambling, 1888 Victorian hotel, whose famous guests have included Edward, the Prince of Wales (said to have met Wallis Simpson, the future Duchess of Windsor, here in 1920), Charles Lindbergh, twelve presidents, and Thomas Edison, who reportedly supervised the incandescent light installation. This is also the locale of *Some Like It Hot* and other films. The "Del" is a grand old showpiece, with its red cone-shaped roof, gleaming white trim, cupolas, and turrets (see other Recommended Restaurants and Lodgings). Take the birdcage elevator to the lower-lobby level and browse the Galleria shops. Wander through the hotel's public rooms, beautiful gardens, and wide beach.

To see more of Coronado's downtown area, from Eighth Street to the "Del," stay on Orange Avenue, the main street of the village and Coronado's "restaurant row." Coronado Visitor Information is upstairs at 1111 Orange Avenue (800) 622–8300; 619–437–8788). Use the convenient sidewalk gondola, crammed with brochures and information.

Coronado is San Diego's resort community, graced by lovely parks and tree-lined streets; it has a relaxed, small-town flavor and offers luxury hotels, golf, tennis, bikepaths, and boating. It also has a history of famous guests and residents, such as millionaire John D. Spreckels, whose former mansion is now the vintage Glorietta Bay Inn, and L. Frank Baum, who wrote the classic *Wizard of Oz*. In 1927 Charles Lindbergh, the "Lone Eagle," took off from Coronado's North Island for his famous solo New York to Paris flight and was feted at the Hotel Del Coronado on his triumphant return.

Continue along Orange Avenue until it ends and then turn right, continuing 2½ blocks to the **Old Ferry Landing,** 1201 First Street at B Avenue, with its Victorian-style white buildings with red roofs. This lively shopping-dining complex and fishing/ferry pier has a grassy park and a small swimming beach fronting along San Diego Bay. Sailboats crisscross the water; there's a great view of the downtown San Diego skyline, as well as of the sweeping Coronado Bay Bridge.

But the best part is watching the passenger ferry arrive at the pier hourly from San Diego. Before the Coronado Bay Bridge was built in 1969, Coronado could be reached only by ferry. The service was discontinued for almost twenty years, but now the popular ferry again carries pedestrians and bikes across the bay.

Drive back to San Diego over the 2-mile-long Coronado Bay Bridge; go north on I–5 to **Seaport Village,** 849 West Harbor Drive at Kettner Boulevard (619–235–4014).

Lunch: **Harbor House,** 831 West Harbor Drive, Seaport Village, on the boardwalk. (619) 232–1141. Along with its stunning harbor view, the Harbor House is noted for mesquite grilled seafood, fresh salads, prime ribs, and steaks. The Topside Gallery lounge offers cocktails and lighter fare.

Afternoon

Enjoy Seaport Village's old-style harbor setting, with a Victorian clock tower and a lighthouse. Cobbled landscaped walks lead around restaurants; shoppers are in heaven with about sixty-five stores to browse for gourmet cookware, Scandinavian imports, and souvenirs. Saddle up on the antique carousel, then stroll the wooden boardwalk along the water.

See the highlights of San Diego aboard **Old Town Trolley Tours,** which include Seaport Village among its ten different stops, for a stimulating, informative, 90-minute city tour encompassing Balboa Park, the zoo, Old Town, and Coronado. You can get off at any place of interest, then reboard another trolley to complete your tour. Knowledgeable drivers sprinkle entertaining commentary with anecdotes, chitchat, and history. Clint Eastwood made his day in *Dirty Harry* at

Seaport Village; Wyatt Earp lived in the Gaslamp Quarter in 1850 and owned the most popular bordello in the West. You note where Charles Lindbergh stayed while his plane *The Spirit of St. Louis* was being built nearby. (Fee; daily tours). (619) 298–8687.

Take Harbor Drive to the Embarcadero at the Cruise Ship Terminal, where the **Maritime Museum**'s trio of historic ships are permanently anchored along the waterfront. The magnificent tallship windjammer *Star of India,* built in 1863, is the oldest iron-hulled merchant ship afloat. Alongside are the 1890 steam ferryboat *Berkeley* and the 1904 steam yacht *Medea.*

Downtown's dynamic **Horton Plaza** dominates a 7-block stretch between Broadway and G Street. This shopping-dining hub houses 4 department stores and some 150 shops, as well as restaurants, theaters, and a multilingual International Visitors Information Center. The **Paladion,** 777 Front Street, dubbed the Rodeo Drive of San Diego, is an enclave of such prestigious designer names as Gucci, Cartier, Tiffany, and Ferragamo.

You're within a few blocks of the historic and lively **Gaslamp Quarter,** bounded by Broadway to Harbor Drive, Fourth Avenue to Sixth. This historic district dates back to the end of the Civil War. After a neglected period it has been restored—its Victorian 1880 buildings now house trendy shops and ethnic restaurants, galleries, and bistros, and is one of the most popular areas in the city. Come for lunch or dinner and stay to hear the jazz the quarter is noted for. Along Fifth Avenue the 700 and 800 blocks appear to have more attractive restaurants. Parking is a problem, though many have valet parking, and the one-way streets make it difficult for hungry visitors.

Dinner: **Panevino Ostario,** 732 Fifth Avenue, San Diego. (619) 598–7959. It's new in the Gaslamp Quarter, small and inviting, with a warm decor of brick walls and small, granite-topped tables. Veal specialties, ravioli, rigatoni. Delicious bread is served with your salad, and you can watch the chef bake your pizza in the small brick oven.

Lodging: Le Meridien San Diego at Coronado.

Day 3

Morning

Breakfast: **Bay Beach Cafe,** at the Old Ferry Landing, Coronado. (619) 435–4900. Just north of your hotel. Dine indoors or enjoy the balmy breeze on the cheery deck overlooking San Diego Bay as sailboats drift past your morning coffee or mimosa. Egg specialties are served with potatoes or refried beans.

Leave for **Old Town.** Cross Coronado Bay Bridge, take I–5 north to the Old Town Avenue exit, turn right, follow the signs, and turn left on San Diego Avenue. As you cross the bridge, the air is so clear you can see far across to the mountains framing the city.

San Diego began in Old Town in 1769, when Father Junípero Serra established California's first mission, Mission de San Diego de Alcala, and the Presidio, a military installation on a hilltop overlooking San Diego Bay. Soldiers' families and early settlers gradually moved down to the flatland, and the old pueblo is the 6-block area of Old Town. The **old central plaza** along San Diego Avenue, the main street, is lined with restaurants, shops, and history. Along here are several cafes, including the Old Town Mexican Cafe, where you can watch the tortilla ladies in the window making fresh tortillas, patting them between their hands. Shopping variety includes Mexican Imports and Apache Indian Art. Free walking tours of Old Town are given daily at 2:00 P.M. from the Old Town State Park Information Center, 4002 Wallace Street.

Around the corner, **Heritage Park** is a delightful cluster of multistory, restored Victorian-era mansions of bright colors, ivory white trim, cupolas, balconies, verandas, and old-fashioned gardens. They house antiques and dolls and offer romantic overnighting at Heritage Park Bed and Breakfast (619–299–6832). From here turn right on Twiggs and left on Juan Street in Old Town to reach Bazaar del Mundo.

Lunch: **Casa De Bandini.** (619) 297–8211. 2660 Calhoun Street, Old Town San Diego. Dine in the courtyard of Juan Bandini's restored 1823 adobe mansion, a State Historic Site. Relax beneath a shady umbrella as you sip a cool margarita in this pretty place near a splashing fountain. Gourmet Mexican and seafood specialties.

Afternoon

Bazaar del Mundo, next door at 2754 Calhoun Street, is a festive dining-shopping garden marketplace of sixteen international shops for handcrafted gifts, Guatemalan fashions, jewelry, pottery, and folk art. Other restaurants here are Casa de Pico, Lino's Italian Cuisine, and Hamburguesa for Mexican/American specialties. Shops are open daily from 10:00 A.M. to 9:00 P.M. (619) 296–3161.

To get to **Sea World,** take I-5 north to the Sea World Drive exit and turn left. The 150-acre marine park is located on Mission Bay. Plan to stay several hours to see the six major shows staged during the day, featuring performing killer whales, seals, otters, sea lions, dolphins, and penguins. Shamu, the three-ton terpsichorean killer whale, is the pride of Sea World. Read your guide map and review the show schedule so you'll know which way to go in this spread-out park. Between showtimes you can visit twenty marine animal exhibits and three aquariums.

Spend the rest of the day in Sea World. Browse the pleasant shops, snack in the cafes, and cool off with ice cream or frozen yogurt. (Open daily, 9:00 A.M. to dusk and to 11:00 P.M. in summer; admission; free parking; 714–939–6212 or 619–226–3901.)

There's More

San Diego Harbor Excursions, 1050 North Harbor Drive at Broadway, San Diego. (800) 442–7847; (619) 234–4111. Take in a one- or two-hour narrated cruise of San Diego Bay; food and drink aboard. Fee.

Cabrillo National Monument and Visitor Center, on the tip of Point Loma, San Diego. (619) 557–5450. The statue of Juan Rodriguez Cabrillo commemorates his 1542 discovery of California. The old Point Loma lighthouse provides an unbeatable panoramic view out to sea and is a prime spot for whale-watching.

Mission San Diego De Alcala, 10818 San Diego Mission Road, San Diego. (619) 281–8449. The first of California's twenty-one Franciscan missions, established by Father Junípero Serra on Presidio Hill in 1769. The mission houses Father Serra's original records and an ecclesiastical art museum. Self-guided tour; services daily; admission.

San Diego Trolley, Santa Fe Depot, Broadway and Kettner Boulevard, San Diego. (619) 231–8549 or 233–3004. The red trolley takes you on a 16-mile trip from downtown to the Mexican border. Every quarter-hour daily, from 5:00 A.M. to 1:00 A.M.; $1.50 each way.

San Diego Factory Outlet Center at the International Border, 4498 Camino de la Plaza, San Ysidro. (619) 690–2999. Well-known manufacturers offer factory outlet prices in designer clothing, housewares, toys, shoes, leather goods, and more. Open daily. Exit I–5 at "Last U.S. Exit" and turn right; proceed 1 block.

Spreckels Park, Orange Avenue between Sixth and Seventh streets, Coronado. Donated by John D. Spreckels, a charming park, with children's playground and nostalgic bandstand for Sunday-evening summer concerts.

Tidelands Park. Twenty-two acres of shoreline below the Coronado Bay Bridge in Coronado. A lively spot to swim, picnic, walk, and bicycle; children's playground.

Art-in-the-Park. Where local artists display work in Spreckels Park, Coronado, the first and third Sunday of the month, from 10:00 A.M. to 4:00 P.M.

Farmer's Market, Old Ferry Landing, First and B Street, Coronado. Open Tuesdays, 2:30 to 6:00 P.M.; fresh fruits and vegetables.

Trolley. Wednesday through Sunday, leaves on the half-hour from

Old Ferry Landing and runs through Coronado, including stops at the major hotels. Fee.

Special Events

Mid-January to mid-May. San Diego Opera Season.
Mid-March. Annual St. Patrick's Day Parade, San Diego.
Early April. Annual San Diego Crew Classic.
Early April through early October. San Diego Padres baseball season home games, Jack Murphy Stadium. (619) 283–4494.
Mid-April. Annual Coronado Flower and Garden Show.
Early May. Annual Cinco De Mayo Festival, Old Town San Diego State Park.
Early June. Annual Greek Festival, the Miss California Pageant, (619) 497–0430, San Diego.
Late June. San Diego International Triathlon. (619) 233–8797.
July 4. Annual Coronado Independence Day Celebration.
Mid-July. Bastille Day Celebration, Balboa Park, San Diego.
Mid-August. Annual World Body Surfing Championships, Oceanside.
Early September. Annual National Bodyboard Championship Pro Am Invitational, Oceanside.
September 6 through December 13. San Diego Chargers football home games. (619) 563–8281.
Mid-September. Annual Greek Festival, Annual All-Star Basketball Classic, San Diego.
September 18 through May 15. California Ballet Season, San Diego.
Late September to early October. Metropolitan Tennis Championships, San Diego.
Early October. Oktoberfest, Zoo Founders Day, free day at the zoo, 9:00 A.M. to 4:00 P.M., San Diego.
Mid-October. Annual Columbus Day Parade, Festa Bella Italian Festival, San Diego.
Mid-November. Annual San Diego International Boat Show.
End of November. Annual San Diego Thanksgiving Dixieland Jazz Festival.
Early December. Coronado Christmas Open House and Parade. Annual Christmas on the Prado, Balboa Park, San Diego.
Mid-December. Annual San Diego Harbor Parade of Lights.
December 15 through February. Whale-watching, Point Loma, San Diego.

San Diego/Coronado   49

Other Recommended
Restaurants and Lodgings

Gaslamp Quarter

La Strada, 701 Fifth Avenue. (619) 239–3400. Chic trattoria, large room, white tablecloths, open kitchen to pizza oven and grill, northern Italian cuisine.

Fio's, 801 Fifth Avenue, on corner. (619) 234–FIOS. Local favorite, sleek and sophisticated. Northern Italian cuisine, homemade pastas, wood-burning pizza oven, calzone, grilled chicken, meats. Valet parking.

Croce's Restaurant and Jazz Bar, 802 Fifth Avenue at F Street. (619) 233–4355. American southwestern and American-international cuisine.

The Horton Grand Hotel, 311 Island Avenue. (800) 542–1886; (619) 544–1886. Belle of the lively Gaslamp Quarter. Guests favor the cozy intimacy of this renovated, 1886 Victorian hotel. All 132 rooms, including 25 suites, have antique decor, cozy fireplaces, and TV (but rather small bathrooms). Suites feature microwave ovens, wetbar, two TVs. Restaurant, lounge, bar, afternoon tea, evening jazz. Overnight parking fee.

Downtown

California Cafe Bar and Grill, 502 Horton Plaza. (619) 238–5440. Great view over the harbor from the top of Horton Plaza. California cuisine, nightly piano entertainment, Sunday brunch.

Coronado

Peohe's Old Ferry Landing, 1201 First Street. (619) 437–4474. Dine on deck or inside beneath the skylight and amid indoor waterfalls and palm trees. Pricey menu features New York steak, grilled citrus scallops, rack of lamb. Sunday brunch.

Hotel Del Coronado, 1500 Orange Avenue. (619) 522–8000. Landmark 1888 Victorian charmer, with distinctive red, cone-shaped roof, as well as dormer windows, turrets, and cupolas. Sprawled along thirty-three beachfront acres; 690 rooms with TV, minibar, some with hair dryers and balconies. Beautiful gardens, two heated swimming pools, spas, six lighted tennis courts. Four restaurants and a deli. Overnight parking fee.

For More Information

San Diego Convention and Visitors Bureau, 1200 Third Avenue, Suite 824, San Diego, CA 92101–4190. (619) 232–3101.

Old Town Chamber of Commerce, 3965 Artista, San Diego, CA 92110. (619) 291–4903.

Tijuana/Ensenada

Mariachis serenade diners in Ensenada.

South of the Border Serenade

———————————— 3 NIGHTS ————————————

Duty-free shopping • Authentic Mexican cuisine
Beaches • Winery • Mariachis • Fishing • Discos

This three-night, four-day adventure south of the border from San Diego to sunny, friendly Mexico affords an interesting change in culture, language, currency, food, drink, and scenery. You don't have to take a plane to get to a foreign country, when Mexico is within a few hours' drive of Los Angeles. U.S. citizens do not need a passport for this short visit to Baja, California, a duty-free zone. In teeming Tijuana, the internationally famous U.S.-Mexican border town, and in Ensenada, a smaller resort town 70 miles farther south, you experience a different life-style as you are serenaded by mariachis; shop for bargains in perfume, cosmetics, and Mexican-made liquor, jewelry, pottery, and other imports; and tour a 104-year-old winery. (*Note:* Each person may bring back $400 worth of purchases; adults may each bring back one quart of alcohol.)

These aren't two sleepy, dusty little Mexican villages. Tijuana is a gaudy, vibrant jumble of noise, traffic, and people. Ensenada, though more laid-back, is a vital, upbeat, friendly port that never wants to sleep.

For a more enjoyable Mexican sojourn, bring along a gallon of drinking water to have on hand. The best way to avoid stomach upsets or traveler's diarrhea is to not drink the tap water. Stick to sealed bottles or cans of beer or soda. (Mexican beers are great.) Drink them right out of the bottle. Never use ice in your drinks. Avoid salads, raw fish, raw meat, and raw vegetables; eat only fruits you can peel. Coffee and tea are safe when made with boiled water. Brush your teeth with mouthwash or bottled water. Tuck some Pepto-Bismol, Lomotil, and/or Imodium in your travel med-kit in the event of any stomach upsets.

Tank up before you cross the border into Mexico. Be certain to purchase Mexican auto insurance, as your U.S. insurance does not cover you for liability or property damage in Mexico.

Day 1

Morning

From Los Angeles drive south on I–5, the Santa Ana Freeway, to San Diego—about 120 miles—and then drive 15 to 20 miles farther to cross the Mexican border, skirting Tijuana now and visiting it on your return from Ensenada, when you can allow whatever amount of time you'd like to spend there. Ensenada can be reached via a free road and also a toll (*cuota*) road. This escape is via the well-maintained, less crowded toll road from Tijuana.

On I–5 south just past Carlsbad, take the Encinitas Boulevard exit to have lunch in this city, an easy freeway exit and return.

Lunch: **Hungry Hunter,** 305 Encinitas Boulevard, Encinitas. (619) 753–8870. Half-hidden by a Texaco station at the edge of a large, unobtrusive shopping center, this enjoyable restaurant is where they create a delicious salad bar at your table, and then you go on to well-prepared sandwiches or steaks. Alternatively, **Allie's** next door offers an inexpensive buffet brunch feast with an extensive variety of delicious hot and cold dishes.

Afternoon

Return to I–5 and continue south through San Diego and to the Mexican border. They wave you right through, but on your return to the United States you must stop for customs inspection, though not every car is inspected. Be prepared for a long wait at that time. Congestion at the border can take more than two hours during the week and longer on weekends and holidays. Try to avoid crossing the border at those times. Although it is not mandatory, you should purchase Mexican auto insurance, since your U.S. insurance does not cover you for liability and property damage in Mexico. You can obtain it through your auto club in advance of your trip or on both sides of the border. It is easiest to buy it on the U.S. side. You'll see many signs along the way; most are near fast-food eateries and convenient to the freeway. Have your auto registration slip in hand, since if you have to trot back to the car for it, you'll lose your place in line. This insurance typically costs about $10 a day for a three-day visit.

At the border leaving the United States, you want to be in the Rosarito/Ensenada lane; stay to the right. You also want the *cuota* (toll) road. If at any time you need to verify directions, do so at the tool booth as you pay your $2.30 for each toll (three times each way). Ask your question quickly, before you pay, as they hustle you right through.

Speed limits and distances are posted in kilometers and easy to convert into miles. Just multiply the kilometers by six and move the decimal point over one space. Watch all road signs carefully for directions or you may wind up in Mexicali or Tecate.

The scenic, well-kept transpeninsular highway curving along the blue-green ocean skims above sandy, lonesome beaches. There is a turnoff to Rosarito Beach, about 17 miles south of Tijuana. If you want to drive through to see this popular beach city, the road intersects back to the Ensenada toll road. Magnificent vistas accompany you all the way down the coast on this uncrowded highway. You pay your last *cuota* at **Ensenada,** 7 miles from town, as you catch a glimpse of beautiful Bahia de Todos Santos (Bay of All Saints).

Check into your hotel to get your bearings, then go on out to explore downtown Ensenada. When driving, you'll soon note that not all streets have names, but some are identified at the big intersections on the horizontal light bars in the center of the street. Remember that Avenida Lopez Mateos is First Street, and Ruiz Street and Castillo are the north and south downtown boundaries. Boulevard Costero, also known as Lazaro Cardenas, is the divided highway along the ocean.

Ensenada's vitality is contagious, marked by the town's liveliness, its friendly, hospitable people, and its endless shopping and dining attractions. Stores and restaurants all accept U.S. dollars. (*Note:* An easy way to figure the peso is to divide the peso by three for an approximate amount and add a bit.) There is a good deal of traffic and not too many parking spaces, so you might prefer wandering about on foot along Avenida Lopez Mateos, the city's main drag.

Dinner: **La Casa Del Abulon** Restaurant and Club, at the end of Boulevard Costero, Ensenada. Phone: 6–57–85. (Take Castillo Boulevard west toward the ocean to Costero Boulevard, the divided highway that follows the bay. Turn left on Costero for about 1 mile to the restaurant at the curve of the road; a large sign out front also says IBIS DISCO.) Casa del Abulon, is one of the city's finest dining places; a comfortable room with ocean views, dim lighting, good food, and attentive service. Patrons dress casually, often in shorts and T-shirts. The moderately priced menu highlights baked abalone, fresh Pacific lobster, prime rib, chicken, filet mignon, and Mexican dishes. Treat yourself to a flaming dessert of delicious crepes suzettes, prepared tableside.

Lodging: **Hotel Villa Marina,** Avenida Lopez Mateos and Blancarte Street, Ensenada, Baja California, Mexico (U.S. mailing address: P.O. Box 727, Bonita, CA 91908). 8–33–21. Attractive, five-year-old twelve-story hotel is a convenient downtown landmark; 146 rooms, well-furnished, nice bathroom; some private balconies have bay views. Cable TV, air conditioning, room service, heated swimming pool, Jacuzzi. Shopping gallery; cafeteria coffeeshop and penthouse restaurant; security parking lot.

Day 2

Morning

Breakfast: Full breakfast at the hotel's coffeeshop. Includes hot cakes, eggs American or Mexican style.

Avenida Lopez Mateos is alive with little shops and restaurants, *Farmacias* (pharmacies) and *licores* (liquor) stores, mariachis strolling along with guitars and trumpets, and busy food vendors on the corners. Merchandise is not as inexpensive as it used to be, though prices are said to be lower than those in Tijuana. You'll find good values in ironwood sculpture, pottery, T-shirts, silver jewelry, Mexican handicrafts, and leather apparel. Sidewalk vendors offer windchimes, jewelry, and novelty items. At the corner of Avenida Lopez Mateos and Avenida Ruiz, in **Plaza Hussong**—a new, attractive, multistory shopping center—Galeria de Perez Meillon displays stunning, quite expensive Indian pottery and also less expensive copies. The legendary Hussong's Cantina, at Ruiz 113, is next door. You'll hear the deafening din before you see it. Hussong's is a tacky hangout, here since 1892, that attracts a loud, youngish crowd.

On the opposite corner across Avenida Lopez Mateos, the modern, glass-walled Guess? store shows its signature jeans and jackets. On Ruiz, Dorian's Department Store is a cool, upscale haven for cosmetics, jewelry, and clothing. D'Isis, next door, offers dressy sequin tops for women.

Lunch: **Las Brasas Restaurant (Pollos Rostizado),** Avenida Lopez Mateos 486, between Avenida Gastelum and Avenida Ruiz, Ensenada. 8–11–95. Here's where they roast 220 chickens a day, and from the sidewalk you can watch the golden birds spinning on the rotisserie (sixty at a time). Dine inside or on the sunny patio. One-half roast chicken is served with fries, tortillas, and beans. Other selections include seafood and Mexican specialties. (Closed Tuesdays.)

Afternoon

Ensenada has delicious bread, *bollilos* (rolls), and pastries to snack on or buy to take home and stash in the freezer. Look for the PANADERIA (bakery) sign. Among others are Panaderia La Mexican, on Castillo Street; Panaderia el Nuevo Cristal, just off Benito Juarez at Calle Sexta (Sixth Street), next to the cathedral; and one on Ruiz, near Hussong's.

Tour **Bodegas de Santo Tomas,** Avenida Miramar 666 (8–25–09), Baja California's oldest winery, established in 1888. Take Lopez Mateos to Miramar and turn right, proceeding about 6 blocks to the sprawling winery. Half-hour guided tours wind up with tastings and assorted breads and cheeses. (Open daily at 11:00 A.M., 1:00 P.M. and 3:00 P.M. but closed at all other times; $2.00 per person.)

In this festive, lighthearted city, the better shopping area on Lopez Mateos is from Blancarte around the Marina Hotel Villa to Castillo Street. Sara's elegant, cool shop features cosmetics and Lladro figurines; clothing is downstairs. Farther along, Casa Colande shows chic clothing and jewelry; Originales Larrac offers pottery and clothing; and La Terraza has handsome leather jackets and jewelry. If you tire of walking around, stop and relax over a refreshing cold beer. Fonart, the large government-run store at 1310 Avenida Lopez Mateos, below the arroyo (the dip), is filled with a variety of handicrafts. (Open weekdays from 9:00 A.M. to 2:00 P.M. and from 3:00 to 6:00 P.M.; Saturdays from 10:00 A.M. to 6:00 P.M.; and Sundays from 10:00 A.M. to 4:00 P.M.)

Dinner: **Las Cazuelas restaurant/bar,** Boulevard Costero and Sangines (next to Casa del Abulon), Ensenada. 6–54–60. Drive to Costero Boulevard, turn left, and continue about 1 mile. This is another locals' and visitors' favorite, with excellent cuisine and service that spoils you. Moderately priced menu features Mexican dishes—delicate burritos, shrimp ranchero, *chipotle,* and so on—also prime rib, filet mignon, lobster, fresh seafood, and New York steak. Live rhythmic lounge music enhances your dinner, as will a dessert of peach Melba prepared and flambéed tableside.

Lodging: Villa Marina Hotel.

Day 3

Morning

Breakfast: **Sorrento Restaurant,** on Avenida Lopez Mateos next to the Cortez Motor Hotel, Ensenada. Regular American breakfast fare of bacon-and-eggs can be recharged with *chiliquiles,* hot red sauce, chorizo, and Salsa Ketchup. But the pancakes are delicious—light and fluffy.

After breakfast, browse around this exciting part of downtown. If you're driving, note that parking meters are not in effect on Saturday and Sunday; the green zones are free to park in while shopping in the nearby stores. The busy sidewalks and roads are clean, and along Avenida Lopez Mateos, arcades protect shops and shoppers from the sun. For cold drinks and snacks, Blanco, a large supermarket, is on Gastelum off Lopez Mateos.

Follow Boulevard Lazaro Cardenas along the blue, crescent-shaped bay to Estero Beach, 6 miles south of Ensenada for lunch at tony **Estero Beach Resort.** You'll pass a military base, groves of olive trees, and roadside stores and vendors selling baskets and pottery. Turn right at the sign for Estero Beach and then left to the resort.

Built in 1937, the resort is a sprawling, cushy complex of villas, elegant shops, a restaurant, and a museum. Drive down the long, impressive entrance road lined with tall palm trees and tropical plantings, and park toward the rear near the restaurant.

Lunch: **Las Terrazas Restaurant,** Estero Beach Hotel and Resort, Ensenada. 6–62–30. Dine on the beachfront cafe's charming patio beneath crisp white parasols. Try the shrimp or lobster cocktail or sample other menu specialties of fried chicken, fish, hamburgers, and Mexican dishes.

Afternoon

Walk past the restaurant, villas, and cottages for a glimpse of the ocean and the stunning blue lagoon. Follow the broad terrace that edges the private bay to its curved viewpoint beneath a large thatched umbrella encircled by stone benches. Relax awhile in this idyllic, tropical setting and watch the swimmers in the bay and the small boats in the ocean beyond.

Your next stop is the Museum or **Exhibition Center** to see the outstanding Mexican Cultural Exhibit, an extensive collection of pre-Columbian sculpture and ancient art. Then take time to explore the hotel's two elegant shops offering fine merchandise totally unexpected in this semi-remote beach area.

Bazar Mexicano is a treasure house of a large variety of selective merchandise from all over Mexico, including handicrafts, ironwood sculpture, art objects, hand-embroidered clothing, silver, and jewelry. Most notable is the beautiful hand-painted pottery from Tonala, Tlaquepaque, and elsewhere in Mexico—pitchers, vases, birds, and other designs in soft, luminous colors and glazes. An adjoining room displays more pottery, enormous paper flowers, and other handicrafts beneath a huge skylight. Prices seem good throughout, but you may do better in the roadside shops en route back to Ensenada.

Near the resort entrance, the striking Mayan-style **Import Shop,** framed by huge stone pillars, showcases exquisite and expensive merchandise, including fine crystal, Rolex watches, silver and gold jewelry, designer clothing, and other imports from Brazil, Portugal, Israel, Italy, Sweden, and India, among other countries as well as Mexican glassware. Both shops are open daily from 9:00 A.M. to 6:00 P.M.

On the way back to Ensenada, look for roadside shops offering lower-priced baskets, pottery, and other native handicrafts. Here's the place to employ your bargaining skills. **Galeria Mexicana** has a large selection of well-priced vases and other pottery, and the owner welcomes your patronage. Across the road, **Bazaar de Mexico** offers clothing, jewelry, and pottery. Additionally, several small roadside markets also sell reasonably priced Mexican art, pottery, and clothing. Look for Ramon's sign for *"hielo"* (ice—and cold drinks), where shelves are stacked with pottery at very good prices.

Dinner: **El Rey Sol,** Avenida Lopez Mateos No. 1000 (corner of Blancarte), Ensenada. 8–17–33. Blue awnings highlight this 1947 landmark French restaurant, long considered Ensenada's finest. Rather expensive gourmet entrees include chicken mole, filet mignon, and New York steak. Service can be indifferent, but—ole!—mariachis serenade diners and the steaks are tender.

On your last evening in Ensenada, stroll along effervescent Avenida Lopez Mateos, which has considerably more car traffic at night than during the daytime. The air is balmy, and lilting music filters from the cantinas and from the radios in the uninterrupted lines of cars. The sidewalk is crowded with people out for an evening promenade. It's a very upbeat scene that will leave you with a warm memory of Ensenada.

Lodging: Hotel Villa Marina.

Day 4

Morning

Breakfast: At the hotel.

Leave Ensenada early, taking the toll road north to **Tijuana.** Allow sufficient time to spend in Tijuana, plus a good couple of hours crossing the border back into the United States. It's a magnificent drive on the divided highway that rolls gently between the tawny cliffs and the peaceful ocean.

As you drive into Tijuana, look for **Avenida Revolución,** the well-known main tourist street. You'll know when you've reached it, because of the crush of cars and people; the restaurants, bars, liquor stores, shopping plazas, sidewalk vendors; and the nonstop movement.

Dynamic Tijuana claims that more Americans visit it than any other foreign city, and, like you, they're all looking for somewhere to park. This vibrant town with twenty-two million border crossings annually is a shopper's best friend, offering lower, duty-free prices in French perfume, cosmetics, liquor, designer clothing, and other imports. It's further noted for sizzling nightlife and lively spectator sports, such as jai alai, horse and dog racing, and bullfights.

Exciting, tawdry, and raucous Tijuana gained notoriety and glamour during the 1920s Prohibition era, when excitement-loving, thirsty Hollywood stars flocked to its bars and gambling casinos. The city was expensively renovated in the 1970s—streets were widened, potholes filled, and street vendors deposited in indoor malls and arcades. Tune up your bargaining skills—this is the major league.

Sara's tony store on Avenida Revolución, at Fourth, is known for discounted cosmetics, perfume, crystal, and Lladro figurines. Take the elevator upstairs for designer fashions and ongoing sales. A parking structure is just up Fourth Street.

Trendy Le Drug Store, with a sidewalk cafe at Revolución and Fourth, is a good source for souvenirs and postcards. Near the corner you can have your photo taken astride a festively clad donkey, for a fee. Ever-popular Caesar's Restaurant, at Fourth Street, the originator of the Caesar salad, serves continental cuisine.

Bargain hunters will find outlet stores located in the large new plazas away from the crowded city center. But there are familiar, prestigious names to shop along Avenida Revolución. Note that in all outlet stores you should examine your selections carefully before purchase to be sure they're in new condition. Further, be aware that some designer names may be bogus or rip-offs.

Guess has two attractive outlet stores, one at 540 Avenida Revolución between First and Second streets diagonally across from the Hard Rock Cafe, and another at 1105 Avenida Revolución between Seventh and Eighth streets across from the Jai Alai Palace. Although these stores are fun to browse, they don't seem to offer any substantial bargains as prices are fairly close to those in Los Angeles.

You'll fare better at **Benetton Factory Outlet**'s very large store, which sprawls between Sixth and Seventh streets on Avenida Revolución. Good values can usually be found in its two floors filled with heavily discounted merchandise.

Ralph Lauren Outlet Store in a mini-plaza on Seventh Street between Avenida Revolución, Madero, and Negrete offers low discounts on its popular polo shirts, cologne, neckties, shirts, and men's suits. Look for women's sweaters, cotton knit dresses, and other items at the rear of the shop.

Ellesse Outlet Shop is in the same mini-plaza as Lauren, on Seventh Street between Avenida Revolución, Madero, and Negrete. It features some Calvin Klein merchandise along with other designer labels, though not all may be the real thing.

Lunch: **Hard Rock Cafe,** Avenida Revolución at Second Street. 85–02–06. This addition to the popular chain, with its distinctive signature red car halfway through its roof as in other locations, opened in May 1992. You'll find the typically long lines of patrons waiting for a table, hamburgers and fries, as well as familiar Hard Rock decor and noise.

Afternoon

Go down Revolución to Second Street, turn right, and continue 2 blocks to **Mexitlan,** 8901D, Ocampo, and Second Street. This fun, fascinating theme park opened in August 1991 and features some 150 miniature replicas of Mexico's famous archaeological sites, plus restaurants, shops, and entertainment. (Open Wednesday through Monday from 10:00 A.M. to 8:00 P.M.; admission; free parking; information, 800–834–4939 in California and 619–531–1112 outside California.)

To visit the striking **Tijuana Cultural Center,** at Paseo de los Héroes and Avenida Mina in the Tijuana Rio Zone, turn right on Second Street to Paseo de los Héroes, go around the circle, go back 1 block, and then turn right on Mina. Easily recognized by its monumental dome and powerful architecture, the center houses Omnimax theater films, exhibit halls, a performing arts theater, a restaurant, and shops. (Open daily except Monday from 10:00 A.M. to 8:00 P.M.)

Across the street, modern **Plaza Rio's shopping mall** has a diversity of restaurants, department and specialty stores, a supermarket, and the popular Suzett Bakery. The unusual **Plaza del Zapata** across the way features only shoes, of all types, from many outlets.

To get to the San Ysidro border, make a right on Paseo de los Héroes and go straight until you see the sign for San Diego, which leads to the crowded border, where you'll find about six lanes of cars crossing to the U.S. side. Watch for signs above the individual gateways indicating the lanes for cars with two passengers or carpools of four people, and get in the correct lane. Otherwise, as you near the gate you'll have to edge your way in line ahead of other drivers, who may not be too gracious about letting you get in front of them.

When you've crossed the border, you are on I–5 north. Stay on it until you reach Los Angeles, or cut over to 405.

There's More

The Riviera Del Pacifico, Boulevard Costero, Ensenada. The sprawling building with graceful arches was a famous 1930s plush gambling casino patronized by Hollywood film stars and is now a social and cultural center. Enjoy a drink to yesteryear on Patio Bugambilia and stroll the lushly landscaped grounds.

La Bufadora, Ensenada's most famous attraction, is 20 miles south to the tip of Punta Banda Peninsula. At this dramatic and natural "blowhole" carved into the cliffs, when the tides are high the ocean crashing into the rocks spouts a geyser of foam and water almost 100 feet high.

Flea markets and swap meets, Ensenada. **Los Globos** is the largest, outdoors on Calle 9, 3 blocks east of Reforma. Open daily; weekends are better. Additional outdoor weekend swap meet at Riveroll and Calle 6.

Chapultepec Hills, Ensenada. Drive north on Calle 2 to the residential area for a stunning, panoramic view of Ensenada and the beautiful bay.

Bullfights are a rich part of Mexico's heritage. Tijuana has two major bullrings, downtown at Plaza de Toros, 100 Caliente Boulevard, and at the Bullring-by-the-Sea. Season runs May through September; open Sunday at 4:00 P.M.; closed in June. For specific dates, call (01152–66) 86–15–10.

Jai Alai Palace, Avenida Revolución and Seventh Street, Tijuana. 800–PIK–BAJA. Watch the fastest sport in the world, year-round, Thursday through Tuesday, 7:30 P.M. Admission.

Racetrack. Just south of Paseo de Los Héroes, Tijuana. Agua Caliente racetrack offers year-round thoroughbred horse racing and greyhound racing. Horse races are held Saturday and Sunday at noon; greyhound racing held nightly (except Tuesday) at 7:45 P.M. Admission. The U.S. information and hotline number is (619) 231–1910.

Golf. Tijuana Golf and Country Club on Agua Caliente Boulevard dates back to the 1920s, when young Arnold Palmer teed off here.

Special Events

End January. Annual Caesar Salad Festival, Tijuana.
January, February, and early March. Whale-watching trips, Ensenada.
Mid-February. Hussong's Centenary Fishing Tournament, two days, Ensenada.
Late February to early March. National Surfing Championship. Caribbean Mardi Gras, Ensenada.
Mid-March. Benito Juárez Birthday, Ensenada.
March 25 and 26. Tijuana-Rosarito-Ensenada Bicycle Race, Tijuana.
Early April and late-September. Rosarito-Ensenada Fun Bicycle Ride. Gastronomic Fair, Ensenada.
Early May. Regatta Newport–Ensenada. Mountain Bike Ride. Batalla de Puebla, Ensenada.
Mid-May. Tecate-Ensenada Bike Ride, two days, Ensenada.
Early June. Baja 500 Off-Road Race, three days, Ensenada.
Mid-June. Tecate Mexican Surf Fiesta, two days. Annual International Karate Championship, Ensenada.
Late June to early July. Expo Ensenada, 18 days, Ensenada.
Mid-July. First Half Marathon by Cross Country, Ensenada.
Early August. Regatta Todos Santos, two days, Ensenada.
Mid-August. Seafood Festival, Tijuana.
Mid-to-end August. Fair of the Californias, Tijuana.
Late August. Gran Carrera de Ensenada, two days, Ensenada.
Early September. Congress of Investigation Sea of Cortez, four days, Ensenada.
September 18. Mexican Food Fair, Tijuana.
Mid-September. Independence Day. Ensenada Discovery, Ensenada.
Early October. Southwestern Yacht Regatta, three days. Mountain Bike Ride Sordomudo Ranch, Ensenada.
Mid-October. Chile Cook-Off. October Fest. Cantina Hussong's Centenary, three days. Ensenada Gran Prix, Ensenada.
Late October. Expo Fiesta Viva. Second Cross Country Biathlon and Mountain Bike Ride, Ensenada.
Mid-November. Baja 1000 Off-Road Race Ensenada—La Paz. Revolution Day, Ensenada.
Mid-December. Club Amigos de Ensenada Christmas Parade, Ensenada.
December 16 to 18. The Christmas Posadas, Tijuana.

Other Recommended
Restaurants and Lodgings

Ensenada

La Cueva de Los Tigres (Tigers' Cave). Acapulco Street and Las Palmas Street in Playa Hermosa District. Romantic seaside hideaway 1 mile south of the city. A steady local and tourist favorite for tender abalone, steaks, and shrimp.

Baja Inn Hotel, Boulevard Costero 1536. 7–22–55. Sunday Mexican-American Buffet Brunch includes fresh fruit platter, egg specialties, *chilaquiles*, refried beans, French toast, 7:00 A.M. to 1:00 P.M. Opened in July 1992; 51 nicely furnished rooms, three suites, satellite TV, heated swimming pool, restaurant, bar, underground garage, twenty-four-hour security guard.

Macho's, Boulevard Costero and Macheros. 4–02–68. Moderately priced and popular for grilled steak, seafood, and *carne asada*.

Corona Hotel, Boulevard Costero 1442 (U.S. mailing address, 482 West San Ysidro Boulevard, Suite 303, San Ysidro, CA 92173). 6–09–01. Sweeping, four-story modern hotel; heated swimming pool, lobby bar, room service.

Cortez Motor Hotel (Best Western), Avenida Lopez Mateos 1089. 8–23–07; (800) 528–1284 (reservations). Excellent location, spacious guestrooms and bathrooms, cable TV, heated swimming pool, restaurant, cocktail lounge, underground security parking.

Estero Beach Hotel Resort, P.O. Box 86. (800) 762–2494. Luxury beachfront resort; 107 rooms, cottages, villas, and suites, with private terraces overlooking Estero Bay. Museum, shops, tennis courts, lagoon, restaurant, exclusive RV park.

Tijuana

Hacienda el Abajeno, 79 Sanchez Taboada Boulevard, in the Tijuana Rio Zone. Good menu; variety of excellent Mexican dishes and fresh seafood.

La Lena, 4560 Caliente Boulevard. 86–29–20. Near the golf club. It's busy because everybody goes for the tender, tasty New York and T-bone steaks.

Pedrin's, 1115 Avenida Revolución. 85–36–03. Locals recommend it for the mixed seafood platter.

Fiesta Americana Hotel, 4500 Caliente Boulevard. (800) FIESTA-1. New, sophisticated, modern, twenty-five-story five-star hotel; 422 deluxe rooms and suites. Heated swimming pool, Jacuzzi, tennis courts; three restaurants, bars; conference center.

For More Information

Note: To phone Mexico from the United States, dial 011–52 plus the city prefix number, unless otherwise noted.

Ensenada State Secretary of Tourism, corner Calle las Rocas and Costero Boulevard, Ensenada. 53–667–6–22–22.

Tijuana Tourism and Convention Bureau, Paseo de Los Héroes, 108 (U.S. mailing address, P.O. Box 434523, San Diego, CA 92143–4523). In California, (800) 252–5363; in Tijuana, 52–66–84–05–37 or 38.

Tijuana Information Booth at the San Ysidro border is open daily from 8:00 A.M. to 7:00 P.M. The information booth for pedestrians is one block past the border on the right-hand side.

Tijuana Information Center Downtown, Avenida Revolución and First. 52–66–85–84–72. Open daily from 8:00 A.M. to 8:00 P.M.

USA Office of Information for Baja California (International Marketing/Promotions Assoc. Inc., 7860 Mission Center Court (#202), San Diego, CA 92108. (619) 298–4105; in California, (800) 522–1516; in the United States, (800) 225–2786.

Disneyland/Anaheim/Buena Park

Bigfoot Rapids offers excitement at Knott's Berry Farm.

Amusement Park Heaven

_____ 1 NIGHT _____

Amusement parks · Theme parks · Shopping · Parades

Though Southern California has many superattractions, this light-hearted escape to two world-famous amusement parks is the ultimate in fun, fantasy, and entertainment. Let the years roll back as you soar on a rocket jet, ride roller coasters upside down, watch parades, and amble through a lively Old West mining town. One visit is never enough, especially for children. You and your family will want to return again and again.

Day 1

Morning

From Los Angeles take I–5, the Santa Ana Freeway, south for the short, 27-mile drive to Buena Park for Knott's Berry Farm and down the road to Anaheim for Disneyland. This area is generally slightly warmer than Los Angeles, so you might dress accordingly. Allow about an hour and a half in travel time, depending on traffic.

To reach Knott's Berry Farm, take the Beach Boulevard exit, turn right, and stay on Beach Boulevard, passing the Movieland Wax Museum, Medieval Times, and the Ripley's Believe It or Not Museum. You'll soon see some of Knott's high-flying amusement rides. Stay to the right, drive beneath the large Knott's Berry Farm banner, and pull into the free parking lot on the left.

Knott's Berry Farm, at 8039 Beach Boulevard in Buena Park (714–220–5200), grew from a mom-and-pop roadside berry stand and small farm in the 1920s to a $5-million, roller-coaster-thriller attraction. Knott's Berry Farm is a story with a happy ending that began when Walter Knott started gathering a few abandoned, derelict buildings from deserted western towns and moved them to the farm around 1940, as a diversion for diners waiting in line for his wife Cordelia's fried chicken dinners and delectable boysenberry pie. Ghost Town, a California mining town, gradually took shape as more rustic buildings were added and the theme further embroidered. Other entertainment areas followed. Visitors still stand in line for the fried chicken, and the berry farm is one of Southern California's leading attractions.

Lunch: **Mrs. Knott's Chicken Dinner Restaurant,** Knott's Berry Farm, Buena Park. (714) 220–5080. You may have to wait for a table (they take reservations), but since there are six dining rooms, it shouldn't be long. They serve one and a half million chicken dinners a year, so go with the favorite: Mrs. Knott's Traditional Chicken Dinner, served from 11:00 A.M. A basket of hot buttermilk biscuits is followed by chunky chicken noodle soup or cherry rhubarb appetizer, a mixed green salad, and then the large, thick-crusted, golden pieces of fried chicken with mashed potatoes, country gravy, and vegetable. For dessert it's boysenberry, apple, or peach pie; ice cream, or boysenberry sherbet.

Afternoon

The country's oldest themed park is actively geared to family enjoyment, offering six distinctive entertainment areas: Camp Snoopy, Fiesta

Village, Roaring 20's, Ghost Town, Wild Water Wilderness, and the new Indian Trails. Each features its own restaurants, specialty shops, exciting rides, shows, and other attractions.

Pick up a map at the entrance to help guide you through the 150-acre park and to check the daily showtime schedule. Go to the right for **Camp Snoopy,** a special wonderland and petting farm for small children. Then work your way around the park. In **Fiesta Village,** with its bright Marketplace and mariachis, zoom on Montezooma's Revenge, a thrilling upside-down-and-backward ride. In the **Roaring 20's,** the high-speed Boomerang roller coaster turns you upside down six times in a minute. If you crave more excitement, strap yourself into the Parachute Sky Jump. Before you can say "Geronimo," you're in a daring, twenty-story parachute fall.

Move on to **Ghost Town,** where lively country music fills the air and rural Main Street, with its covered wagons, Old West saloon, and blacksmith-at-the-forge, evokes a sense of history. Browse for knickknacks at the General Store. Tall, leafy eucalyptus trees provide generous shade, and masses of bright flowers soften the one-hundred-year-old weathered wooden buildings, with their wide verandas and sagging doorways, moved here from forgotten towns. Though there may be hundreds of people about, somehow you don't feel crowded in this low-key, comfortable ambience.

Just beyond Ghost Town, **Indian Trails** explores the heritage of American Indians from four geographic areas. Artisans from each region demonstrate handcrafts, including canoe carving, mask and totem pole making, beadwork, weaving, and pottery. While storytellers spin legends, kids can have their faces painted. The Native American food is good here, particularly the Indian fry bread and the Navajo tacos.

It's wise to visit **Wild Water Wilderness** last, as you do get wet in this turn-of-the-century California river wilderness park. The highspot is Bigfoot Rapids, a wet and wild ride where passengers are bounced and splashed as they ride down a long, turbulent, man-made river, spinning in fast-moving currents and shooting under waterfalls. (Hours: Memorial Day weekend to Labor Day weekend, open Sunday through Thursday from 9:00 A.M. to 11:00 P.M. and Friday and Saturday to midnight; Labor Day weekend to Memorial Day weekend, open weekdays from 10:00 A.M. to 6:00 P.M., Saturday to 10:00 P.M., and Sunday to 7:00 P.M. Closed Christmas Day; admission; free parking.)

Leave Knott's Berry Farm and drive to Disneyland Park and the Disneyland Hotel, about 10 miles away. The easiest route to the Disneyland Hotel is to get back on I–5 south and take the Ball Road exit. Turn right to West Street, then turn left; the Disneyland Hotel is on the right, at the corner of Cerritos and West (check-in is after 3:00 P.M.). Stop in the main lobby to purchase your tickets/passports to Disneyland and then board the tram, which drops you at the Main Gate, or ride the monorail, which deposits you in Tomorrowland. Both go round-trip all day until the park closes.

Disneyland is the most popular attraction in the world—a must-see, ever since it opened in 1955, for statesmen, royalty, celebrities, and just about everyone else who visits or resides in Southern California. It offers more than sixty adventures in eight different themed lands. Wandering through its eighty acres is not just another stroll in the park; in *this* park you take your imagination along to visit Tomorrowland, Fantasyland, Adventureland, Critter Country, Frontierland, New Orleans Square, Mickey's Toontown, and Main Street U.S.A., a nostalgic prototype of a circa-1900 small town, where the streetlamps are 150 years old.

The folks at Disneyland recommend that no matter the season, the best times to see the most popular attractions are before noon and after dinner. Restaurants are busiest at lunch and dinner hours—same as at home—so try to eat early or late. You'll also find weekdays less crowded than Saturday and Sunday.

Enter the park and receive your free *Disneyland Today* schedule of daily entertainment. Pick up a free guidebook as well, which has a handy map showing attractions plus dining and shopping in each area. Board a double-decker minibus or a horse-drawn trolley or else stroll up Main Street to romantic Sleeping Beauty Castle, the entrance to **Fantasyland.** As you cross the drawbridge over the moat where swans glide elegantly, keep looking for Mickey and Minnie Mouse, Goofy, Pluto, and Chip 'n' Dale, Disneyland's official greeters, who love to have their picture taken with visitors.

Along Main Street stop at the inviting plaza, with benches, flowers, and trees, to relax, people-watch, and listen to the ragtime pianist expertly playing old tunes in toe-tapping rhythm. You'll find musicians throughout the park, playing various instruments to entertain visitors.

There's certainly no place like Disneyland—big, sunny, clean, and busy, where people of all ages amble in different directions to browse, eat, shop, snack, board another ride, and greet a new adventure. There's happy music, flowers, and lots of smiling children. If you find lines too long at your favorite ride, you can soon find another and return later. Listen and watch for the parade of elaborate floats down Main Street, with Mickey and other Disney figures singing and swaying to rollicking music.

Dinner: At Disneyland Park, Anaheim. There are satisfying, healthful eating places throughout the park. Consult your guidebook if you don't spot someplace you'd like to try. At Cafe Orleans in New Orleans Square the dinner menu features beef Bourguignonne, Seafood Parisienne served over rice, or spicy chicken with pasta.

Lodging: **Disneyland Hotel,** 1150 West Cerritos Avenue, Anaheim, CA 92802. (714) 788–6600 or (213) 636–3251; (800) 647–7900 or (714) 956–6400 (reservations). Newly refurbished, this sixty-acre, tropical garden resort features 1,131 rooms, 62 suites, and 2 concierge floors. Color TV has closed-circuit channel and free Disney Channel. Snack/beverage bar in room. Three heated swimming pools, Jacuzzi, marina playground, sandy beach, ten lighted tennis courts. Eleven restaurants and lounges. Shops, nightly entertainment, family video game center. Complimentary monorail and tram service to Disneyland Park; overnight parking fee. Seasonal one- and two-night packages include Disneyland Passports and hotel parking.

Day 2

Morning

Breakfast: In hotel, at **Goofy's Kitchen.** Children enjoy meeting Minnie Mouse, Goofy, and other Disney favorites who visit at tables. All-You-Can-Eat Buffet features waffles, egg specialties, cereals, and fruits. Kids receive a special memento.

Take the tram or the futuristic monorail back to Disneyland Park to enjoy a full day of fun and adventure. Just past the entrance, walk up the wide staircase to ride the **Disneyland Railroad,** pulled by a genuine steam locomotive. The train visits all the different lands in a restful, fifteen-minute narrated ride during which you can see the cars ahead as you round a curve and hear the nostalgic train whistle. You can get off at any stop or stay aboard until you're back at your station.

Lunch: **Plaza Inn on Main Street,** Disneyland Park, Anaheim. This busy buffeteria has a Victorian decor of pink umbrellas and white furniture. Attractive, wholesome-looking foods include baked chicken, spaghetti, salads, and meat-and-cheese sandwiches with pasta salad; children's menu. It's pleasantly cool inside, but you can also tote your tray out to the terrace.

Afternoon

Spend the rest of the day and evening or as long as you like visiting other themed areas. Ride the **Matterhorn** bobsled that zips in and around the tall mountain in a fast roller-coaster ride. Tuck into **It's a Small World,** a delightful child-oriented ride, and sail around a glitzy ornamental world while festively costumed figures sing a happy tune. Embark on **Star Tours,** a thrilling, flight-simulated spaceship journey into space.

During summer evenings the perennial **Main Street Electrical Pa-**

rade is worth waiting for. The musical procession of floats is outlined in twinkling lights and followed with fireworks accompanied by rousing music. After dark go to Frontierland, to experience **Fantasmic,** Mickey Mouse's imaginative new musical spectacular of fire-breathing dragons, laser storms, heroes, and villains.

From mid-June to mid-September, the park is open daily from 8:00 A.M. to 1:00 A.M. From mid-September to mid-June, hours are Monday through Friday, 10:00 A.M. to 6:00 P.M., Saturday and Sunday, 9:00 A.M. to midnight. Special holiday hours are offered; to verify them, call (714) 999–4565. Passport/ticket admission includes unlimited use of the attractions (except Arcades); one-, two-, and three-day Passports are available as are seniors, annual, seasonal, and summer passports. There is a parking fee.

Return to Los Angeles via I–5 north.

There's More

Medieval Times Dinner and Tournament, 7662 Beach Boulevard, Buena Park. (714) 521–4740; (800) 899–8600 (nationwide). Enjoy a hearty, four-course feast in a huge (1,134-seat), indoor ceremonial arena of an eleventh-century-style castle. Dine while watching a lively two-hour pageant of knights in colorful raiment astride costumed horses competing in daring equestrian tournaments, sword fights, and jousting. Dinner, served by friendly "serfs" and "wenches," begins with a fruit wine cocktail and appetizers. No silverware was used in A.D. 1539 so drink your tasty vegetable soup from its small metal bowl and tear your hot and tasty whole roast chicken, spare ribs, and potato apart with your fingers, just like Henry VIII. Dinner includes two rounds of beer, a wine cocktail, or soft drinks, as well as a pastry dessert and coffee. There's lots of encouraging shouts and cheers for favorite knights as they gallop heroically through the arena. Performances seven nights; matinees Saturday and Sunday. Phone for showtimes; reservations are required. Free parking; ask your hotel about bus service.

Movieland Wax Museum, 7711 Beach Boulevard, Buena Park. (714) 522–1134. One block north of Knott's Berry Farm. Everyone wants to see movie stars, and after a visit here you can brag about seeing plenty of Hollywood favorites, along with more than 270 other celebrity wax figures wearing movie costumes in authentic soundstage sets. Take a two-hour self-guided tour through the dimly lighted, mirrored corridors, where you'll hear recorded music and voices of some of the stars: Mae West singing in a sequinned gown, W. C. Fields telling stories. Clint Eastwood emerges from a saloon, gun in hand.

Judy Garland, in *Wizard of Oz* costume, is flanked by the Tin Man and Scarecrow. Nearly every famous movie star is here, portrayed life-size with realistic facial likeness. Open daily, including holidays (in summer from 9:00 A.M. to 9:30 P.M. and in winter from 10:00 A.M.). Box office closes one-and-a-half hours earlier. Admission. Combination tickets available for Ripley's Believe It or Not Museum across the street.

Ripley's Believe It or Not Museum, 7850 Beach Boulevard, Buena Park. (714) 522–7045. One block north of Knott's Berry Farm, across from the Movieland Wax Museum, you'll see an amazing, entertaining collection of curiosities that are true, strange, and bizarre, from Ubangi women whose lips are pierced to have saucers inserted to a Chinese shrunken head about the size of a lemon. These and many other oddities displayed in glass showcases were accumulated by Robert Ripley, TV and radio pioneer and syndicated newspaper columnist, during his world travels.

Anaheim Stadium, 2000 State College Boulevard, Anaheim. (714) 937–6750. This 70,000 seat stadium hosts events year-round. Two miles east of Disneyland, the stadium is home to two professional sports teams.

Baseball: The California Angels season runs from April through September. Tickets are usually available before each game. (714) 634–2000.

Football: The Rams play professional football August through November. Includes eleven home games, three in preseason. (714) 937–6767.

Golf. H. G. "Dad" Miller, 430 North Gilbert Street, Anaheim. (714) 774–8055. Eighteen-hole public course with natural lake. Night-lighted driving range, restaurant, cocktail lounge. Reservations recommended.

Miniature Golf. Golf 'n' Stuff, 1656 South Harbor Boulevard, Anaheim. (714) 778–4100; (213) 868–9956. Across from Disneyland, two 18-hole miniature golf courses with an arcade center. Open daily. Birthday groups and family rates.

Special Events

Early April. Freeway Baseball Series, Anaheim Stadium, Anaheim. (714) 634–2000. California Angels Baseball Opening Day, Anaheim Stadium.

June to September 8. Disneyland opens summer season with Main Street Electrical Parade and Fantasy in the Sky, Anaheim.

August. Rams Football, Anaheim Stadium, Anaheim. (714) 937–6767. Third Annual Disneyland Pigskin Classic preseason college football. (714) 999–4445; (213) 626–8605.

Early August to early September. Camp Snoopy Days, Knott's Berry Farm, Buena Park.

Mid-August. Thirty-eighth Annual Southern California Home and Garden Show, Anaheim Convention Center, Anaheim. (714) 978–8888.

October 9–10, 16–17, 23–25, and 29–31. Halloween Haunt, Knott's Berry Farm, Buena Park.

Late October. Orange County Fall Festival and Anaheim Halloween Parade, downtown Anaheim. (714) 999–5191.

November 26. Thanksgiving Day, New Year's Week, Very Merry Christmas Parade, Disneyland, Anaheim. (714) 999–4565.

Late November. Anaheim Harvest Festival, Anaheim Convention Center, Anaheim. (800) 321–1213.

Late November to December 24. Knott's Berry Farm Christmas Crafts Festival, Buena Park. (714) 827–1776.

December. Freedom Bowl, Anaheim Stadium, Anaheim. Ninth-year college football game, Anaheim Stadium. (714) 634–1984.

Note: Dates are subject to change. For timely information, call the Visitor Information Line at (714) 635–8900.

Other Recommended Restaurants and Lodgings

Anaheim

The Anaheim Hilton and Towers, 777 Convention Way. (714) 750–4321; (800)–Hiltons; (800) 233–6094 (in California). Has 1,600 deluxe guestrooms and 100 suites, cable TV, three rooftop recreation gardens, sundecks, heated swimming pool, four spas, pool bar, 25,000-foot sports and fitness center with pool and basketball court, golf center, pitching range, putting green. Concierge service. Post office. Eleven restaurants and lounges. Free shuttle to Disneyland Park all day until closing. Various packages. Overnight parking fee.

Anaheim Marriott, 700 West Convention Way, Anaheim. (714) 750–8000; (800) 228–9290 (reservations). Has 1,039 guestrooms, including 72 suites, 2 concierge levels. AM/FM radio, cable TV, in-room pay movies. Heated indoor and outdoor swimming pools, two hydrotherapy pools, fitness facility and sunning decks, video game room. Giftshop, two restaurants, two lounges. Complimentary trolley to and from Disneyland Park. Family vacation and other packages. Overnight parking fee.

For More Information

Anaheim Area Visitor and Convention Bureau, 800 West Katella Avenue, Anaheim, CA 92802. (714) 999–8999.

Visitor Information Line. (714) 635–8900.

Anaheim Convention Center, 800 W. Katella Avenue, P.O. Box 4270, Anaheim, CA 92803. (714) 999–8963; (800) 321–1213.

Temecula and Wineries

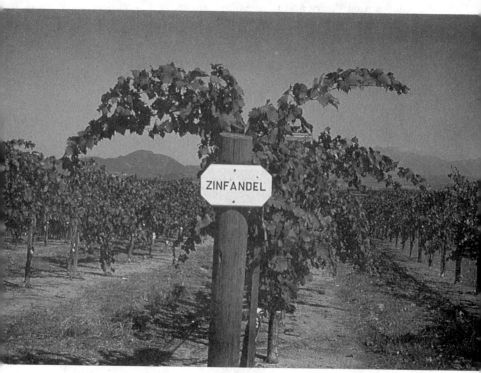

Vineyards flourish in fertile Temecula Valley.

The Old West and The Wine Road

_____ 2 NIGHTS _____

Antiques · Dining · Museum · Golf
Resort · Wineries · History · Tennis

In this two-night itinerary you wander through a restored 1890 cowboy town with a colorful past of Indians and the Butterfield Overland Stage; walk through historic buildings and visit a museum filled with mementos of the city's beginnings and Old West life-style; hunt for antiques and collectibles; have lunch in a bank vault; taste-tour nearly a dozen wineries and learn the romance of the grape; play golf and tennis; and spend the night in a casual/luxe resort.

Day 1

Morning

From Los Angeles take I–5 south to Riverside Freeway 91 (before Fullerton). Head east on 91 (past Corona) and pick up I–15 south to **Temecula,** about 90 miles. Take the Rancho California Road exit to Old Town Temecula/Front Street and turn right.

Park your car and then amble down **Front Street,** the main thoroughfare of rambling wooden buildings with thick wood-plank verandas out front. The new buildings are skillfully designed to blend in well with the old 1890s structures. Temecula is curb-to-curb antiques shops and a collector's mecca, with all manner of memorabilia. In addition to many individually run stores, groups of dealers are housed together in various antiques malls. Even if you're not an antiques maven, you will enjoy the stores. Each has something different and appealing to offer and the furniture, in particular, gleams in richly polished woods and is nicely displayed.

Old Town Temecula is a pleasant, relaxing, and happy place to browse; walk around and poke into its shops. The small, 6-block-long area along Front Street and some sidestreets retains its flavor of the Old West between the 1800s and the 1900s. The city is often called Southern California's "New Frontier"; its first inhabitants, the Shoshonean Indian tribe, christened it "Land Where the Sun Shines through the Mist," or Temecula.

Temecula's history began in 1797, when its Indian village was discovered by Father Juan Santiago from San Juan Capistrano, who was looking for a new mission site. Santiago wrote to King Charles IV describing the Indian village. The king named the area Rancho Temecula, and it became one of several Spanish land grants.

In 1845, during the Mexican-American War when the missions were secularized, Rancho Temecula was given to Felix Valdez and the great ranches were divided into smaller parcels with private ownership. This was the beginning of the romantic era of the rancheros and vaqueros of early California.

After the first Butterfield Overland Stage arrived in September 1858 and became a regular stop on the route between St. Louis and San Francisco, new homesteaders began settling in. Mail service began, and in April 1859 the first inland Southern California post office was established in Temecula. The Civil War brought an end to the Butterfield Overland Stage service, and transportation was limited until January 1882, when a rail line was completed from National City to Temecula. As large numbers of people began migrating west, the city's business and population increased, but a series of floods in the late 1880s destroyed the railroad tracks and the old Temecula depot was abandoned.

Temecula dozed until 1904, when Walter Vail came to town and purchased most of the land in the valley (87,500 acres) for Vail Ranch, his cattle empire headquarters. The great cattle drives began, and the city became a focal point for shipping cattle and grain. For the next sixty years, Temecula was a lusty, prosperous cow town with a population of about two hundred and a western life-style of ranchers and cowboys hanging out at the Swing Inn, Long Branch Saloon, and other watering holes. In 1964, when the Los Angeles–San Diego Freeway, I–5, was completed, the Vail Ranch was sold to developers. It was subdivided as a master-planned community and became incorporated as a city in 1989.

With its fertile soil and mild climate, the vast grazing land has been planted in vineyards and in citrus and avocado groves. It's still a noted horse-raising area.

Lunch: **The Bank of Mexican Food,** corner of Front and Main streets, Old Town, Temecula. (714) 676–6160. Built in 1914, it housed the First National Bank of Temecula for thirty years, until it closed in 1941 and became an antiques shop. In 1978 it was refurbished as an authentic home-style Mexican restaurant. Despite the building's rather hideous green exterior color, it's pleasantly cool inside the tall wood-beamed dining room with comfy booths, and the food is good. Menu selections include tostadas, crab enchiladas, burritos, and luncheon specials.

Afternoon

After lunch you can check into your hotel and play a round of golf or stay and browse **Old Town Temecula's shops and antiques stores.** Strolling down Front Street, you'll come to Temecula Market and Bakery and Barbeku, 28693 Front Street, with its wide wooden verandas. Here you can purchase local farmers' fresh produce, buy some baked goods, and snack outside on the veranda facing Front Street and watch the dudes go by.

Farther along are several antiques stores and giftshops; Rocky Mountain House features crystal, American Indian art, and jewelry. The Welty Building, between Third and Main streets, was a former store and saloon built by the Welty family in 1902. It later became the Ramona Inn, then a prizefighters' gym where Sharkey, Dempsey, and other heavies worked out. Now it's an antiques store and deli. More antiques are around each corner and in the malls. ABC Trading Company features bottles and other collectibles; Far East Collection shows Oriental imports; and A to Z Antiques and Country Seller highlights country curtains, antiques, and furniture. The large, impressive Welty Temecula Hotel, on Main Street, was built in 1882 by the Welty family. It is now a private residence.

Across the street, Temecula Mercantile, at 42049 Main Street, is a marvelous place to browse. Built in 1891, it was a general store patronized by local ranchers for sixty years. Now it's a fascinating antiques store to explore for dishes, crystal, furniture, pottery, bric-a-brac merchandise, and jewelry. Most regular customers are collectors; the upstairs room is for special-interest collectibles.

Between Main and Fourth streets, Calico Coffee Company is the place for fine gourmet coffee, candy, aprons, and well-priced wines from local wineries. Old Town Antique Faire houses thirty antiques dealers. Chapparal Antique Mall, at 28645 Front Street, distinguished by a large wooden wagon out front, is a complex of more than seventy dealers, offering pottery, china, folk art, toys, quilts, and many more old-time collectibles.

Stroll both sides of Front Street. The Machados store is another historic site, built by the owner in 1892 as a general store. It later became the local post office, with the owner as postmaster; had a good life as the Long Branch Saloon for many years; and now is a mall of about eighteen antiques dealers.

Stop by the **Temecula Museum,** 41950 Main Street, in the small red-brick building at the north end of town in Sam Hicks Park. Like a visit to great-grandmother's attic, this is a gem to visit, with artifacts dating back to the days of the Indians and old-fashioned household and farm items of the 1800s and early 1900s, collected locally. Wall shelves display interesting turn-of-the-century items, including an old telephone, grand old typewriters and cameras, irons, a treadle sewing machine, buckets, pottery, branding irons, and old saddles. In the center of the room is a large diorama of the town in about 1914; browse through the large scrapbooks of photos of Temecula now and way back then. (Open Wednesday through Sunday from 11:00 A.M. to 4:00 P.M.; donations accepted.) A Visitor Information Center is here too.

Dinner: **Temecula Creek Inn,** 44501 Rainbow Canyon Road, Temecula. (800) 962–7335; (714) 676–5631. Intimate dining room with cathedral ceiling overlooks the golf course. Southwestern cuisine offers variety in appetizers like crab corn cakes, tortillas with smoked salmon or chicken. Grill favorites are steaks, prime ribs, T-bone veal chop with wild rice; wines from local vineyards and elsewhere.

Lodging: **Temecula Creek Inn,** 44501 Rainbow Canyon Road, Temecula, CA 92593. (800) 962–7335; (714) 676–5631. Centered atop

300 acres, eighty-four large, well-furnished rooms in soft colors, each with sitting area and all with fairway views, are tucked into five low-rise lodges. Honor bar, minirefrigerator, coffeemaker, hair dryer, cable TV, compartmented bathroom, two phones; three 9-hole golf courses, putting green, driving range, two tennis courts, heated swimming pool with hydro spa; dining room, lounge with nightly entertainment; conference facilities. Dinners and breakfasts included in two-night golf packages; outstanding Sunday champagne buffet brunch.

Day 2

Morning

Breakfast: At the inn. Full breakfast is included in the golf package and is served in the sunny dining room overlooking green fairways and energetic golfers. Try the scrambled eggs with smoked salmon and toasted bagel with cream cheese or the avocado-and-green-chili burrito with scrambled eggs and salsa covered with melted cheese, served with refried black beans and excellent coffee.

After breakfast golfers will want to get out on any of Temecula Creek Inn's three challenging 9-hole **golf** courses: the Creek, the Oaks, or the Stone House. Wine lovers will want to visit the nearby wineries, about 4 miles east of the city.

Temecula Valley is a prime Southern California wine-growing area. Its soil and climate, in addition to the vintners' skill, produce award-winning wines served in the White House as well as to the Queen of England and the rest of us. **Temecula wine country** was first discovered in the 1840s by the legendary wine master Jean Louis Vignes and was rediscovered in the 1960s. The first vines were planted in 1967.

Obtain a "Wine Country Tour Map" from the hotel. Take I–15 north to first exit and follow the circular wine trail along Rancho California Road (about 4 miles east of the city). Continue past Palomar Village, follow the sign to "Temecula Wine Country" straight ahead, pass a golf course on the left, and you'll soon see the vineyards and hilly terrain on both sides of the highway.

The eleven wineries whose twelve vineyards cover about 4,000 acres in the rolling hills of the valley's eastern region are close together on a scenic road and easily visited in a day or half-day outing. Most offer daily or weekend tasting and tours; hours and days vary; some charge a small tasting fee.

Be sure to check the winery guide and map for the days and hours each winery is open to avoid disappointment after long uphill drives (some are on dirt roads). Frequently, fast traffic behind you may not allow you sufficient time to slow down enough to turn into the narrow winery driveways. In that case, it may be better to continue on along the road and catch that one as you circle back. Learn to speak Chardonnay as you sample the wines and talk to the proprietors or winemakers about the various wines. Attractive giftshops feature gift-packs and mementos; some have cheese and deli items to gather together for an impromptu picnic beneath fragrant grape arbors.

Your first stop on the left side of the road is **Calloway Vineyard and Winery** (32720 Rancho California Road; 714–676–4001). Atop 750 acres, it's the largest premium Southern California winery. On the long uphill drive, vines and flags frame the road. White wine is all they make—Queen Elizabeth favors the White Riesling. Visitor center/gift-shop; informative hourly tours daily from 11:00 A.M. to 3:00 P.M. Large tasting room open daily from 10:00 A.M. to 5:00 P.M.; $2.00 fee.

Farther along is **Piconi Vineyard and Winery** (33410 Rancho California Road; 714–676–5400). Be careful turning onto the narrow road to this small family winery perched at the top of a hill. Daily tasting at friendly winebar, 10:00 A.M. to 5:00 P.M. They sell only estate wines; most popular is Christmas Carbel all year round. The $1.00 tasting fee is applied to purchases. No tours.

Continue on the same side of the road, drive uphill to **Mount Palomar Winery** (41220 Calle Contento; 714–676–5250), passing vineyards and picnic tables. Tasting Bar, $2.00 for four samples, 9:00 A.M. to 5:00 P.M. Tours are at 1:30 and 3:30 P.M. weekdays and 11:30 A.M. Saturday and Sunday. Riesling and White Cabernet are the most popular wines. This is the only winery in Temecula making Cream Sherry. Giftshop. Purchase bread, cheese, and deli fare and enjoy a picnic under the grape arbor.

Go back and across the road to **John Culbertson Winery** (32575 Rancho California Road, 714–699–0088). Attractive Mediterranean-style buildings with a wide courtyard and a large fountain overlook the sweet valley of vineyards. Six award-winning sparkling wines are produced in the *methode champenoise.* Twenty-minute tours Saturday and Sunday at 10:00 A.M., 4:00 P.M. and 6:00 P.M. Champagne bar tasting, $6.00 for four champagne tastings. Pretty giftshop.

Lunch: **Cafe Champagne,** in the courtyard of the John Culbertson Winery. Intimate, with open kitchen, overlooks vineyards. A popular luncheon destination offering California cuisine of mesquite-grilled steaks, salads, and sandwiches.

Afternoon

Continue along the route de vin to **Maurice Carrie Winery** (34225 Rancho California Road; 714–676–1711). The large, white, Victorian-style tasting building set back on a broad lawn is bordered with roses. Patio tables and chairs and a little gazebo are inviting for picnics.

Good-looking interior has a large chandelier, ceiling skylight. Tasting 10:00 A.M. to 5:00 P.M. daily. Most popular wine is Sara Bella Cabernet. Giftshop, deli items.

Back down the road again is **Baily Winery** (33833 Rancho California Road; 714–575–WINE). A wonderfully scenic hilltop location for wine sampling with panoramic view of vineyards and Mount Palomar from the veranda. Tastings daily 10:00 A.M. to 5:00 P.M. Picnic area; giftshop.

Dinner: Temecula Creek Inn. If you enjoy music with dinner, the lounge presents nightly entertainment, and the food service is good. The filet mignon is delicious, with a spicy, creamy Charon sauce. Linger over brandy and dessert—a surprisingly good bread pudding or ice cream sundaes.

Lodging: Temecula Creek Inn.

Day 3

Morning

Breakfast: At the inn.

After breakfast lounge around the pool, play another round of golf on the uncrowded courses, hit some tennis balls, visit more wineries, or return to Old Town Temecula.

To visit more of the valley's fine wineries start with **Hart Winery** (32500 Rancho California Road; 714–676–6300). This hospitable winery in a red, barnlike building is usually closed during the week, but you're welcome for tasting and tours weekends from 9:00 A.M. to 4:00 P.M.

Continue to **Cilurzo Vineyard and Winery** (41220 Calle Contento; 714–676–5250). This family-run operation was the first vineyard in Temecula and specializes in red wines, with Petite Sirah heading the list. Tasting and tours daily 9:00 A.M. to 5:00 P.M.; picnic area.

Drop in at **Keyways Vineyard and Winery** (37338 De Portola Road; 714–676–1451). Ten acres of this three-year-old winery are planted in varietal grapes; the most popular wines are Chardonnay and Muscat Canelli. This eclectic winery has llamas out in the pasture, a miniature train running through the property, antiques, antique cars, and a giftshop. Tasting room open weekends 1:00 to 5:00 P.M., may be open other days. $1.00 fee to sample six wines.

A bit farther along is **Filsinger Vineyard and Winery** (39050 De Portola Road; 714–676–4594). The white stucco building with red tile cupola is adorned with a colorful flower-bordered gazebo. Here since 1980, twenty-five acres are planted in varietals producing seven wines and three champagnes. Most popular are the Gewurztraminer and

Blanc de Blanc Champagne. Tasting and tours weekends from 10:30
A.M. to 5:00 P.M., weekdays by appointment; $1.00 to taste five wines is
refunded on purchase. Gift items; picnic area.

Lunch: Pick up some lunch fixings along the way and snack on
Filsinger's pretty picnic patio.

Afternoon

Retrace your route from Old Town Temecula back to Los Angeles.

There's More

Sam Hicks Park, Mercedes and Moreno streets, at the north end of
Old Town. This small, historic park features Temecula's Monument
Rock, a massive (twenty-ton) granite marker with fifty-six names of pi-
oneers sandblasted on its surface, in tribute to former settlers.

Hot-air ballooning. DAE Flights, P.O. Box 1671, Temecula, CA
92390. (714) 676–3902. Soar over the valley in an eight-stories-high
balloon. Daily one-hour flights begin at 6:30 A.M., with preflight continental breakfast. Brunch with champagne ceremony served after the
flight. Phone for reservations.

Temecula Shuttle, 28657 Front Street, Suite A, Temecula. (714)
695–9999. Narrated tours and tastings of wine country, souvenir wine-
glass, appetizer party tray, Culbertson Champagne toast; $30.00 per
person, in luxury air-conditioned vans. Advance reservations required.
Senior discount.

Baily Vineyard and Winery (36150 Pauba Road; 714–676–WINE)
is the second location for this family-owned winery. Baily makes the
wine here on 60 acres of varietal grapes. Tastings are Saturday and
Sunday, 10:00 A.M. to 5:00 P.M. This winery started in 1986 and now
produces eight wines, with Blush Cabernet Blanc and Cabernet Sauvignon the most popular. They sell only from the winery and tasting
room. $1.00 fee to taste five of the eight wines is refunded on pur-
chase.

Santa Margerita Winery is on Madeira del Playa, just past Cilurzo
Winery. Turn right on Madeira del Playa for this new winery, which
opened in 1991. Tasting and touring weekends only for its Cabernet
Sauvignon and Sauvignon Blanc.

Special Events

Last weekend in February. Early Times Mid-Winter Road Run,
Old Town Temecula.

Last weekend in April and last weekend in August. Semiannual Western Days, Old Town Temecula. (714) 676–4718.
Early May. Temecula Valley Annual Two-Day Balloon and Wine Festival. (714) 676–4713. Two days. Daily liftoff, entertainment, wine tasting, children's fair. Lake Skinner.
Fourth of July. Parade, Old Town Temecula.
First weekend in October. Annual Great Temecula Tractor Race. (800) 800–4038; (714) 676–4718. Temecula Showgrounds. Three days; mudboggin' obstacle course for kids, pig race, fair, country-western music.
Fourth weekend in October. PRCA Rodeo and ICS Chili Cook-Off, Temecula Showgrounds. (800) 800–4038.
Early November. Pumpkin Run 5K and 10K. (800) 800–4038. Costumes, children's events. Old Town Temecula.

Other Recommended Restaurants and Lodgings

Rosa's Cantina, 28636 Front Street, corner of Main, Old Town. (714) 695–2468. Popular for good Mexican food, serve yourself, casual dining inside or on patio. Moderate-priced specialties include tacos, burritos, chimichanga, nachos, tostados, and *combinaciones.*

Texas Lil's Mesquite Grill, 28495C Front Street, Old Town. (714) 699–5457. A lively, local favorite for steak and ribs and good chili.

Swing Inn Cafe, 28676 Front Street, Old Town. (714) 676–2321. Popular since the cowboys and ranch days, cozy, and busy; home-style cooking—spaghettis, soups, sandwiches, and daily specials.

Rustlers Bar and Grille, 27789 Front Street, between Rancho California Road and Winchester, (714) 699–5789. Gourmet menu features excellent steaks and beef dishes. With western bar and dance floor, it's a popular nightspot that fits right in this western town.

Doubletree Suites, 29345 Rancho California Road and I–15. (800) 528–0444; (714) 676–5656. Lake setting of 136 luxurious suites with wetbar, refrigerator, microwave, TV, VCR, stereo, heated swimming pool, spa, fitness center, restaurant, lounge.

Loma Vista Bed and Breakfast, 33350 La Serena Way, Temecula. (714) 676–7047. Set high on a hilltop, it overlooks citrus groves and vineyards. All rooms have air conditioning and private baths with tubs/showers. Rates include a champagne breakfast, served in spacious dining room. Rooms are named after wines—Champagne, Chardonnay, and so forth—and individually furnished.

For More Information

Old Temecula Merchants Association, P.O. Box 1981, Temecula, CA 92593. (714) 676–2322.
Temecula Valley Chamber of Commerce, 27450 Ynez Road #10, Temecula, CA 92391. (714) 676–5090.
Temecula Valley Vintners Association, P.O. Box 1601, Temecula, CA 92390. (714) 699–3626.

Note: The (714) area code listed in the phone numbers for this escape has changed to (909).

Escondido/Lake San Marcos

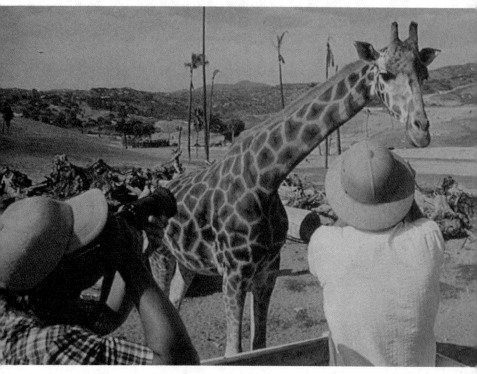

Visitors on safari at Wild Animal Park meet a Ugandan giraffe.

Wine, Pontoons, and Safari

1 NIGHT

Wild animal park • Wineries • Antique cars • Lake
Ethnic and gourmet dining • Resorts • Boating

This varied, two-day itinerary takes you off the beaten track, with plenty of change of pace and scene. Using Escondido as a convenient hub to explore the rural area, you visit and taste-tour local wineries, see a marvelous collection of classic restored antique cars, go on a safari through an 1,800-acre wildlife preserve, view a historic battlefield, and go boating on a peaceful, secluded lake.

Day 1

Morning

Drive south from Los Angeles on I–5 to Oceanside. Take Highway 78 east to I–15 north. Exit at Mountain Meadow Road; turn right to the stop sign and left on frontage road, Champagne Boulevard, proceeding for about 2.5 miles to Lawrence Welk Resort.

Lunch: **Lawrence Welk Resort,** 8860 Lawrence Welk Drive, Escondido. (800) 932–9355. The enticing Buffet du Chef in the resort's large dining room overlooking the inviting golf fairways features carved-to-order roast beef, roast chicken, or fish fillets, plus another entree, as well as an extensive salad bar assortment. The buffet is served Sunday, Tuesday, Wednesday, and Thursday from 11:15 A.M. to 1:15 P.M. Regular popular luncheon menu is available other days.

Afternoon

Continue along the frontage road, Champagne Boulevard, a very short distance to the **Deer Park Wine Tasting Car Museum,** 29013 Champagne Boulevard (619–749–1666). This place is perfect for car nostalgia buffs and wine enthusiasts, who can taste wines from the surrounding vineyard and from the Napa Valley at this family-owned and -operated winery tasting room. As you tour the winery, you can view the large collection of antique cars and convertibles.

The Market Deli, giftshop, wine-tasting room, and a dozen classic cars share space in the large Market Building. After sampling the wines, guests take a self-guided tour of the winery (tours offered daily from 10:00 A.M. to 5:00 P.M.). The gourmet Market Deli's sandwiches are named for cars: the Ford is roast beef, the Chevy is ham, the Edsel is turkey, and so forth. Order a sandwich, buy some wine, and picnic in the winery's beautiful, fifteen-acre park (the deli closes at 3:00 P.M.). The giftshop's selection includes car models, books, posters, wine accessories, and wineglasses, plus T-shirts and other items. The Wine Boutique offers California premium wines from limited-production wineries.

The gleaming cars on display include a 1928 Ford that sold for $550, a 1935 Packard, and a 1931 Chrysler Deluxe that sold for $1,545. Each car is fully identified. In the new Mission-style Winery Building, with a collection of autos of the 1950s, the prize is the triple black, 1953 Cadillac Eldorado. The Car Museum, in another building, displays open roadsters, touring cars, and nostalgic convertibles, resembling everyone's dream car (the Car Museum closes at 4:00 P.M.).

Leave Deer Park and drive back past Lawrence Welk Resort, go up the hill to the four-way stop, and turn right on I–15 south to Highway 78, about 7 miles. Stay on Highway 78 to the Rancho Santa Fe exit. Turn left and continue for about 2 miles to Lake San Marcos Drive; turn left and go downhill to the end of the street to your hotel, Quails Inn, in **Lake San Marcos,** a small, exclusive, nontouristy city in a rural resort setting.

After checking into your lakefront hotel, you'll have time for a refreshing **boat ride** on Lake San Marcos. Ask the desk clerk to arrange a ride for you, and walk or drive to the boathouse, just past Quails Dinnerhouse. Here a small lawn tapers down to the lovely lake, where swans pose elegantly and ducks quack as they paddle around close to shore. After receiving easy instructions to operate the electric gondolas or open-air pontoon boat, you'll soon be out on the cool, secluded, 1.25-mile-long lake, gliding around the little inlets to the dam and back. (Hourly boat fee.)

Dinner: **Quails Dinnerhouse at Quails Inn,** Lake San Marcos Resort, Lake San Marcos. (619) 744–2455. Overlooking the lake, the restaurant is a town favorite for the spectacular seafood/salad bar and other entrees. For faster service take the stairway down to the convivial Lakeside Lounge, which also overlooks the water. Happy Hour, Monday through Friday from 4:00 to 7:00 P.M. with lower-priced drinks, features an extensive variety of hot and cold complimentary hors d'oeuvres. The regular dinner menu offers fish-and-chips, Cajun chicken, cheeseburgers with terrific cross-fries (basket-weave), and different nightly specials.

Lodging: **The Quails Inn Hotel,** Lake San Marcos Resort, 1025 La Bonita Drive, Lake San Marcos, CA 92069. Reservations: (800) 447–6556; (619) 744–0120. You'll appreciate this quiet and romantic lakeside setting of 142 nicely appointed large rooms, plus suites and apartments, some with patio overlooking the private lake. In-room coffeemaker, separate bathroom pullmans with roomy storage, bathtub and stall shower, fresh flowers, complimentary continental breakfast served in the lobby Monday through Friday, daily newspaper. Three restaurants; cocktail lounge with disco and entertainment nightly. Boating on the lake; 18-hole Championship Country Club golf course and access to 18-hole executive course; four tennis courts, four paddle-tennis courts; four heated swimming pools; large conference center. Weekend Dinner Theatre, Sunday brunch.

Day 2

Morning

Breakfast: **Lake San Marcos Country Club Dining Room,** 1750

San Pablo Drive, Lake San Marcos. (619) 744–9385. The pretty dining rooms overlook the lush fairways. You don't have to be Jack Nicklaus to enjoy the Golfer's Tee-Off breakfast of eggs with ham or bacon, potatoes, and muffins; other options include waffles and buttermilk pancakes.

Investigate the good-looking **Village Center** across from the hotel with coffeeshop, small market, liquor store, pharmacy, and shops. Hotel guests may charge purchases to their rooms. Then walk down to the lake and enjoy a quiet stroll alongside the tranquil water. Relax and watch the ducks and the swans and the little children who chase the ducks across the lawn and into the water as they offer them food. If you have time, go for another sail around Lake San Marcos. It's a wonderful experience. You may want to have lunch early today since there are lots of activities scheduled for the afternoon.

Drive up San Marino to Rancho Santa Fe Road, turn right to San Marcos Boulevard, and turn right again several blocks later to San Marcos's famous **Restaurant Row,** on the left. Here's an exciting variety of twelve fine restaurants in one convenient location (see Other Recommended Restaurants and Lodgings).

Lunch: **Bruno's Italian Restaurant & Pizzeria,** 1020 San Marcos Boulevard, San Marcos. (619) 744–7700. Recommended enthusiastically by fussy diners, the lunch buffet, served Monday to Saturday, features ten items, including veal parmigiana, several different pizzas, seafood, and pasta. Other menu selections are hearty sandwiches and a salad bar. (*Note:* If you like to share portions, there's an extra plate charge of $1.50.)

Afternoon

To visit the San Diego Wild Animal Park, take San Marcos Boulevard past Restaurant Row to Freeway 78; go east to I–15, then south to the Via Rancho Parkway exit. Turn left onto San Pasqual Road, and follow it until it becomes Highway 78, leading to the Wild Animal Park (about 6 miles).

San Diego Wild Animal Park, 15600 San Pasqual Valley Road (Highway 78) in Escondido (619–747–8702). It's almost a culture shock on the Wgasa Bush Line Monorail's fifty-minute narrated safari, where you skirt the 5-mile perimeter of Asian and African animal habitats. As your guide describes many of the 2,500 animals living in the 2,100-acre preserve—a haven for vanishing wildlife species—you may feel as though you've been deposited in Africa, as you see animals roaming freely in dramatic open plains.

In addition to Asian and African elephants, you'll see giraffes, Persian gazelles, flamingos, zebras, ostriches, Arabian oryx, Sumatran tigers, wild horses, 4,000-pound white rhinos, many species of antelope, and numerous other wild animals and birds. You won't always see the tigers and other animals that sleep throughout the day, and many are too far away. A zoom lens for your camera is useful, as are binoculars. The right-hand side of the monorail affords better viewing. When your safari ends, visit the 17-acre Nairobi African Village, with its restaurants, snackbars, and shops. Check the map you received at entry for schedules of the engaging bird, elephant, and other daily shows. Youngsters adore the Petting Kraal and Animal Care Center, where they can cuddle the koalas and watch nursery feedings. Lush botanical gardens, a wooden bridge, a waterfall cascading down boulders, a treehouse, and large, colorful macaws all enhance your exit (if you can find it) from the park. (Open daily from 9:00 A.M. to dusk; seasonal events and special exhibits; admission and parking fee; entry ticket includes monorail, animal shows, and exhibits.)

To get to the Thomas Jaeger Winery, turn left on San Pasqual Road; go 3 miles, passing a large produce stand, Old San Pasqual Road, and a Christmas tree farm. Look for vineyards on the low hillside at the left of the road, and continue to the large Thomas Jaeger Winery sign, turning left through the gates past a picnic lawn to the wine-tasting room.

In the rather bare but deliciously cool tasting room of **Thomas Jaeger Winery** (13455 San Pasqual Road in Escondido 800–929–9463, 619–745–3535), you sample award-winning wines of San Diego's largest premium winery. Then join daily half-hour tours of the winery, held at 11:30 A.M. and at 1:30, 3:00, and 4:00 P.M. Many visitors purchase luncheon foods and wine in the Gourmet Vineyard Kitchen and picnic beneath the grape arbor overlooking the vineyards and the beautifully scenic San Pasqual Valley. Jaeger moved here from Napa in 1988. On its 120 rolling acres, the winery has 30 acres of estate vineyards producing Chardonnay grapes, while its 60-acre vineyard in nearby Fallbrook produces a variety of other grapes. The giftshop sells cheese, giftpacks, wineglasses, and wines. Wine tasting is offered daily from 10:00 A.M. to 5:30 P.M.

To reach I–15 north to Los Angeles, go west on San Pasqual Road to San Pasqual Valley Road/Highway 78. Stay on 78 west for 7 to 10 miles until you come to I–15. From I–15, take Beach Cities/Riverside 91 exit to the left. Then look for I–5 north just past Anaheim and take it into downtown Los Angeles.

There's More

Ferrara Winery, 1120 West 15th Avenue, Escondido. (619) 745–7632. San Diego County's oldest grape-growing winery is a designated State Historical Point of Interest. If you enjoy the challenge of finding Ferrara, the tasting room offers a selection of premium wine, Monday through Friday from 9:00 A.M. to 5:30 P.M. and from 10:00 A.M. on Saturday and Sunday. The deli makes sandwiches to enjoy in the hundred-year-old vineyard. Enter the winery, with its two red-brick pillars and machinery out front, from the parking lot next to number 1160, in a residential street.

Palomar Observatory, forty-five minutes northeast of Escondido on Palomar Mountain. (619) 742–2119. The home of the 200-inch Hale Telescope offers two kinds of tours. On the third Saturday of each month, four one-hour free tours are given on a reserved basis for groups; call or write for reservation forms. Additionally, the Reuben H. Fleet Space Theater and Science Center in San Diego offers six tours yearly, May through October; reserve through them at (619) 238–1233. Fee.

The observatory is open daily, except Christmas, from 8:00 A.M. to 4:30 P.M. Visitors may take a free self-guided tour and view the Hale Telescope from the gallery in the dome; there is no viewing through the telescope. The giftshop is open daily during July and August and then only on weekends. Take Highway 76 to County Road S6 and wind up the mountain to the observatory gate.

San Pasqual State Historic Park and Museum, east of the San Diego Wild Animal Park on Highway 78, 115808 San Pasqual Valley Road, Escondido. (619) 489–0076. For history buffs; the fifty-acre hillside park overlooks the site of the Battle of San Pasqual, December 6, 1846, between U.S. forces and Mexico, during the Mexican-American War. The visitor center presents a short video of the war, a map, and a description of the battle. Open Thursday to Monday, 10:00 A.M. to 5:00 P.M.

Heritage Walk Museum Complex, Grape Day Park, 321 North Broadway, Escondido. (619) 743–8207. For a quick glimpse into Escondido's past, take Highway 78 east, turning left on Washington to Grape Day Park, with tall, beautiful shade trees. Heritage Walk museum complex includes buildings preserved from Escondido's beginnings in 1888. Stroll around to see the town's first library, a little 1894 yellow cottage with brown trim, the 1900s Red Barn with wagon and windmill, a two-story 1790 country house, a blacksmith shop currently used for restoring stagecoaches, and the 1888 Santa Fe Railroad Depot, which ended passenger service in 1945 and is presently used by the local historical society. Buildings are open Thursday through Saturday from 1:00 to 4:00 P.M. but can be viewed at any time.

Bates Nut Farm, 15954 Woods Valley Road, Valley Center. (619) 749–3333. About fifteen minutes northeast of Escondido, here's where to stock up on packages of dried fruits, candies, and fresh-roasted nuts from all over the world. Kids get to feed ducks and geese and pet the sheep and goats. Gift boutique; freshly ground peanut butter; special festive events during the year. Open daily, 8:00 A.M. to 5:00 P.M.

Special Events

Mid-April, early August, mid-to-end of October, mid-November, late November, and mid-December. Bates Nut Farm Fairs and Shows, Valley Center.
Early June. Chili cook-off, San Marcos.
Early June, mid-to-late June, early August, and late December. San Pasqual Battlefield events, Escondido.
Mid-to-late June. Concours d'Elegance Annual Car Show, Deer Park Winery, Escondido.
Late July. Mission San Luis Rey Fiesta, Oceanside.
Mid-August. San Diego Symphony Concert, Kit Carson Park, Escondido.
Mid-to-end of October. Downtown Street Festival, Escondido Historical Society's Harvest Festival, Escondido Street Fair, Escondido.
Mid-December. Christmas Parade, Escondido.

Other Recommended Restaurants and Lodgings

San Marcos

Fish House Vera Cruz and Rancho Vera Cruz. In restaurant row. (619) 744–8000. The two restaurants share the same building, with separate entrances and dining rooms. The Fish House is popular for tasty, fresh, mesquite-broiled seafood. Rancho Vera Cruz is equally popular for fine steaks.

Acapulco Mexican Restaurant and Cantina. (619) 471–2150. A local hangout for its variety of Mexican dishes, lively Happy Hour with complimentary hors d'oeuvres, and Sunday brunch.

Escondido

The T-Bird Diner, 601 North Broadway. (619) 480–2473. Guests enjoy the 1950s decor and familiar menu of chili, hamburgers, meatloaf, and fare from the soda fountain; beer and wine.

The Brigantine Restaurant, 421 West Felicita Avenue. (619) 743–4718. South of Grape Day Park. Another reliable choice for seafood entrees.

Cocina del Charro, 625 North Quince. (619) 745–1382. Serves authentic Mexican specialties, *carne asada* burritos, and enchiladas for lunch and dinner; Sunday brunch.

Lawrence Welk Resort, 8860 Lawrence Welk Drive. (800) 932–9355; (619) 749–3000. Sprawling, 1,000-acre resort with three 18-hole golf courses established by the late orchestra leader has 134 spacious rooms, 6 suites, and two-bedroom villas, all with views of the golf course, some with patios. In-room coffeemaker and TV; galleria, market/deli, beauty shop; three swimming pools with spas. Restaurant and lounge; Wednesday- and Thursday-evening Happy Hour offers free hors d'oeuvres. Conference facilities; live theater performances.

Fallbrook

Alexander's, Pala Mesa Resort, 2001 Old Highway 395. (619) 728–5881. The knockout Sunday brunch buffet, with free-flowing champagne, is served in the large dining room overlooking the fairways. The extensive, inviting array of foods features carved-to-order baron of beef, several hot entrees, cold salads, and omelet, shrimp, and seafood stations. Treat yourself to dessert by creating your own ice cream sundae. Sunday brunch served from 10:30 A.M. to 2:00 P.M.

Pala Mesa Resort, 2001 Old Highway 395. (800) 722–4700; (800) 822–4600 (outside California); (619) 728–5881. Framed by avocado groves, this rural retreat of two-story, ranch-style buildings is surrounded by one of Southern California's most beautiful 18-hole championship golf courses, with 133 well-furnished rooms with 54 condominiums overlooking the fairways. In-room coffeemaker, TV, honor bar/minirefrigerator, nightly turndown service; golf course, driving range, putting green, pro shop; four night-lighted tennis courts; swimming pool, Jacuzzi. Restaurant and lounge, with live music and dancing weekends. Terrific Sunday champagne buffet brunch. Conference center; golf and tennis packages. All public space, lobby, and restaurant were redecorated at the end of 1992.

For More Information

Escondido Convention and Visitors Bureau, 720 North Broadway, Escondido, CA 92025. (800) 848–3336; (619) 745–4741.

San Marcos Chamber of Commerce, 144 West Mission Road, San Marcos, CA 92069. (619) 744–1270.

Julian/Anza Borrego/ Borrego Springs

Julian's town hall is a center for year-round events.

Gold Rush and Desert Grandeur

——————————— 1 NIGHT ———————————

Fruit orchards · Gold-mining town · Museum · Horse-and-buggy ride
Country shopping · Historic trails and nature walks
Wildflowers · Bighorn sheep

There's plenty of change in this two-day itinerary that gets you off the fast track. It takes you high up in the mountains of north San Diego

County to a small, historic gold-mining town still reflecting its aura of the 1870 Gold Rush days, then down to the mighty Anza Borrego Desert to explore the natural wonders of the nation's second largest state park. You'll also stay overnight in a luxurious, desert-oasis resort and browse a small, upscale resort community surrounded by spring wildflowers.

Day 1

Morning

Leave Los Angeles via I–5 south through Oceanside, then head east on Highway 78 into Escondido, continuing on 78 up the mountains to Julian, about a three-hour drive. Following Highway 78 on the scenic drive up to Julian, the backcountry road borders a woodsy stream as it climbs and weaves through broad, rolling plains where cattle graze in sunny pastures. In fall the open fields tumbled with fat golden pumpkins are bucolic treats for city dwellers. Look for roadside stands selling eggs, cider, pears, and apples (in fall) and buy as you go along. Better yet, wait until the return trip to purchase fresh produce to take home. About 7 miles from Julian, you'll pass **Dudley's Bakery and Restaurant** on the left near Highway 79, noted for baking twenty varieties of bread daily and for its long lines. It's so popular that it has a toll-free number so customers can call in a pickup order: (800) 225–3348, 8:00 A.M. to 5:00 P.M. (Closed Monday and Tuesday.)

Julian, a former Gold Rush mining town and a National Historic Site, is a sleepy, 4-block-square rural community. At 4,235 feet high in the oak-and-piney hills, Julian's apples and cider lure thousands of visitors to its Fall Harvest Festival in October and November. The town celebrates other seasons too, with festivals and arts and crafts shows. Cafes and restaurants feature fresh apple pie year-round by the slice, or you can lasso a whole pie.

In our harried, computerized age, visitors come to Julian for more than apples. They come for its atmosphere and nostalgic reminders of simpler times and for the romance of an exciting, lusty era they missed.

Julian has about 500 residents, and, adding in the surrounding suburbs, the population hits 2,000. There are no movie houses, glitz, or shopping malls in this rustic, pint-size village that dozes all week and hums with tourists on the weekend. Most stores close between 5:00 and 6:00 P.M., and all are open weekends.

Lunch: **Romano's Dodge House,** 2718 B Street, Julian. (619) 765–2265. Around the corner from Julian Lodge. Considered the best Italian food in town; they treat you like one of the family, except you don't have to help with the dishes. Sample the lasagna, pizza, and veal and pasta selections. (Sorry, no apple pie here.) There's a small bar. Closed Tuesday and Wednesday.

Afternoon

Julian is a true success story, one that began in 1869, when miners found placer gold in a nearby stream. Searching farther upstream, they discovered gold ore in 1870. As claims were staked out and mines multiplied, the exciting Gold Rush began. One of the local residents, Mike Julian, helped record and lay out the town site, and the towns-people named it after him.

In a dizzying boom, gold seekers, prospectors, and miners showed up from all over the West, by sea from Northern California and by stage from San Diego. Within a month nearly 1,000 gold hunters arrived to work the town's mines. Julian expanded rapidly, as buildings sprang up along bustling Main Street. In its prime the town had four general stores, fifteen hotels, a dozen saloons, and two stage lines to San Diego.

The bonanza ended ten years later, when the rich veins of gold in the mines were exhausted after producing millions of dollars worth of gold. The stampede ended when the migrant miners rushed off to a new boom in Tombstone, Arizona, in 1880.

Julian didn't become a ghost town, as did so many others. Farmers found the rich soil and pleasant mountain climate ideal for growing apples and pears. A ragtag bunch stayed on and homesteaded the fertile valley and hills. Julian soon became an active farming-trading community.

Drop in at the **Town Hall,** at the corner of Washington and Main, in a historic 1913 building—it's the center of all year-round activities. Take a look at its historic photos and pick up a list of special events. The Chamber of Commerce is located here (see "For More Information").

Around the corner, **Julian Pioneer Museum,** 2811 Washington Street (619–765–0227), is the city's oldest building. Built in 1875, it was originally the town's brewery and later on a blacksmith shop. Restored and enlarged, townsfolk call the museum "Julian's Attic." It's filled with a jumble of old furniture, photos and historical records, mining equipment, a gleaming old square Weber grand piano, a Victorian carriage, and many other items depicting the city's life in the Gold Rush days of 1869. (Open daily April through November from 10:00 A.M. to 4:00 P.M. and then on Saturday, Sunday, and legal holidays; closed Thursday, Christmas, and New Year's Day; donation.)

Among the shops and cafes at this historic part of **Main Street** near the site of the Washington Mine around the Fire Station are several antiques stores tucked in small cottages. Mosey down Main Street, with its wooden, 1800s buildings to Mom's Cafe, where you can watch the bakers making hundreds of apple pies daily. Next door, Painted Pony Native American Arts is a treasure to browse, with its perky country music and old-fashioned but trendy country-style antique items, like Coca-Cola signs, baskets, and tins of Lipton's tea. Check out the great-looking Indian pottery, baskets, Kachinas, and jewelry in the rear of the store, all authentic and rather expensive. Near the end of Main Street, Julian Cider Mill, a family-owned local institution, offers welcome cups of its hot cider in winter and sips of cold boysenberry apple cider in summer. From about October through March, you can watch apples being pressed into cider. Additionally, you'll always find a nice assortment of dried fruit, honey, nuts, candy, and popcorn.

Across the way on B Street, take time to browse **K. O. Corral's rustic courtyard shops.** To tour Julian's only remaining 1897 operating gold mine, drive up hilly C Street about 6 blocks to the **Eagle and High Peak Gold Mines** (619–765–9921). Take the hour-and-forty-five-minute guided tour through 1,000 feet of underground tunnels, and relive the gold-fever days. Daily tours start at 10:00 A.M.; the last tour is at 2:30 P.M.; the site is closed before 10:00 A.M. and after 4:00 P.M. (Picnic area; closed Christmas and Easter; fee.)

Among the two dozen or more remaining historic structures in town, the 1869 **Julian Hotel,** 2032 Main Street (800–734–5854), on the National Register of Historic Places and the sole survivor of the town's fifteen hotels in its heyday, began as a restaurant owned by a freed Georgia slave whose wife's delectable southern cooking attracted hungry travelers on the Butterfield Stage. They built a successful hotel around it, and it's now a popular B&B with sixteen rooms, most with baths down the hall, and a separate honeymoon cottage.

When you have explored Julian, drive through to the end of Main Street for the 28-mile, one-hour drive down the mountainside to Borrego Springs and Anza Borrego Desert State Park. Be advised to leave in daylight, as this is a very curvy, very dangerous mountain road. The road is cut right through the low mountains, with pure desolation on both sides toward the flat desert plains below. It's a hair-raising ride down Banner Grade, with many curves as the road descends to the desert floor, where the vast, 600,000-acre park stretches to the soft, sensuous foothills, as you wind and twist through Yaqui Pass. Just after Rams Hill you arrive at La Casa del Zorro Desert Resort Hotel, a welcome oasis of palm trees, lush green grass, and fountains.

Check into your hotel, and if there's time and daylight, get back on S3, Borrego Springs Road, to explore the little town of **Borrego Springs,** and plan to visit the huge state park tomorrow. Follow the green Christmas Circle turnaround along Palm Canyon Drive to the

good-looking, smartly landscaped mall of shops and restaurants—
Willie's Bar and Grill, Borrego Jewelers, Union Bank, and others.
Across the street a smaller shopping complex includes the Live Theater, a restaurant, a library, a gas station, and the Borrego Springs
Chamber of Commerce (see "For More Information"), if you need any
information or brochures. All stores close between 5:00 and 6:00 P.M.,
earlier in summer.

Borrego Springs's population of 3,000 increases in winter to about
8,000. This peaceful little community is often compared with Palm
Springs of the 1930s. But residents know there is no danger of urban
sprawl or crowding, as the city is completely surrounded by the magnificent desert park.

Its enviable life-style of peace and quiet in the warm, clean, desert
air includes golf, tennis, swimming, and other good-life amenities.
Temperatures can rise in the summer from 107 degrees to around 124
degrees, but evenings are cooler. Accommodations range from luxury
resorts to smaller hotels.

Dinner: **La Casa del Zorro,** 3845 Yaqui Pass Road, Borrego
Springs. (800) 824–1884; (619) 767–5323. Two dining rooms feature
varying Early Bird Special entrees from 4:00 to 6:00 P.M. On Monday
and Tuesday evenings, many guests gather in the lively bar and lounge
for the All-You-Can-Eat Buffet (generally $1.00 or $1.50 per person).
Monday is Spaghetti Night; Tuesday, Taco Night. Weekday Happy
Hour from 5:00 to 7:00 P.M. includes complimentary hors d'ouevres.

Lodging: **La Casa del Zorro,** 3845 Yaqui Pass Road, Borrego
Springs, CA 92004. (800) 824–1884; (619) 767–5323. This luxury desert
hideaway, a *Mobil Travel Guide* four-star resort, offers seventy-seven
elegantly decorated rooms, deluxe suites, and casitas on thirty-eight
acres of lush desert landscaping. Rooms feature clock alarm, coffeemaker, hair dryer, daily newspaper, terry robes, large fireplace, TV,
comfortable lounge chairs, and good lighting. Complimentary coffee
in the lobby; three swimming pools and spas, six night-lighted tennis
courts, tennis pro shop, putting green, fitness room; salon, giftshop;
two restaurants, bar and lounge, Saturday and Sunday Buffet Brunch,
jazz weekends. Seasonal rates, special events, conference center,
country club golf nearby.

Day 2

Morning

Breakfast: At the hotel. In two dining rooms, elegantly served continental breakfast includes a generous bowl of fresh fruit or yogurt plus
muffins, toast, or croissants, juice, and coffee. Full breakfast features
Belgian waffles and egg specialties

Drive to Borrego Springs, and, following the green Christmas Circle turnaround on Palm Canyon Drive, continue on S22 to the state park, past the shopping village, about a 7-mile drive through the vast, serene desert. In spring, after the winter rains, thousands of tourists arrive from early March through mid-April to marvel at the spectacular view of wildflowers carpeting the arid desert floor and hillsides.

Anza Borrego Desert State Park, the largest park in California, covering more than a half-million acres, attracts close to a million visitors in the winter season, from October through May. These visitors explore and experience the park's open wilderness beauty, taking self-guided auto tours to many points of interest, and hiking, camping, mountain biking, and backpacking amid the palm-studded canyons, plains, and desolate badlands. Elevations range from 15 feet to more than 7,000 feet of the towering Santa Rosa Mountains.

The park is named for Spanish explorer Juan Bautista de Anza, who led an expedition for Spain from Mexico through Cahuilla Indian territory in 1774 and discovered the first overland route to California. Markers commemorate the historic event. *Borrego* is the Spanish name for the elusive peninsular bighorn sheep that take refuge here.

The area resembles a surreal desert moonscape and is as natural and rugged as when the Spaniards first arrived hundreds of years ago. Surrounded by the tall cinnamon mountains, it is a scene of desolation and solitude, absolutely haunting in its stark, lonely beauty and grandeur. Park rangers advise visitors to carry plenty of water and to wear a hat and sunblock. It can be very hot.

Drive up to the Visitor Center. The entrance is not visible from the road, in its underground building sheltered beneath a low hillside with a desert sand roof dotted with low native plants. The center provides slide shows on the hour and the half-hour; these explain the desert's history and variety of more than 600 species of plants and 300 species of reptiles and birds, including the fast little roadrunner. Among native animals are the bobcat, coyote and kangaroo rat.

The center offers naturalist talks, guided walks, hikes, and tours, and it provides brochures and maps of the most scenic places. *Note:* The Visitor Center (619–767–4205) is open daily *only* from October through May, from 9:00 A.M. to 5:00 P.M., and open weekends and holidays *only* from June through September. The Administration Office (619–767–5311) has opposite hours, open weekdays from 8:00 A.M. to 5:00 P.M. and closed weekends and holidays.

The favorite and most scenic hike is the Palm Canyon Nature Trail, a 1.5-mile hike up through the hills to an oasis of a grove of about 1,000 palm trees thriving in the rocky canyon. Other trails cover the historic routes traveled in the 1840s and 1850s by Kit Carson, the Mormon Batallion, adventurers, gold seekers, the first transcontinental mail service, and the famous Butterfield Overland Stage traveling from St. Louis to San Francisco, a twenty-four-day journey of extreme hardships wherein passengers frequently had to get out and help push the stagecoach over steep mountain passes. Today's visitors on self-guided auto tours can follow the deep wagon-wheel ruts along the road, look across the incredible shimmering desert, and reclaim a bit of history in the Old West for themselves.

To return to Los Angeles, you need to retrace your way, driving back up the mountain and through Julian and down Highway 78. From Anza Borrego Park go back on the road to Casa del Zorro, following the curve to the right on S3. This is the same very winding and curvy road you drove down from Julian, only now it winds sharply up and up around the mountains. The spectacular views make up for all the curves, with the mountains covered in various shades of green.

Afternoon

You can spend time browsing again in Julian, have lunch or more apple pie, or continue through town on Main Street, turn left on Washington and on to Highway 78, a rolling pleasant road. You'll pass many fruit orchards on the way (see There's More). Continue on Highway 78 to I–5 north to Los Angeles.

There's More

Country Carriages, available in front of Julian Drug. (619) 765–1471. Offers romantic, old-fashioned buggy rides. Fee.

If you like to buy fresh fruit, look for apple and pear orchards located throughout Julian. Pears are available in different seasons, with a good crop in September; apples are usually harvested in October, and peaches in August.

The following fruit markets are on Highway 78 three miles west of Julian just past Wynola Road (on the right). They're usually open daily from 9:00 A.M. to 5:00 P.M. and sell, depending on the season, apples, pears, peaches, cider, jams and jellies, and other items.

Farmers Mountain Vale Ranch, 4510 Highway 78, Julian. (619) 765–0188. In addition to the fresh fruits, this ranch also bakes and sells delicious apple pies.

Manzanita Ranch, 4470 Highway 78, Julian. (619) 765–0102.

Meyer Orchards, 3962 Highway 78, Julian. (619) 765–0233.

Redding "R" Ranch, 3265 Old Cuyamaca Road, Julian. (619) 765–0200.

Julian Orchards, 1255 Julian Orchards Drive, Julian. (619) 765–0111. Apples only, no cider. You can pick your own apples here or buy those already bagged.

Julian Apple Mountain Orchard, 1125 Farmer Road, Julian. (619) 765–1906. Here's where you can actually rent a tree (fees vary), which entitles you to all the produce for the harvest season. Come up and pick your own apples. Additionally, you'll find cider presses, a country giftstore with gourmet goodies, and family recreational activities. **Menghini Winery,** 1150 Julian Orchards Drive, Julian. (P.O. Box 1359.) (619) 765–2072. Enjoy wine tasting and a guided tour of this family-run winery with picnic area. Open Friday, Saturday, and Sunday from 10:00 A.M. to 4:00 P.M., weekdays by appointment.

Special Events

Note: All events take place in Julian Town Hall unless otherwise noted.
January through mid-December. Art shows and crafts shows. Contact Chamber of Commerce for schedule.
February, March, and end of April. Spring wildflowers, Borrego Springs.
Late March to early April. Grapefruit Festival. Arts and Crafts Show, Borrego Springs.
Early May. Spinning and Weaving Show.
Early to mid-May. Annual Wildflower Show.
Late June to early July. Annual Heritage Quilt Show.
Fourth of July. Deep-Pit Barbecue Dinner, American Legion Hall, Second and Washington streets.
Late August-to-early September. Annual Weed Show.
Mid-September. Lions Club Banjo/Fiddle Contest. Lane Field Annual Woodturners Show and Sale.
Mid-September through November. Julian Apple Harvest time.
Every weekend in October. Triangle Club Melodrama.
Early October. Back Country Arts Festival, Methodist Church, 1 mile west on S78/79.
Last weekend in October to early November. Desert Festival, street parade. Borrego Springs.
Late November. Christmas Craft Show.

Other Recommended Restaurants and Lodgings

Julian

Rongbranch Restaurant and Boar's Head Saloon, 2722 Washington Street. (619) 765–2265. This perennial favorite is well known for hearty sandwiches, charbroiled burgers—also buffalo burgers made of lean ground buffalo meat. Variety of pies, convivial saloon, and attractive giftshop.

Kendall's Korner, Third and B Street. (619) 765–1560. Specializes in omelets and pancakes for breakfast and lunch. Open daily: Monday through Friday from 6:00 A.M. to 3:00 P.M., Saturday and Sunday to 7:30 P.M. Patio dining.

Bar-B-Q Dinner Theatre, Pine Hills Lodge, P.O. Box 701, Julian, CA 92036. (619) 765–1100. Join the fun Friday and Saturday evenings. Bar-B-Q at 7:00 P.M.; curtain at 8:00 P.M. Enjoy baby-back pork ribs, chicken, zesty beans, salads, Dudley's bread.

Julian Lodge Bed and Breakfast, Fourth and C Street. (800) 542–1420; (619) 765–1420. Two-story, modern; twenty-three rooms with bath, cable TV, air conditioning, and heat. Continental breakfast served in homey lobby.

Borrego Springs

Note: Summer hours and days are subject to change.

George and Ernie's Little Italy, The Center. (619) 767–3938. Open Wednesday through Sunday, 11:00 A.M. to 2:00 P.M. and 5:00 to 9:00 P.M. Closed Monday and Tuesday.

Kendall's Cafe, The Mall. (619) 767–3938. Open Monday through Wednesday from 6:00 A.M. to 2:00 P.M. and Thursday through Saturday until 8:00 P.M.; Mexican food served Thursday through Sunday, from 11:30 A.M. to 8:00 P.M.

Rams Hill Country Club Restaurant, Yaqui Pass Road. (619) 767–5006. Lunch Monday through Saturday from noon to 2:00 P.M.; dinner nightly from 6:00 P.M.; Sunday Minibrunch from 8:00 A.M. to 2:00 P.M.

Palm Canyon Resort, 22 Palm Canyon Drive. (800) 242–0044; (619) 767–5341. Fourteen-acre complex includes forty-four-room hotel, deluxe RV park, two swimming pools and spas, restaurant, lounge, minimarket, bike rentals.

Rams Hill, 4343 Yaqui Pass Road, P.O. Box 2190. (619) 767–5028. Rentals of privately owned, well-furnished homes, with weekly, monthly, and group rates. Championship eighteen-hole golf course, pro shop; swimming pool, Jacuzzi; restaurant, lounge.

Villas Borrego, P.O. Box 185. (619) 767–5371. One- and two-bedroom villas with patios, swimming pool.

Road Runner Golf and Country Club, 1010 Palm Canyon Drive, P.O. Box 3081. (619) 767–5374. Family-owned, luxury mobile home retirement community, with 18-hole executive golf course, clubhouse, tennis courts, and large therapeutic swimming pool.

For More Information

Julian Chamber of Commerce, Town Hall, P.O. Box 475, Washington and Main streets, Julian, CA 92036. (619) 765–1857. Open from 11:00 A.M. to 4:00 or 5:00 P.M. Monday, Tuesday, and Friday. Closed Wednesday and Thursday.

Borrego Springs Chamber of Commerce, P.O. Box 66, 622 Palm Canyon Drive, Borrego Springs, CA 92004. (619) 767–5565.

Santa Catalina Island

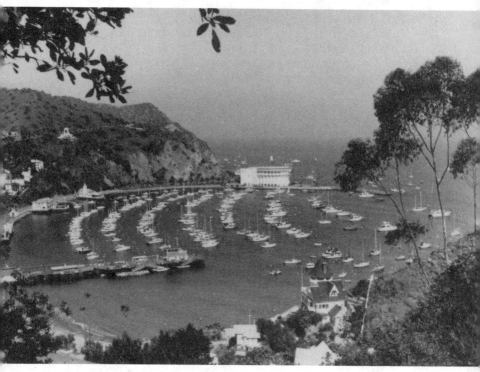

Beautiful Santa Catalina Island's Avalon Bay

Island Getaway

_____ 1 NIGHT _____

Ocean cruise to island · Beach · Pier · Scuba/snorkel diving
Boating and fishing · Hiking · Island and harbor tours
Glass-bottom boat · Wilderness · Dance casino · Horseback riding

On your two-day Santa Catalina Island escape, which begins with a
brisk ocean voyage, you'll soon be seduced by an entirely different
environment.

The island air, surrounded by the sea, is clearer, the sun is brighter, and there are no automobiles. Sunbathe and swim in a small, protected beach area; scuba and snorkel in translucent waters; go sailing, fishing, or biking; and join a variety of scenic tours around the island, from the sparkling, peaceful harbor to the undeveloped wilderness interior where buffalo and deer roam freely. Enjoy a glass-bottom boat trip, visit the dance casino of the Big Band era, and dine in fine style at water's edge.

Day 1

Morning

From Los Angeles the fastest way to get to Catalina by boat (fifty-five minutes) is from Long Beach via the Catalina Express boats, which make frequent daily departures year round from the *Queen Mary* port alongside the legendary ocean liner whose celebrity passengers included royalty, Hollywood stars, and millionaires.

Head south on Santa Anna Freeway I–5 to Long Beach Freeway 710 south to Long Beach. Follow signs to the *Queen Mary,* which lead you to the Catalina Express Port and parking lot; it's advisable to arrive twenty minutes or more before departure time. Lock up your car (daily rates) and board the *Catalina Express,* double-deck, one-hundred-passenger cruiser. It's best to keep your luggage light or in small bags that you can stow in the ship's hold as you board or carry on with you to place under your airline-style seat. This saves waiting for your luggage when you arrive in Catalina.

The 21.8-mile crossing may be a bit rough in a few spots but on the whole is fairly smooth sailing, as the fast boat seems to skim across the waves. Pretty soon you spot the tall, jagged hills of **Catalina Island** rising dramatically out of the limitless ocean; then you see the tall, graceful, round Casino building in the blue bay encircled by small boats, and you're disembarking in **Avalon.**

Beginning in the 1920s and through its heyday of the 1930s and early 1940s, visitors sailed to Catalina Island from Los Angeles aboard either of two Great White steamers, the S.S. *Avalon* and the S.S. *Catalina,* which carried 2,000 passengers on a never-to-be forgotten adventure. Orchestras played for dancing, and there were food, romance, and the thrill of a two-and-a-half-hour ocean voyage, even though the crossing was frequently rough. (The *Avalon* retired in 1956, and the *Catalina* discontinued its sailings in 1976. Both stopped service during World War II, when they were commandeered by U.S. forces.)

The big ships were welcomed at the pier in Avalon by entertaining, costumed mariachis, as well as by island residents and visitors, since meeting the boat was a high spot of the day. When you left the island on the Great White steamer, your departure was sentimentally serenaded by the mariachis, and folks lined up waving good-bye. During the glamorous Big Band era, all the famous names—Benny Goodman, Count Basie, Harry James, Freddy Martin, Ray Noble, Tommy Dorsey, Jan Garber, Jimmy Dorsey, and others—played nightly for thousands of enthusiastic dancers at the elegant Casino overlooking Catalina Bay. The Casino made history in May 1940, when 6,200 people came to swing and sway to the lilting music of Kay Kyser and his orchestra.

Nowadays high-speed cruisers make multiple sailings to and from Catalina Island daily, with service from five different ports during summer and from four during winter. You can also reach Catalina by helicopter and airplane.

Most hotels arrange to meet their guests at the pier and transport them to the hotel via golf cart as a courtesy service. Upon arrival you may as well check in if your room is ready. You should inquire about check-out time, which is usually quite early, around 10:30 or 11:00 A.M.

Investigate **Crescent Avenue,** Avalon's main street, with its shops and cafes, palm trees, and postage-stamp-size beach that could probably fit in your backyard. The population in Avalon—the only city on the 21-mile-long, 8-mile-wide island—is about 2,470. Summertime visitors increase this to 6,000, and on weekends up to 10,000 crowd the tiny, 1-square-mile city, feeling lucky to find a place to stand on the beach, let alone sprawl on the warm sand.

You'll soon be aware of the pleasant absence of cars. No automobile traffic is permitted, and only a few service-oriented cars are allowed on side streets. Automobile use is limited. There are no rental cars on Catalina Island. Vehicle permits are tightly restricted by the city, and the waiting list is said to be about ten years. In Avalon you mostly walk, ride a bike, use a golf cart, or board a tram.

There's no traffic, no noise or congestion, no smog, and no freeways here—truly an island paradise. You'll really feel on vacation in this happy-go-lucky little seaside resort. There's a vague European Riviera feeling in its compactness, tall palm trees, and jumble of cottages covered with flaming bougainvillea climbing up the steep hillsides. Church bells chime from a hilltop; small boats rock in the sunny bay. The air is soft, and the fragrant, caressing breeze is balmy. It's a bit funky, a bit scruffy—and relaxed, friendly, romantic, carefree, and disarming.

Lunch: **Antonio's Pizzeria and Cabaret,** 230 Crescent Avenue, Avalon. (310) 510–0008. Select a window table overlooking the blue postcard bay or out on the deck in this large, casual local hangout with 1950s decor and sawdust and peanut shells on the floor. Made-to-order thick-crust pizza with four cheeses is served hot and tasty. There're also pasta, steaks, and chicken. Individual jukeboxes at each table is where all the good 1950s music is coming from.

Afternoon

Crescent Avenue, sometimes called Front Street, is made for leisurely window shopping or relaxing on a bench watching the action in the yacht-filled harbor. As the only offshore mooring for Southern California yachtsmen, Catalina originally gained popularity as a yacht haven and sportfishing mecca and is still a prestigious yachting anchorage. John Wayne and other celebrity outdoorsmen used to sail their yachts over to fish for swordfish and marlin. Author Zane Grey, who lived up in the hills for many years, was an ardent fisherman as well. The tall, stately Casino Building dominates the far side of the bay. Shops and restaurants line both sides of the busy, broad, red-bricked street. Stores feature beachwear, casual attire, souvenirs, T-shirts, and kitsch you never dreamed of. Catalina Island Department Store carries active sportswear; the good-looking bookstore has magazines, gifts, and postcards. The staff at the Visitors Information Center, across from the green Pleasure Pier, will be happy to help you line up sightseeing tours convenient to your busy schedule.

A leading island attraction is the twelve-story, landmark art deco **Casino Building,** which opened in 1929 and is where all the Big Bands played·during the swinging years. During the 1930s the famous Casino Ballroom vibrated with 3,000 to 5,000 dancers on an average night. During a forty-minute guided tour of the historic Casino Building, you're waltzed out on the circular dance floor for a nostalgic twirl, then onto the broad terrace for photogenic views of the harbor, city, and mountains. This tour also includes the **Avalon Theater,** the **Catalina Island Museum,** and the **Catalina Art Association Gallery** in the building (fee for tour).

Dinner: **Cafe Prego,** 403 Crescent Avenue, Avalon. (310) 510–1218. Considered Avalon's finest Italian cuisine. Try to snag a streetside window table or one facing the water so you can watch the lights twinkling in the harbor. You could be in a small, romantic seaside cafe in Portofino. Dinners include soup, crisp salad, and a basket of bread. Try the richly flavored pasta combo: manicotti and cannelloni with aglio olio linguini. Dinner only; casual dress; best to reserve.

Lodging: **Pavilion Lodge,** on Crescent Avenue, Avalon, CA 90704. (800) 4–AVALON (from California, 8:00 A.M. to 5:00 P.M.); (310) 510–1788 (twenty-four-hour service). Opposite the beachfront, seventy-one rooms cluster around a sunny, grassy courtyard. Newly remodeled and refurbished, the lodge is sparkling clean, with cable TV, minirefrigerator, in-room coffeemaker, complimentary coffee in the lobby, and courtesy baggage service to and from the boat terminal (no in-room telephone). Two-person, two-night packages from Sunday to Wednesday include round-trip boat transportation and choice of two island tours.

Day 2

Morning

Breakfast: **The Busy Bee,** 306 Crescent Avenue, Avalon. (310) 510–1983. If the sun's shining, you'll want breakfast outdoors at one of Catalina's oldest restaurants. At a deckside table over the shining water, you can savor pancakes and eggs, New Orleans Scramble with Cajun sausage, and other specialties.

In summer Avalon is a splendid place to lounge on the beach or go for a swim. But after breakfast you'll probably have to check out of your room. The Pavilion Lodge will store your luggage and transport it to the boat in time for your departure. (Not all hotels include this courtesy service.)

To see more of Santa Catalina Island than just the downtown area, opt for the **Avalon Scenic Tour,** which takes you on a 9-mile, fifty-minute narrated tour from the waterfront up into the hills high above the harbor. Your driver tells the history of Catalina Island, which was discovered in 1542 by Juan Cabrillo, a Portuguese explorer, who named it San Salvador. It was rediscovered sixty years later by Spanish explorer Sebastian Viscaino, who renamed it Santa Catalina in honor of St. Catherine's Feast Day. Both explorers claimed the island for Spain, which did not attempt to colonize it.

During the 1880s Yankee sailors and Russian fur traders from Alaska began a thriving, illegal sea-otter fur trade. Additionally, there were cattle and sheep raising, smuggling, and a gold stampede, all of which ended during the Civil War, when U.S. Army (Union) troops arrived and took possession of the island. Their barracks building, which remains in the small village of Two Harbors at the other end of the island, is now home of the Isthmus Yacht Club.

The tour-guide driver then fills you in about the island's many owners. At the end of the Mexican War in 1848, Pio Pico, California's last Mexican governor, allegedly deeded the island to an American, Thomas Robbins, in exchange for a horse and silver-trimmed saddle. There was a succession of private American owners before the island was sold to the Banning Brothers, who formed Santa Catalina Island Company to develop the island as a pleasure and fishing resort.

Outside of Avalon the rest of the island's 74 square miles are largely uninhabitable and pretty much the same as they were when the island was discovered 450 years ago, thanks to the foresight of William Wrigley, Jr., the chewing-gum magnate who purchased Catalina Island in 1919 and began improvements and conservation programs to preserve its natural beauty. In 1972 the Wrigley family established the Santa Catalina Island Conservancy to protect and preserve Catalina for future generations. The conservancy now owns about 80 percent of the island's 76 square miles.

Among other high spots brought to passengers' attention is Zane Grey's "Pueblo Hotel." Built in 1926, it is the former hillside home of the prolific author of eighty-nine books, including *Riders of the Purple Sage, Call of the Canyon,* and other western novels. Also pointed out is the former Wrigley estate, now a popular hillside B&B. The bus winds up around the hills, and you have passed absolutely no other car on the road, which overlooks Catalina's 9-hole golf course, tennis courts, stables, and the baseball field where, from 1921, Wrigley's Chicago Cubs held their annual spring baseball training for about twenty-six years. View stops and photo opportunities are plentiful on this tour (tour fee).

Lunch: **Armstrong's Fish Market and Seafood Restaurant,** 306 Crescent Avenue, Avalon. (310) 510–0113. Sit inside the small, cheery dining room with blue-and-white checkered tablecloths or out on the broad deck over Avalon Bay. Lunch favorites are mesquite-charbroiled fresh swordfish and seafood specialties that include rice pilaf, cole slaw, or steamed vegetable.

Afternoon

Stroll the green **Pleasure Pier,** where the Chamber of Commerce can answer any questions and make suggestions. Along the pier you'll find boat rentals and Catalina Diver's Supply Shop. Eric's is known for burgers, sandwiches, and ice cream. At the end of the pier where the seagulls convene, Earl & Rosie's Seafood snack bar has, since 1967, been dispensing burgers, fries, and its specialty abalone burgers with tartar sauce and melted cheese.

About midway along this pier, board the **Glass Bottom Boat,** where you can see through Catalina's crystalline waters below the surface of the sea to a marine preserve of brightly hued fish and giant beds of kelp. This cruise is best on a sunny day when visibility is generally 70 to 80 percent. The iridescent orange Garibaldi, California's state marine fish, is easy to spot. Sleek baby California sea lions do somersaults beneath the glass floor, so close you can count their whiskers. Occasionally, you might see a cormorant, a large feathered bird that swims underwater, greedily feasting on fish as fast as it can catch them in its long beak. Night trips are also available (trip fee).

If there's time before you leave the island, browse Avalon's fascinating side streets. **Catalina Design Center,** 125 Sumner Avenue, is a stunning shop, with contemporary handmade jewelry, mobiles, art objects, and T-shirts. On Metropole Street are Von's grocery and the multilevel **Metropole Market Place and Hotel,** a rambling complex of small shops and restaurants around a pretty courtyard.

Head for the boat pier about fifteen to twenty minutes before departing the storybook island to claim your luggage, if it's been forwarded by your hotel. The cruise back to the mainland is frequently smoother sailing than coming over. Disembarking in Long Beach, pick up your car and head for the 710 Freeway north to Los Angeles.

There's More

Santa Catalina Island Company Discovery Tours, P.O. Box 737, Avalon, CA 90704. (800) 322–3434 nationwide); (310) 510–2500. This company offers a variety of island tours. The extremely popular Inland Motor Tour is a three-and-three-quarter-hour scenic adventure that includes an Arabian horse show and visits the rugged and unspoiled wilderness interior, where you can see rare native plants and free-roaming buffalo herds, descendants of those brought over in 1924 for the filming of Zane Grey's book *The Vanishing American.* Inquire about other exciting island tours.

Wrigley Memorial and Botanical Garden, 1400 Avalon Canyon Road, honors William Wrigley, Jr's., lifework in preservation of the island. The huge memorial is the almost forty-acre showcase of Catalina native plants. Open daily, 8:00 A.M. to 5:00 P.M. Tram service from Island Plaza, or inquire at Visitors Center.

Two Harbors at the Isthmus is a casual, secluded, small village for camping and hiking; it has swimming beaches and a B&B as well. Among many movies filmed in this scenic area are *Hurricane, Mutiny on the Bounty,* and *MacArthur.* For information, call (313) 510–0303.

Catalina Safari Bus supplies daily scheduled transportation between Avalon and Two Harbors, with stops throughout the island. Call (310) 510–2800.

West End Divers offers daily scuba and snorkeling trips. Call (310) 510–0303.

Brown's Bike Rentals and Sales, 107 Pebbly Beach Road, Avalon. (310) 510–0986. Across from the basketball court. Open 9:00 A.M. to 5:00 P.M. Permit required outside of Avalon or Two Harbors.

Boats to Catalina from different ports. Catalina Express. (310) 519–1212; (800) 540–4573.

Catalina Cruises. (800) 888–5939 (in California); (310) 253–9800.

Seajet Cruise Lines in San Diego. (619) 696–0088.
Island Express Helicopter. (310) 510–2525; (800) 228–2566.

Special Events

Early January. Benefit 50-Mile Run, Avalon to Two Harbors.
Mid-February. Sunday Afternoon Dance, Casino Ballroom.
Mid-March. Annual Catalina Marathon, Avalon.
Early May. Cinco de Mayo Celebration, Two Harbors.
Mid-May. Silent Film Classic, Casino Theater.
July 4. Fireworks Display over Avalon Bay.
Mid-September. Annual Catalina Festival of Art, Avalon.
Early- to mid-October. Annual Catalina Jazz Trax Festival, Avalon.
Mid-October. Plein Air Painter's Show, Avalon.
End of October. Halloween Costume Ball, Casino Ballroom.
End of December. Annual New Year's Eve Celebration, Casino
Ballroom. New Year's Eve Gala, Two Harbors.

Other Recommended
Restaurants and Lodgings

Avalon

Note: Catalina Island hotels offer various midweek and seasonal
rates and packages. The high-rate summer season is mid-June to mid-
September. Some packages include round-trip boat passage, island
tours, a courtesy taxi to and from the boat dock, and continental
breakfast. It's best to inquire when making reservations.
   Channel House, 205 Crescent Avenue. (310) 510–1218. Noted for
savory European cuisine. Lunch and dinner specialties feature
schnitzel, chicken pasta Cabo San Lucas; Sunday brunch.
   Ristorante Villa Portofino, 111 Crescent Avenue. (310) 510–0508.
This classy dining room with flowers on white tablecloths opens to
the beachfront street. A dinner favorite for northern Italian dishes of
homemade pastas, lasagna, ravioli filled with pheasant, Penne Arrabi-
ata. Reservations recommended.
   Sally's Waffle Shop, on the beachfront opposite the green Pleasure
Pier. (310) 510–0355. Breakfast headquarters for islanders and visitors
who fancy its variety of omelets and waffles.
   Casa Mariquita, 229 Metropole Avenue. (800) 545–1182; (310)
510–1192. AAA, new Spanish-style hotel, ¾ block from the beach, with
nineteen rooms, cable TV, minifridge, and complimentary coffee, tea,

and hot chocolate. Two-night, midweek packages include boat trip and tours.

Hotel Metropole, 123 Crescent Avenue. (800) 541–8528; (310) 510–1884. Opened in 1990 in attractive Metropole Market Place; entrance is on Whitley Avenue. Forty-seven custom rooms, cable TV, complimentary continental breakfast in the lobby, welcome bottle of house wine. Various two-night, midweek seasonal rates and packages include round-trip boat passage.

For More Information

Catalina Visitor's Information Center, P.O. Box 737, Avalon, CA 90704. (800) 4–AVALON (in California); (310) 510–3000.

Catalina Island Chamber of Commerce and Visitors Bureau, P.O. Box 217, Avalon, CA 90704. (310) 510–1520.

Northern Escapes

Malibu

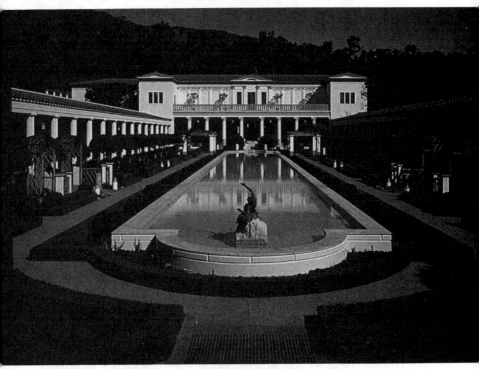

Classic pool at entrance of J. Paul Getty Museum

Surf and Celebrities

_____ 1 NIGHT _____
Watersports • Celebrities • Museums
Shopping • Parks • Hiking • Horseback riding

Malibu is a magical name forever identified with the romance and glamour of movie stars and celebrities, golden beaches, bronzed sunbathers and surfers, partying, and rich, famous, and beautiful people with extravagant beach houses and fancy, expensive cars—the epitome of everything the California good life stands for.

In reality, Malibu is a small, unpretentious, and informal residential community, situated on a stunningly expensive and scenic beachfront that stretches 27 miles up the gold coast to the Ventura County line.

In a two-day outing to the seductive beach kingdom, you'll soak up the same sun on soft, sandy beaches as the Academy Award winners who live nearby; stroll the water's frothy edge; walk on Malibu Pier and watch sportfishing boats set out and anglers cast their lines over the rail; follow the fearless, easy-riding surfers as the big rollers overtake them; goggle for celebrities (check the markets, bookstores, and cafes); visit the world's richest museum; go surfing at a world-famous surfing beach; and go scuba and skin diving. Learn to speak Malibu, the most beautiful word in Southern California.

Day 1

Morning

Drive out Sunset Boulevard west of San Diego Freeway 405 for a scenic, curving drive past Bel Air, Brentwood, Mandeville Canyon, the Riviera (with all Italian street names), the Riviera Country Club, and beautiful estates and lush landscaping along the way.

Sunset Boulevard winds down and curves past Rustic and Sullivan canyons, and tall eucalyptus trees grace the scenic road, adding to its rural look. On weekends there's another look: one of traffic and slow-moving cars going to and from the beaches, as Sunset is the main thoroughfare. Try to visit Malibu during the week, when traffic is light and you'll find more parking spaces at the beach.

You pass **Will Rogers State Historic Park,** formerly the ranch of the American humorist and movie star. His 137-acre estate, with a polo field and a picnic area, is open for tours.

Drive through the Pacific Palisades area, where former President Reagan used to live; it has the only business section on Sunset Boulevard. Continue past Temescal Canyon and Marquez Knolls, winding down again as you approach the ocean around the Self-Realization complex and its small lake. You arrive at the beach at Pacific Coast Highway, where you can see the blue bay and the surfers dotting the water.

You're at your first stop as you turn into the driveway for the **J. Paul Getty Museum,** 17985 Pacific Coast Highway (310) 458–2003, atop an ocean bluff on a sixty-five-acre estate, the first or second signal past Sunset Boulevard. Admission and parking are free, but you must phone ahead for a parking reservation. There is no drop-in visiting.

If you miss the driveway, take the next right and follow through the wide stone arches up the hill to "Visitor Parking" in the underground garage. Take the elevator to the second floor, turn left, walk up a few marble steps, and you're viewing the long, serene pool and main peristyle garden, with its formal plantings leading to the vestibule entrance and the museum. Plan to spend several hours touring the Getty's treasures.

The Getty, a private museum built in 1974, is said to be the richest museum in the world. The building is a re-creation of an ancient Roman country villa that was buried, along with Pompeii, in the eruption of Mount Vesuvius in A.D. 79. Archaelogists rediscovered the villa during the eighteenth century, 60 feet below the earth. Their notes and copies of its floor plan were the basis for the design of the museum.

Its prestigious permanent collections include Greek and Roman antiquities, found on the main level. Upper galleries house pre-twentieth-century drawings, European paintings, sculpture, rare illuminated medieval manuscripts, decorative arts made for French nobility, and American and European photographs from the early 1840s to the 1950s. The small, busy bookstore, on the main level, just to the left as you enter the vestibule, contains many art publications, books, posters, postcards, and color slides. The Garden Tea Room, through the vestibule and to the left, offers moderately priced, cafeteria-style lunches of sandwiches, salads, soups, and desserts from 11:00 A.M. to 2:30 P.M. and light refreshments from 9:30 A.M. to 4:30 P.M. Changing exhibitions, lectures, films, courses, and programs are part of the museum's ongoing offerings. (Open Tuesday through Sunday, 10:00 A.M. to 5:00 P.M.; closed Monday and all major holidays.)

When the new J. Paul Getty Center is completed in West Los Angeles in 1996, all collections except antiquities will be moved there. The villa in Malibu will become the country's only museum devoted exclusively to Roman and Greek art.

Leaving the museum, you see the ocean glittering through the trees. Turn left to Pacific Coast Highway and then turn right, past Topanga Canyon and the beginning of Malibu, past the Reel Inn Restaurant (18661), noted for fresh fish. Continue along past Big Rock Beach, Las Flores Beach, and Surf Riders State Beach to the famous **Malibu Pier** and hope for some roadside parking.

Lunch: **Alice's Restaurant,** 23000 Pacific Coast Highway, Malibu. (310) 456–6646. Tucked alongside Malibu Pier, this congenial, casual, and elegant landmark offers windows facing the beach and ocean. The door at the left of the bar is open to the pier, and everywhere you look is beach and ocean. The rather high-priced California cuisine menu includes smoked chicken quesadillas, a good Cobb salad, and daily lunch specials of fresh fish, pastas, sandwiches, and hamburgers.

Afternoon

Walk out on the famous 870-foot-long, privately owned Malibu Pier, or drift onto the sand at **Surf Riders Beach,** considered the best surfing beach in Southern California, to watch the surfers riding the long rollers in to shore. This beach is also excellent for swimming; restrooms and showers are here too.

You're at Malibu Lagoon and the **Malibu Lagoon Museum,** 23200 Pacific Coast Highway (310–456–8432; giftshop, 310–456–9378). The small museum is part of the Adamson House, built in 1929 for the Rindge family's daughter and her husband. Any Malibu buff will tell you that the house has always been here on the surfers' beach. May and Frederick Rindge originally bought the entire 13,000-acre Malibu Rancho in 1891 for around $10.00 an acre. Years later, during the 1920s May Rindge fought winning battles to keep Southern Pacific from running tracks through her backyard. Finally, in 1925, the state of California built the Pacific Coast Highway through Malibu. The Adamson House has been designated a national Historic Site as well as a Califonia landmark.

The small house is furnished with beautiful old Spanish Colonial Revival–style pieces. At first glance the seashore seems a strange place for an elaborate fringed Persian carpet. But after a careful second look, you realize that the floor is made entirely of the old "Malibu Potteries" ceramic tiles of the 1920s, in the intricate, floral design of a Persian carpet, complete with fringe. The clear orange, bright yellow, and jade green colors have not lost their jewel-like richness after so many years. (Open Wednesday through Saturday, 11:00 A.M. to 3:00 P.M.)

Movie stars began arriving in Malibu in the early 1920s and established an exclusive, private enclave. **Malibu Colony** is still home to many celebrities, including Johnny Carson, Barbra Streisand, Cher, Ali McGraw, Burgess Meredith, Carroll O'Connor, and a roster of directors, producers, writers, and other creative people who live, work, and cherish their privacy in the area where Chumash Indians lived for 4,000 years.

You can't really see the stars' homes, because they front on the beach. With their closed garage doors facing the road, you can't check out the Mercedes, BMWs, and Rolls-Royces or even the Land Rovers. With a scarcity of beachfront property, all of it extremely expensive, houses are packed tightly together.

Unfortunately, Malibu is periodically subjected to nature's terrible rampages and destructive forces, with raging fires sweeping through the area, fueled by heavy winds. Disastrous landslides and flooding during a heavy rainy season cause lavish beachfront homes to slide and wash partly away into the roaring sea, and million-dollar profiles are seen on the late news piling sandbags around their homes attempting to protect them from damage. Residents seem to accept nature's ravages, and many consider it a small price to pay for the privilege of living in beautiful exclusive Malibu.

Hikers and equestrians explore richly scenic canyons and parks in the Santa Monica Mountains, where many movies and TV series are filmed. Most of these areas provide overlooks for exceptional panoramic coastline viewing.

Back on Pacific Coast Highway, drive to the 23700 block to Malibu Colony, where most of the stars reside. Turn left at the signal on Webb Way to Malibu Road and **Malibu Colony Plaza.** This attractive, sprawling complex of coral buildings with red-tile roofs is surrounded by a tropical landscape of hanging flower baskets, a fountain, and benches. Besides popular restaurants, among the numerous shops are Campbell-Tolstad stationers, Theodore's chic sportswear, handsome SavOn Drug, Hughes Market, and Nikki's clothing. To drive along the famed Malibu Beach colony road to see where the stars live, turn left on Webb Way and left again at Malibu Road and drive until you come to the gatehouse, where the rest is a private road. Public-access stairways to the beaches are between 24300 and 24700 Malibu Road.

As you continue along Pacific Coast Highway, you pass unobtrusive Pepperdine University on the inland side and also Mulholland Road to the valley and Freeway 101/Calabasas. Traffic is fast and can be relentless behind you, allowing little time to pause and look around as you drive. You go past the Malibu Fish/Seafood restaurant, then past Corral and Latigo Canyon, where huge boulders loom in the waters close offshore. At **Malibu Bluffs Community Park,** the emerald grass leads to playground equipment, a soccer field, and groups of active youngsters. You curve down toward several beautiful bays along this scenic highway under a blue Malibu sky, and—who needs the French Riviera?

Drive past Paradise Cove, where they filmed "Gilligan's Island" and some of the "Rockford Files" series. At **Point Dume State Beach,** you'll find a big, beautiful beach that has volleyball facilities and is excellent for swimming, diving, and fishing. Point Dume was named by English explorer George Vancouver, sent by King George III to explore America's West Coast in 1792. The explorer named the point after Father Dumetz, a padre he met at San Buenaventura to the north (now Ventura).

After Point Dume you come to **Zuma Beach,** the most popular beach in the area, covering 105 acres and offering a volleyball court and playground. It's a broad, clean expanse of sand, and there's a strong surf with high waves. Zuma has good swimming but also has dangerous riptides in the summer, though there's plenty of skin diving and good fishing. Street parking is available, and you can step from the busy roadside onto the warm, soft sand.

Next is **Trancas Beach,** at about 31800 Pacific Coast Highway, where many celebrities live. Drive along rural Broad Beach Road, noting its expensive beachfront homes; here tall sand dunes act as windbreaks. Public-access stairways to beaches are in the 31200 to 31300 block.

After Encinal Beach continue around the curving bay past Nicholas Beach, with its dramatic ocean bluffs, to the very popular **Leo Carrillo Beach State Park,** practically at the Ventura County line. There's good skin and scuba diving here, as well as good swimming. Sailboarders love it, and you'll sometimes see about 200 of them out on the water at one time. This state park has two campgrounds; for information, call (818) 706-1310.

Returning from Leo Carrillo Beach, drive back toward Malibu Pier. Turn off the highway and drive down some of the quiet oceanside streets to the water and prowl the uncrowded beaches.

Continuing east, turn left, inland across the highway, at Cross Creek Road and Malibu Creek Plaza, 3800 Cross Creek Road, to a large shopping and dining center that includes Wherehouse, Crown Books, Super Care Drugs, Malibu Cinema, and other shops and eateries.

There's more across the narrow street at Malibu Country Shops, on Civic Center Way, and at Malibu Country Mart, 3835 Cross Creek Road, an upscale, inviting shopping-dining complex that rambles around lawns, pathways, and a children's play area. Browsers especially like to explore the bakery, clothing and jewelry store, Gallery Millieu, and Cosentino's Nursery.

Dinner: **Malibu Adobe Restaurant,** 23410 Civic Center Way, Malibu. (310) 456-2021. Good-looking, friendly local favorite, with patio dining. Appetizers include Cajun chicken and Ahi tuna tacos. Daily specials highlight grilled salmon with black beans and rice, mesquite-grilled New York steak, and pastas. Happy Hour offers complimentary hors d'oeuvres, and there's dancing to live-band music Thursday to Saturday evenings. The Santa Fe–style decor is by Ali McGraw.

Lodging: **Malibu Beach Inn,** 22878 Pacific Coast Highway, Malibu, CA 90265. (800) 4-MALIBU; (310) 456-6445. Steps from Malibu Pier, fairly new, handsome Spanish-style hotel on the beach features forty-seven rooms, including three suites, all with beachfront balconies and panoramic views right on to Hawaii, wetbar, refrigerator, fireplace, TV and VCR, clock radio, coffeemaker, hair dryer, personal safe, and nightly turndown service. Complimentary California continental breakfast is served in the lobby, on the oceanfront patio, or in your room. On weekends there is a two-night minimum stay, though there's the occasional exception.

Day 2

Morning

Breakfast: At the inn. Festive complimentary continental breakfast served in the lobby includes bagels, muffins, English muffins, assorted fresh melons and fruits, cereal, and tea, coffee, and hot chocolate.

This is going to be a beach day. Malibu's beaches are clean and beautiful and you'll welcome the chance to enjoy them at a relaxed pace. Swim, sunbathe, or stroll along the water's edge and watch the lively action in the surf.

Lunch: **Malibu Inn Restaurant,** 22969 Pacific Coast Highway, Malibu. (310) 456–6106. Across from Malibu Pier; a local hangout, with wooden floor, booths, old-fashioned glass, mirrors, and photos decor. Southwestern specialties include fajitas and tacos; pizza, pasta, and hamburgers served as well. Funky bar in adjacent room.

Afternoon

Enjoy the rest of the day at sunny and peaceful Malibu beach. Retrace your route back to Los Angeles.

There's More

Golf. Malibu Golf Course, 901 Encinal Canyon Road and Mulholland Highway. (818) 889–6680.

Horseback riding. Arabians for rent. (310) 456–2173.

Red Barn Stables. (818) 707–9395.

Tennis. Malibu Racquet Club, 23847 Stuart Ranch Road. (310) 456–3313.

Malibu Riding & Tennis Club, 33905 Pacific Coast Highway. (310) 457–9783.

Sportfishing. Malibu Pier Sport Fishing, 23000 Pacific Coast Highway. (310) 456–8030.

Wylie's Bait & Tackle, 18757 Pacific Coast Highway. (310) 456–2321.

Nursery. Cosentino's Nursery, 21201 Pacific Coast Highway. (310) 456–6707.

Camping, RV parks. State of California Department of Parks and Recreation, 1925 Las Virgenes Road, Calabesa, CA 91302–1909.

Malibu Beach RV Park, 25801 Pacific Coast Highway. (310) 456–6052.

Special Events

Last full weekend in July. Art Festival.
Last weekend in November and three full weekends in December. County Christmas Village, Calamigos Ranch, 327 Latigo Canyon Road.

Other Recommended
Restaurants and Lodgings

Malibu

Granita, 23725 West Malibu Road, Malibu Colony Plaza. (310) 456–0488. More discreet than an unlisted phone number, this place has no name sign identifying it as Wolfgang Puck's posh restaurant, but its expensive decor is a giveaway, from the glass-screened patio to the marble entrance. The trademark open kitchen features scallops appetizers, entrees such as roast Sonoma lamb with artichoke mousse, and for dessert it's the pecan tart.

Geoffrey's Restaurant, 27400 Pacific Coast Highway. (310) 457–4519. On an ocean bluff, with terrific views and attractive gardens. Expensive continental cuisine items favor grilled steak, creative gourmet salads, and fresh fish.

Beaurivage, 26025 Pacific Coast Highway. (310) 456–5733. Across from the ocean; the red-tiled roof makes it easy to spot. Recently remodeled, light and flowery decor feels just right in this Mediterranean restaurant. Menu offers Italian, Greek, and Spanish foods, as well as porterhouse steaks. Dinner only, plus Sunday champagne brunch. Good service, expensive, dressy.

Coogie's Beach Cafe, 23755 West Malibu Road, Malibu Colony Plaza. (310) 317–1444. High-tech, large, bright, casual family place where, along with salads and charbroiled hamburgers, specialties include Szechuan-style mahi-mahi and linguini with shrimp.

Charley Brown's, 21150 Pacific Coast Highway. (310) 456–2810. The Sea Lion has been gone since December 1991, but the same tables overlook the broad expanse of ocean. Green Grocer salad bar is an extensive array of cold appetizers, a meal in itself or an addition to entrees. Sunday champagne brunch.

Casa Malibu on the Beach, 22752 Pacific Coast Highway. (800) 831–0858; (310) 456–2219. Twenty-seven rooms around a sunny courtyard, some with beachfront decks, all with coffeemaker, refrigerator, cable TV, clock radio. You'll need to book a month in advance for summer weekends.

Malibu Shores Motel, 23033 Pacific Coast Highway. (310) 456–6559. On the inland side; two-story typical motel, small bedroom, small bath.

For More Information

Malibu Chamber of Commerce, 23805 Stuart Ranch Road (extension of Webb Way), Suite 100, Malibu, CA 90265–4897. (310) 456–9025.

The Santa Monica Mountains Conservancy. (800) 533–PARK. Provides park and hiking information.

Malibu Creek State Park. (818) 706–1310. Provides campsite, hiking, and fishing information.

Ventura/Oxnard

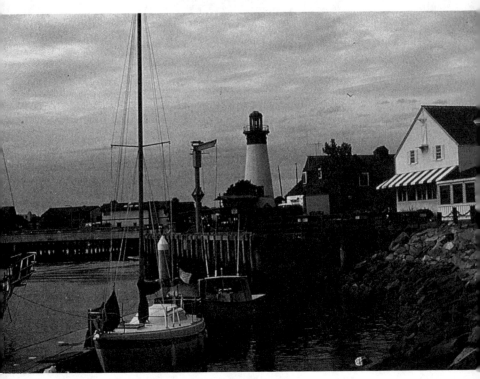

Lighthouse at Oxnard's Channel Island Harbor

Harbor Hopping

1 NIGHT

Historic sites · Beaches · Waterfront dining · Local produce
Harbor and island cruises · Whale-watching · Antiques · Watersports

This two-day, one-night escape to a nearby pair of small, friendly coastal cities offers refreshing harbor and marina activities and lifestyles, a famous mission, historical sites, museums, and adventure cruises to scenic offshore islands. You'll shop, dine, and snack at the bubbling waterfronts; purchase fresh produce at its source; and stretch out on splendid, sunny, uncrowded beaches.

Day 1
Morning

Drive north on Ventura Freeway 101 through the San Fernando Valley. Along the Conejo Grade you can see the flat valley spread out to the foothills. Though much of the time the air is misty, you can still see across acres of citrus groves and farms and frequently spot workers in the fields picking the strawberries for which the area is famous—like a painting by Millet. Ventura County is a leading producer of lemons and strawberries and has a great deal of open space. In Oxnard, from the freeway and along roads leading to the ocean and beaches, are miles of lemon groves and fields of strawberries and celery, which flourish in the rich soil of the Oxnard Plain. After passing Oxnard, continue a short distance north to Ventura, alongside richly cultivated farms. Ancient, leafy eucalyptus trees with trunks as thick as a barn door stand tall astride the freeway.

In **Ventura** exit the freeway at California Street, turning right on Main Street and then left on Main for the historic downtown area. The city's noted **San Buenaventura Mission,** 211 East Main Street (805–643–4318), where the city of Ventura began, is a few blocks farther along Main, between Junipero and Palm.

You enter the mission a few doors away, through its giftshop, at 225 East Main Street, which sells religious artifacts and cards. The giftshop leads to the small Museum of Vestments, which displays clothing worn by the missionary fathers over a 200-year period. Walk through the pleasant mission garden, with its Spanish-style fountain and tall, shady trees. The small church, graced by a tall beamed ceiling, wrought-iron chandeliers, wall paintings, and lighted candles at the altar, holds services every Sunday. San Buenaventura Mission, founded in 1782, was the ninth of twenty-one California missions built during Spain's occupation of California, and it was the last mission founded by Father Junípero Serra. The mission, open from 10:00 A.M. to 5:00 P.M. daily, offers self-guided tours (50-cent admission fee).

Next door to the church, the red-tile-roofed **Albinger Archaeological Museum,** 113 East Main Street, (805–648–5823), exhibits some of the 30,000 artifacts discovered in a 1974–75 dig. The oldest treasure is a bowl dating back 2,500 years. (Open Tuesday through Sunday from 10:00 A.M. to 4:00 P.M.; free.)

Across the street the **Ventura County Museum of History and Art,** 100 East Main Street (805–653–0323) houses three galleries. The Smith Gallery features the George Stuart Historical Figures Collection

of some 197 miniature figures in rotating exhibits. Authentically detailed and elaborately costumed, the figures represent leading historical persons, including Abraham Lincoln, Queen Victoria, Marie
Antoinette, and Louis XIV. The Native American Room displays Chumash Indian pottery and a small, glass-enclosed statue of Father
Junípero Serra. The Hoffman Gallery's changing exhibitions range
from fine arts to local history. The giftshop is nicely stocked with ethnic jewelry, as well as a variety of art, travel, and local history books.
(Open Tuesday through Sunday from 10:00 A.M. to 5:00 P.M.; docent-
led tours Sunday at 1:30 P.M.; free.)

About 5 blocks from the mission, **Ortega Adobe,** 100 West Main
Street (805–654–7837), is the last of the downtown area's small
adobes. Built in 1857, this is the site where Emilio Ortega began fire-
roasting his chiles and started the popular Pioneer Ortega Chili Company, said to be the first commercial food manufacturing venture in
California. The furnishings and interior of this small, red-tile-roofed
home offer insight into family living during the era.

Before driving down to the waterfront for lunch and sightseeing,
check out some of Ventura's noted **antiques dealers** on Main Street.
Heirloom Antiques, 494 East Main Street (805–643–6050), ensconced on
the corner in what formerly was the First National Bank of 1926, claims
to have the largest selection of French antique furniture in the tricoun-
ties. Marge's Antiques, at 451 East Main, shows costume jewelry, glass,
china, and primitives. (Open Tuesday through Saturday from noon to
4:30 P.M. and Sunday till 4:00 P.M.). Nicholby Antiques, 404 East Main, is
a group of forty dealers of glass, toys, furniture, and collectibles.

To get to the waterfront and Ventura Harbor Village, turn right on
California Street, and continue to Harbor Boulevard and the Promenade.

Lunch: **Berto's Ristorante,** 1591 Spinnaker Drive, Ventura. (805)
658–8800. On the marina. A gourmet Italian gem, with white tablecloths, period-style chairs, and waiters sporting gondola-type outfits. It
is an elegant choice for veal specialties and freshly caught local
seafood. Patio dining; Happy Hour; Sunday champagne brunch.

Afternoon

Ventura Harbor Village, spread along thirty-three waterfront
acres, is the area's largest harborside dining-shopping-entertainment
showcase. Tall, red-roofed spires and arches envelop shops, galleries,
restaurants, theater, and a carousel, amid bright flowers, colorful sailboats, and yachts swaying in the sparkling marina. For a spin across
the water, board the *Harbor Queen* or the *Bay Queen* for forty-minute
cruises, which leave hourly Tuesday through Sunday, from 1567
Spinnaker Drive, Slip 14 (805–642–7753).

Drop by the gray, weathered, three-story **Channel Islands Na-**

tional Park Headquarters and Visitors Center, 1901 Spinnaker Drive (805–644–8262). Park rangers offer information on what you'll see on trips to the five rugged, primeval Channel Islands, lying just 14 miles off Ventura's coast. Tidepool displays and topographic island exhibits point out the characteristics of each island. The elevator whisks you to the top-floor deck tower for a tremendous panoramic view of the harbor, the mountains, and the Channel Islands out in the Pacific. (Open daily from 8:00 A.M. to 5:00 P.M., later in summer; free). For more detailed and firsthand information on year-round excursions to the islands, visit Island Packers, the only commercial charter permitted to land on the Channel Islands. 1867 Spinnaker Drive (805–642–7688).

If you want to get out on the sand and in the water, practically next door to the Channel Island National Park Headquarters is **Marina Cove Beach,** the city's safest swimming beach, protected by a breakwater and offering a children's play area and restrooms. **Surfer's Point,** at Seaside Park, is one of the most popular surfing and sailboarding beaches. Closer by, the 1,200-foot-long **Ventura Pier,** completed in 1872, had its heyday when the harbor was filled with steamships whose passengers and cargoes waited to be loaded and unloaded. Nowadays visitors strolling the long, peaceful pier can watch fishermen casting their lines for bass and bonita.

Dinner: **Alexander's Restaurant** in Harbortown Marina Resort, 1050 Schooner Drive, Ventura. (805) 658–1212; (800) 622–1212 (in California). Alongside the boat-filled marina, this intimate room is a favorite rendezvous for fine (albeit pricey) dinner specialties, such as New York steak stuffed with Roquefort cheese, tournedos with whiskey peppercorn sauce, prime rib, grilled swordfish, and broiled lobster; all include choice of Alexander's Caesar salad or seafood chowder.

Lodging: **Harbortown Marina Resort,** 1050 Schooner Drive, Ventura, CA 93001. (805) 658–1212; (800) 622–1212 (in California). An AAA, four-diamond resort 1 block from the beach and edging the marina. The dynamic, rambling architecture was designed by the Frank Lloyd Wright Foundation. Offers views from each of its 160 rooms and suites, cable TV, complimentary in-room coffee; heated swimming pool, three tennis courts, spa, and nearby golf. Rates include breakfast buffet daily in Alexander's Restaurant and unlimited cocktails between 5:00 and 7:00 P.M. with complimentary hors d'oeuvres in the Dockside Lounge of Alexander's Restaurant. Sunday Brunch.

Day 2

Morning

Breakfast: At the resort. Breakfast buffet in Alexander's Restaurant

offers ample selections, from omelets, any-style eggs, and cold cereal
to bagels and lox.

Oxnard, 60 miles from Los Angeles and the "Strawberry Capital of
the United States," is just minutes away along the scenic Gold Coast.
Follow Harbor Boulevard south along the beautiful stretches of pale,
near-deserted beaches from San Buenaventura State Beach, which begins at Ventura Pier, passing McGrath State Beach, with its sand dunes
and lagoons, and Mandalay Beach to Channel Islands Boulevard and
Channel Islands Harbor, a lively waterfront resort, recreation, and
dining marketplace. Chumash Indians fished and hunted here in the
dramatic, lonely marshes you can see from the highway.

The horseshoe-shaped **Channel Islands Harbor** complex com-
prises **Harbor Landing,** the **Marine Emporium,** and **Fisherman's
Wharf,** flagged by its white lighthouse and home to the **Ventura
County Maritime Museum.** In this bustling area, a variety of specialty shops, restaurants, and sidewalk cafes add to the appeal of this
special and sunny seaside setting.

Oxnard Harbor, considered to be one of California's finest full-
service facilities, has 2,600 boat slips, four yacht clubs, and nine full
service marinas. It also offers beautifully landscaped parks with attractive picnic areas and barbecues.

Stroll around the terra-cotta-colored buildings of **Harbor Landing
Promenade** (2800 South Harbor Boulevard), and watch the masts of
boats and small craft bobbing in the pristine harbor. Along here you
can buy a yacht, charter a sportfishing or cruise boat, take sailing
lessons, rent a bike or a boat, and go whale-watching from December
through March when the Pacific grey whales pass through the channel
on their annual migration from Alaska to Baja. For a change of scene,
board the Harbor Hopper ferry for a tour of the harbor, by dialing (805)
985–HOPP, as you would call a taxi (various rates, closed Monday).

From Harbor Landing, drive or walk alongside the water a few
blocks to the **Marine Emporium,** 3600 South Harbor Boulevard
(805–984–3677), a grey-and-white trimmed waterfront shopping-dining
complex of New England style clapboard architecture. Among the numerous shops, **Coast Chandlery** features traditional nautical items
and supplies, which are in sharp contrast to the unique clothing and
gift boutique—**Dress Canvas Loft**—upstairs.

Fisherman's Wharf, just across the water, is your next destination.
To get there, turn right on Channel Islands Boulevard, go across the
bridge to Victoria Avenue, turn right and park.

Lunch: **Reuben's** in Fisherman's Wharf, 3910 West Channel Islands
Boulevard at Victoria Avenue, Oxnard. (805) 985–3922. A popular
steakhouse and seafood grill, in the shadow of the picturesque lighthouse. Salads, sandwiches, fresh seafood, prime ribs, and lemon herb

chicken are all equally delicious on the sunny cobblestone patio or in the attractive dining room overlooking the water. Happy Hour, 4:30 to 7:00 P.M., with complimentary hors d'oeuvres. Sunday champagne brunch.

Afternoon

On **Fisherman's Wharf,** the striking, white lighthouse stores icing equipment for the commercial fishing boats that unload their catch at the dock. Pleasure boats also tie up here for provisioning.

Walk along the boardwalk to the **Ventura County Maritime Museum,** 2731 South Victoria Boulevard (805–984–6260), located in a large square behind the small waterfront buildings. This new museum is a seafarer's Valhalla. On display are 24 models of historic ships, including the *Golden Hinde, Old Ironsides,* the *Mayflower,* and the *Bounty,* as well as antique ship models and many other sailing exhibits and artifacts. (Open Thursday through Monday, 11:00 A.M. to 5:00 P.M.; admission.)

En route back to Los Angeles, visit the **CEC-Seabee Museum,** in the Naval Construction Battalion Center in Port Hueneme, a commercial and military port. Drive east on Channel Islands Boulevard to Ventura Road, turning right on Sunkist to the museum. The Seabees is the branch of the U.S. Navy that goes overseas and builds bridges, runways, and other immediate needs for the armed forces. The museum was established in 1947 to preserve its history and achievements.

Among the museum's exhibits of U.S. and foreign military memorabilia from World War II collected by the Seabees on foreign shores and donated to the museum are unusual musical instruments, coins, weapons, and World War II posters. Dioramas feature Seabee major construction jobs throughout the world; a giftshop sells logo Seabee T-shirts, caps, and souvenirs. (Open daily until 4:30 P.M., weekdays from 8:00 A.M., Saturday from 9:00 A.M., and Sunday from 12:30 P.M.; closed holidays; free; (805–982–5163.)

When you leave the museum, follow Ventura Road to Surfside Drive and **Port Hueneme Beach Park,** a beautiful, quiet beach ideal for swimming and surfing, with palm trees, a playground, a fishing pier, barbecue pits, picnic areas, and restrooms. **Port Hueneme Historical Museum,** nearby at Market and Hueneme Road, displays the early days of the historic port (open Monday through Friday, 10:00 A.M. to 3:00 P.M.). Port Hueneme is the only deep-water facility between Los Angeles and San Francisco, a thriving international port where, among other goods, imported automobiles are unloaded for U.S. distribution.

To return to Los Angeles, take Fourth Street to Pleasant Valley Road, turn right, and follow Pleasant Valley Road as it angles up toward Highway 34; turn right (south) on 34 until it intersects Freeway 101 south to Los Angeles.

There's More

Olivas Adobe, 4200 Olivas Park Drive, Ventura. (805) 644–4346. Built in 1847 by wealthy Don Raimundo Olivas for his family on his 4,700-acre rancho, when early California life revolved around working farms and ranches. Listed on the National Register of Historic Places, the spacious, two-story, Monterey-style home is furnished with antiques of the period. Grounds open daily, 9:00 A.M. to 4:00 P.M.; house open weekends, 10:00 A.M. to 4:00 P.M. A major portion of adjacent land is now Olivas Park Golf Course.

Ventura Certified Farmers' Market. (805) 529–6266. Held twice weekly, these fairly small markets offer good prices on fresh fruits and vegetables, eggs, seafood, plants, and flowers. Two outdoor locations: Montgomery Ward Parking Lot, Mills Road and Main Street, Wednesday, 10:00 A.M. to 1:00 P.M.; corner of Santa Clara and Figueroa streets, Saturday, 8:30 A.M. to noon. For more information, call (805) 654–7846.

Amtrak. Since 1992, Ventura has been an Amtrak stop for trains traveling between San Diego and Santa Barbara, with four stops daily at the platform located on Harbor Boulevard near the Ventura County Fairgrounds. For information, call Ventura Commerce and Visitor's Bureau, (800) 333–2981.

Golf. Olivas Park Golf Course, 3750 Olivas Park Drive, Ventura. (805) 642–4303. Next to Olivas Adobe; 18-hole golf course, driving range (night-lighted), pro shop, restaurant, and lounge.

Buenaventura Golf Course, 5882 Olivas Park Drive, Ventura. (805) 642–2231. Public 18-hole golf course, pro shop, restaurant, and lounge.

Jim Hall Kart Racing Schools, 1555G Morse Avenue, Ventura. (805) 642–1329.

Ventura Sportsfishing, 1516 Anchors Way, Ventura. (805) 650–1255.

Produce stands: Olivas Park Drive and Telephone Road; also along Victoria south of Gonzales and also south of Olivas Park Drive.

Oxnard Carnegie Art Museum, 424 South C Street, Oxnard. (805) 984–4649. On the National Register of Historic Places, this neoclassical-style museum with stately pillars houses a permanent collection of more than 200 paintings and sculptures focusing on California painters from the 1920s to the present; important changing exhibits. Open Tuesday through Friday, 10:00 A.M. to 5:00 P.M.; Saturday and Sunday, 1:00 to 5:00 P.M. Admission.

Alongside is **Gull Wings Children's Museum,** 418 West Fourth Street, Oxnard. (805) 483–3005. Children love hands-on, touchable exhibits and activities. Giftshop. Open Wednesday through Friday from 1:00 to 5:00 P.M., Saturday from 10:00 A.M., and Sunday from noon. Admission.

Special Events

March. Whale-watching, Ventura.

End of April. Annual California Beach Party. Food, entertainment, crafts, Ventura.

Early May. Cinco de Mayo, Oxnard.

May-June. Fiesta Del Sol, Harbor Village. Weekend activities, Ventura.

Mid-May. Offshore Power Boat Races, Ventura.

May 19-29. Annual California Strawberry Festival. A statewide food event at Channel Islands Harbor. Gourmet strawberry foods, contests, entertainment, Oxnard.

End of May. Earth Day. Kite Festival, Ventura.

July 4. Street Fair. Dawn's Early Light Fireworks, Ventura. Fireworks Street Fair. Music Extravaganza, Oxnard.

Early July. Point Mugu Air Show, Point Mugu Naval Air Test Center, Oxnard.

July. Oxnard Sports Festival.

August 19–20. Ventura County Fair.

Early September. Oxnard Air Show, Oxnard Airport.

Mid-September. Ventura Music Celebration. Fiestas Patrias Parade and Celebration, Oxnard.

Early October. Annual Maritime Days, Channel Islands Harbor. Nautical celebration, classic yacht races, exhibits, food, entertainment, Oxnard.

Early December. Holiday Street Festival. Food, entertainment, arts and crafts, Ventura.

December 8. Parade of Lights and Harborfest, Channel Islands Harbor. Parade of lighted decorated boats, Oxnard.

Mid-December. Parade of Lights, Ventura.

Other Recommended Restaurants and Lodgings

Ventura

Hungry Hunter, 2046 East Harbor Boulevard. (805) 648–5146.

Choice steaks and seafood; innovative salad bar created and served at your table.

Yolanda's, 2753 Main Street. (805) 643–2700. Award-winning Mexican fare, great margaritas, salads, tacos, burritos, refried beans.

Doubletree Ventura, 2055 Harbor Boulevard. (805) 643–6000; (800) 528–0444. Offers 285 luxurious guestrooms, including 14 suites. Adjacent to San Buenaventura State Beach. Heated swimming pool, whirlpool, fully equipped health club with saunas. Restaurant and Lobby Bar; AAA rate includes full breakfast daily. Special rates available.

Holiday Inn Beach Resort, 450 East Harbor Boulevard. (805) 648–7731; (800) 842–0800. At the beach, 260 rooms with balconies, satellite TV; two restaurants, three cocktail lounges; heated swimming pool, exercise room. Just 1 block from the Ventura Pier; special and seasonal rates. AAA rate includes discount.

Lobster Trap, 3605 Peninsula Road. (805) 985–6361. Overlooks Channel Islands Harbor; trendy and popular for steak and seafood entrees, salads, shrimp, crabcakes. Sunday buffet brunch.

Oxnard

Mandalay Beach Resort, 2101 Mandalay Beach Road. (805) 984–2500; (800) 582–3000 (nationwide). On the beachfront; 250 suites, each with two full bathrooms, wetbar, refrigerator, microwave ovens, two TVs. Large heated pool, two spas, two lighted tennis courts. Restaurant, lounge; complimentary cooked-to-order breakfast, plus two hours of complimentary cocktails nightly. Special packages.

For More Information

Ventura Visitor and Convention Bureau, 89C South California Street, Ventura, CA 93001. (805) 648–2075; (800) 333–2989 (in California). Open Monday through Friday from 8:00 A.M. to 5:00 P.M. and weekends from 10:00 A.M. to 4:00 P.M.

Ventura Parks Division, City of San Buenaventura, P.O. Box 99, Ventura, CA 93002. (805) 652–4550.

Ventura Recreation Division, City of San Buenaventura, P.O. Box 99, Ventura, CA 93002. (805) 658–4726.

Oxnard Visitor Center, Channel Islands Harbor Assoc., 3600 South Harbor Boulevard, Suite 234, Channel Islands Harbor, Oxnard, CA 93035. (805) 985–4842.

Ojai

Putting green at Ojai Valley Inn & Country Club

Country Getaway

_____ 2 NIGHTS _____

Golf • Tennis • Parks • Orange and avocado groves • Museum
Hiking and biking • Antiques • Galleries • Fishing and boating

This sleepy little country village has a special tranquillity perfect for
unwinding in a three-day outing. Creative people as well as fugitives
of Los Angeles's fast lanes have long been drawn to Ojai (pronounced
"O-hi") for its quiet, unhurried pace. Tucked in a deep coastal valley,

extending from the 6,000-foot Topa Topa Mountains at the edge of Los Padres National Forest to the ocean, Ojai's miles of orange groves brim with golden fruit. Avocado trees drape the rolling foothills, and the hectic world seems far away. Small wonder that Ojai was the setting for the mystical, beautiful valley of Shangri-La in the movie *Lost Horizon,* starring Ronald Colman.

In this cozy town you can tee off at two championship golf courses, play tennis, browse and shop at fine galleries and boutiques, tour artist studios, and pedal a bike along a meandering creek down country lanes where horses graze in sunny pastures. You can visit a museum, "take it off" in style at a chic health spa resort, picnic in uncrowded parks, purchase just-picked oranges and avocados to tote home and stay in a legendary world-class inn. Camping, fishing, and boating are available in nearby Lake Casitas, site of the 1984 Olympic rowing and canoeing events.

Day 1

Morning

Drive north on Ventura Freeway 101 to **Ojai,** 76 miles through the rural San Fernando Valley. Traveling over the Conejo Grade, you see the vast fertile plain spread out below. Both sides of the highway are checkerboarded with farms, row crops, and citrus groves.

Immediately after seeing the signs for Ventura, exit to the right on Highway 33 north to reach Ojai, 14 miles inland along a divided country road framed by voluptuous hills that turn chartreuse in spring and are sere in winter.

After Foster Park follow the one-lane rural road past Casitas Springs and small houses; you'll see bikers and horseback riders on the bike and equestrian paths that follow the road. Stop at the **Big Red Barn** roadside stand, at Rancho Arnaz, 9504 North Ventura (Highway 33) (805–649–2776), to buy fresh apple cider, fresh produce, jams, nuts, and olives. In fall this is a popular spot to pick your own apples at the adjacent orchard.

As you drive through Oak View, make note of **Oak Pit Barbeque,** on the right side of the road, to return to for sandwiches to eat there or take out on your way home (see Other Recommended Restaurants and Lodgings).

Continue through the small village of Mira Monte, along Ojai Avenue, to the Ojai Valley Inn & Country Club, on the right, and turn onto the private road to the inn.

Lunch: **Ojai Valley Inn & Country Club,** Country Club Drive, Ojai. (805) 646–5511; (800) 422–6524. Dining on the broad Oak Terrace beneath billowy umbrellas surrounded by the lush golf course marks a carefree beginning to your holiday. Relax in the beautiful surroundings over creative sandwiches—croissant club, roast beef melt, salads, soups, hot entrees; moderately priced.

Afternoon

Golfers won't waste any time teeing off on Ojai Valley Inn's renowned, challenging course. Nongolfers enjoy tooling around this very scenic, impeccably maintained course in a golf cart, rattling over rustic wooden bridges spanning picturesque creeks, and cruising fairways lined with giant sycamores and oaks. Tennis enthusiasts will soon be racing across the courts, and swimmers are equally at home in the sunny, uncrowded pools.

Others can drive, take the trolley, or borrow a bike from the inn and pedal about 1 mile into downtown Ojai. **Libbey Park,** with its splashing fountain smack in the center of town across from the Arcade, is the showcase for most local events and activities. In the charming, small, oak-studded park, the secluded bowl beneath an ancient sycamore tree is the delightful setting for the city's prestigious annual Ojai Music Festival at the end of May, concerts, and theater. Libbey Park is also the site of the April Ojai Tennis Tournament and public courts.

Alongside, the post office, with its landmark 65-foot bell tower, was built in 1917, at the same time as the shaded, Spanish-style shopping Arcade across the street. There are no parking meters, and you'll find plenty of parking places.

The best way to see Ojai is to stroll the small downtown area. **The Arcade,** between Signal and Montgomery streets, is the city's main shopping stretch of stores, galleries, and some restaurants. You'll find more of everything on the small side streets, across from the Arcade and behind it.

Rains, at 218 East Ojai Avenue (805–646–1441), is Ojai's largest store and family-owned since 1917; an attractive, well-stocked, upscale emporium, featuring men's and women's apparel, giftware, kitchenware, pottery, and hardware. A few doors away, Tottingham Court, Ltd., 242 East Ojai Avenue (805–646–2339), is a unique place to shop or have brunch or both. Its small tearoom offers quiche, sandwiches, salads, pastries, and true English scones with Devonshire cream from England. Among its multitude of import gift items are china, crystal, silver, babywear, and tiny collectibles. The Ojai Chamber of Commerce, at the end of the Arcade, is where you can pick up maps, brochures, and other visitor information.

A bit farther down, The Ojai Indian Shop, at 318 East Ojai Avenue (805–646–2631), has since 1968 been a popular source for authentic

Indian artifacts, baskets, masks, moccasins, turquoise jewelry, coins, and full feather headdresses for young chiefs and squaws.

Across from the Arcade, **Barbara Bowman stores,** at 139 East Ojai Avenue, make their own exclusive and handsome clothing and accessories. Follow Ojai Avenue east to Montgomery Street and turn right for the small **Ojai Valley Museum,** 109 South Montgomery Street (805–646–2290), located in an old firehouse built by the WPA during the Great Depression. You get a glimpse of the city's past from the displays of Indian artifacts discovered in nearby excavations of the Oak Grove and Chumash tribes, who settled here thousands of years ago. View the lifelike birds and animals, together with memorabilia depicting Ojai's early pioneer life. The museum's giftshop offers T-shirts, postcards, and great children's books. (Open daily except Tuesday, from 1:00 to 4:00 P.M.)

Next door stop by the **Massarella Pottery & Gallery,** 105 South Montgomery Street (805–646–9453), a good-looking showroom and factory displaying the owners' classic stoneware and porcelain made on the premises. If you're lucky, you can watch the potters throwing the clay and firing it. (Closed Monday.)

Dinner: At the Ojai Valley Inn & Country Club. The elegant, candlelit **Vista Dining Room**'s gourmet dinners are frequent incentives for players to hurry through the back nine. Highlights include smoked duck a l'orange with tangy pink peppercorn sauce, followed by grilled veal tenderloin in savory port wine sauce, followed by luscious desserts you've only dreamed about until now. Your dinner is enhanced with entertaining piano music. Reservations suggested. Casual dining in the **Oak Grill** (Tuesday through Saturday) focuses on such Italian specialties as veal saltimbocca and pizza; steak and fish entrees are also available.

Lodging: Ojai Valley Inn & Country Club, Country Club Drive, Ojai, CA 93023. (805) 666–5511; (800) 422–6524. Deluxe award-winning resort atop 200 rolling acres; 218 guestrooms and suites, each with private balcony or terrace overlooking the fairways; hair dryer, coffeemaker, television, honor bar, minirefrigerator, turndown service; 18-hole championship golf course, driving range, putting green, golf shop; eight tennis courts (four lighted), tennis center; two swimming pools, whirlpool, exercise facility; two restaurants, lounge; conference center; concierge service; children's playground; complimentary bikes and Ojai trolley shuttle to town. Outstanding Sunday buffet brunch. Member of Historic Hotels of America. Site of Annual GTE Classic Senior PGA event. Full breakfasts and dinners are included in two-night golf, tennis, and fitness packages. Other seasonal packages are available.

Day 2

Morning

Breakfast. At the inn. Generous buffet breakfast (included in two-night packages) in the glass-walled Vista Dining Room overlooking the sunlit golf course and the Topa Topa Mountains begins your day with beauty. Place your order with the obliging chef at the Omelette Bar for eggs just the way you like them, prepared with all the fixings. Then serve yourself with fresh juice, fresh fruits, quiche or crepes, eggs Benedict, waffles, French toast, ham, bacon, sausage, hash-browned potatoes, hot and cold cereals, and freshly baked blueberry muffins, breads, and pastries. Hot coffee is brought to your table.

After breakfast, golfers will soon be breaking par on the front nine. Or you can drive into and through the village for about another 2 miles east, to see the beautiful acres of orange groves and avocado groves, and then drive up into the foothills for spectacular vistas across the rich valley.

This most easterly end of town is where you can see the famous Shangri-La view. At Boccali's Pizza Place, 3277 Ojai Avenue, turn right and drive partway up the hill to Dennison Grade. Stop at the stone bench on the right side of the road. The panoramic view down into the valley on a clear, bright day, as well as when the mountain ranges seem to be floating in clouds and mist, is gorgeous.

Return to Ojai Avenue and turn left to **Ventura County Soule Park,** off Highway 150 on Boardman, adjacent to Soule Golf Course (pronounced "sole").

The spacious park, edging squiggly San Antonio Creek, provides shady picnic tables, barbecue pits, a playground, tennis courts, and serene expanses of lawn and trees. Local equestrian groups hold weekend shows in Soule's horse arena, considered one of the country's finest.

Lunch: **The Ranch House,** South Lomita and Besant, P.O. Box 458, Ojai. (805) 646-2360. Follow Ojai Avenue west to the "Y" intersection signal. Turn right on El Roblar, turn left at Lomita, then turn left to the restaurant. This flower-filled garden restaurant is a longtime special favorite for Ojai residents and visitors. Luncheon suggestions include homemade fettucine with crab, Gorgonzola cheese, snowpeas, and mushrooms. Breads are baked daily; desserts are made in the kitchen; the wine list is notable. Garden luncheons served from April 22 to September, Wednesday through Saturday; dinner served Wednesday through Saturday; Sunday brunch and dinner served at 1:00 P.M. Phone for reservations and information.

Afternoon

Driving around this rural area of Meiners Oaks, you are apt to find fresh produce for sale at private homes. Try those along La Luna, with its groves of orange trees, and those along Cuyama. Look for little stands of oranges, avocados, and berries in front or side gardens available for you to purchase on the honor system, according to directions given there.

Return to the Ojai Valley Inn for golf, tennis, or swimming and sunning. Later you might want to drive back into the village or pedal in for shopping or further sightseeing. **Bart's Books,** on Matilija at the corner of Cañada (805–646–3755), is a collector's delight and a town pride. Go inside to browse this unusual open-air bookmart, built around a huge oak tree and offering some 100,00 new and used books, magazines, and sheet music. Shelves of bargain-priced used books line the exterior walls to accommodate after-hours book lovers, who can buy them by tossing the marked price over the wall onto the patio.

A few blocks away are the **Biblical Gardens,** on the grounds of the graceful old Presbyterian Church, 304 North Foothill Road at the corner of Aliso (805–646–1437), featuring fifty varieties of plants mentioned in the Bible; all have been authenticated, and you're in for a few surprises. Join a guided tour or pick up a map and wander about on your own. All plants are labeled, making them easy to identify.

If antiques hunting is part of your fun in visiting small villages, check out the **Antique Collection,** 236 West Ojai Avenue at Cañada (805–646–6688). A group of about twenty-five antiques dealers share a large building, with space divided into small rooms and areas. You'll find all kinds of bric-a-brac, furniture, objets d'art, books, kitchen collectibles, sterling silver items, memorabilia, and varied accessories.

Dinner: At the Ojai Valley Inn & Country Club. The creative chef's prix fixe dinner menu in the sleek Vista Dining Room changes about every two weeks. Among its variety of appetizers, entrees, and desserts to choose from are tournedos of beef, rack of lamb, and Lake Superior whitefish. Or you can happily enjoy an encore of last night's gastronomic pleasures.

Lodging: At the Ojai Valley Inn & Country Club.

Day 3

Morning

Breakfast: Another splendid buffet breakfast at the inn.

Golfers will want to play another round on this well-manicured course, hit some balls on the driving range, or sharpen up their game on the putting green near the dining terrace, with Ojai's warm sun on their backs.

Afternoon

On your return to Los Angeles, try to allow time to stop at lovely **Lake Casitas.** Follow Highway 33 to its junction with Highway 150; west from Mira Monte turn right (north) and drive about 3 miles to the entrance. The gleaming man-made reservoir, with 60 miles of shoreline, is surrounded by lush avocado groves.

Recreation is unlimited at Lake Casitas. Here at one of the area's largest campgrounds, visitors can rent a boat; ride a bike; fish for trout, bass, or catfish; picnic and barbecue—but no swimming. Admission; (805–649–2233). After your visit to Lake Casitas, take Highway 33 back to 101 and follow it south to Los Angeles.

There's More

Golf. Soule Park Golf Course, 1033 East Ojai Avenue. (805) 646–5633. 18-hole public course, threaded with old oaks and pine trees. Golf shop, driving range, carts; Clubhouse Restaurant; seniors weekday rates.

Tennis. Tennis is a large part of Ojai's life-style. Besides courts at Libbey and Soule parks, you can play at Nordhoff High School, .5 mile north of the "Y" intersection on Highways 150 and 133, or at Matilija Junior High, just off El Paseo Road.

The Oaks at Ojai, 122 East Ojai Avenue. (805) 646–5573. Health and fitness spa resort run by noted fitness expert Sheila Cluff, who can help you take it off and stay that way. Various programs and packages.

The Sunday Art Show is a tradition wherein local artists show and sell their work at Security Pacific National Bank parking lot, on Ojai Avenue, till noon.

The Ojai Trolley takes you for a ride through town from Soule Golf Course to the "Y" shopping center. Daily schedule; varied modest rates.

Bike riding is one of the most pleasant ways to see the Ojai Valley, riding either through the downtown area or along the 10-foot-wide, paved bikepath separated by a fence from the road and equestrian path. A 6-mile trail begins at Fox Street and leads through scenic backroads, ending in Oak View. Pick up trail maps at the Chamber of Commerce or at rentals. The Bicycle Doctor, 212 Fox Street (805–646–7554), is at the beginning of the Ojai trail; get on your bike and follow the path. Or rent a bike from Bicycles Collectables, 108 Cañada Street (805–646–7736).

Friend's Ranch Market, (new downtown location), 469 East Ojai Avenue, corner of Fox Street. (805) 640–0995. You'll spot the large wooden wagon out front, piled with bags of oranges, apples, and avocados delivered daily from local growers and packers. Small giftshop inside offers preserves, sauces, breads, pasta, and pottery. Friend's original longtime location, 15150 Maricopa Highway, 2.5 miles north of the "Y" intersection, is a scenic drive but may be a bit out of the way. It sells fresh orange juice, oranges, avocados, nuts, and lemons and will ship all over the United States.

Ojai's "Pink Moment." At day's end look toward the soaring Topa Topa Mountains to watch the pink-orange sunset radiate over the peaks. It bathes the sky and mountains in a luminous, blushing glow that gradually diffuses and fades. Strictly an Ojai phenomenon.

The Pottery, studio gallery of Vivika and Otto Heino, 971 McAndrews Road. (805) 646–3393. Internationally acclaimed potters welcome visitors Tuesday through Sunday. Go east on Ojai Avenue, past Soule Park; turn left on Reeves Road to McAndrew Road.

The Krotona Institute School of Theosophy, 46 Krotona Hill, Highway 33 and Hermosa Road. (805) 646–2653. Courses and workshops are conducted in its serene, one-hundred-acre hilltop setting. Library houses the largest theosophical collection on the West Coast. Bookshop and library open daily from 10:00 A.M. to 4:00 P.M. and Sunday from 1:00 to 4:00 P.M. Ojai was the foundation headquarters and residence of the late philosopher Jidda Krishnamurti and was the sanctuary of author Aldous Huxley.

Krishnamurti Library, 1130 McAndrew Road. (805) 646–4948. The works have a large following, with frequent gatherings. Books and tapes for sale. Open Wednesday through Sunday, 1:00 to 5:00 P.M.

The **Beatrice Woods Studio gallery,** on Highway 150 in Upper Ojai, is worth a visit to see this ceramicist's work and collection of international folk art in a spectacular view setting. Look for the pink mailbox about a mile past the top of Dennison Grade on Ojai–Santa Paula Drive. Open daily from 11:00 A.M. to 4:00 P.M.

Special Events

Note: Call for admission fees.

March 20. GTE West Classic Senior PGA Event. (805) 646–5796. Senior golf superstars play the demanding course of Ojai Valley Inn & Country Club.

Last weekend in May. Annual Ojai Music Festival, at Libbey Park. (805) 646–2094. Day and evening concerts.

Mid-June. Annual Ojai Wine Festival. Lake Casitas. (800) 548–4881. Live jazz, food, art.
Last Sunday in June. Annual Ojai Country Music Festival, Libbey Park Bowl. (805) 646–8126.
August 7–9, 14–16, 21–23. Annual Ojai Shakespeare Festival, Libbey Park Bowl. (805) 646–WILL. Afternoon and evening performances; preshow entertainment.
Beginning of October. Annual Bowlful of Blues Festival, Libbey Park Bowl. (805) 646–7230. World's top artists.
End of October. Annual Ojai Studio Artists Tour. (805) 646–8126. Tours of private studios.

Other Recommended Restaurants and Lodgings

Ojai

L'Auberge Restaurant, 314 El Paseo. (805) 646–2288. Between Cañada and Rincon; entrance on Rincon to this vintage 1910 white house, half-hidden by oak trees. L'Auberge enjoys an excellent reputation for noteworthy French Belgian cuisine; specialties such as New York pepper steak flambé, *poulet cordon bleu,* and desserts of raspberry ice cream dipped in chocolate. Lunch, Saturday and Sunday; dinner, Wednesday through Monday; closed Tuesday.

The Clubhouse Restaurant at Soule Park Golf Course, 1033 East Ojai Avenue. (805) 646–5685. Wrapped around a dramatic fireplace in a dining room overlooking sunny fairways. Medium-priced continental menu includes sandwiches, pasta, seafood, salads, fresh pastries. It's quite busy weekends; best to reserve. Closed Monday.

Casa Ojai Best Western, 1302 East Ojai Avenue. (805) 646–8175. Across from Soule Park Golf Course; forty-five units, in-room coffeemakers, cable TV, nonsmoking rooms available; heated pool and spa; complimentary continental breakfast of muffins, pastry, orange juice, and coffee in lobby.

Los Padres Motel, 1208 East Ojai Avenue. (805) 646–4365; (800) 228–3744. Thirty-one units in attractive, Spanish-style architecture; kitchen units available. Cable TV; swimming pool and hot Jacuzzi; complimentary coffee in lobby; senior citizen rates. One block from Soule Park Golf Course.

Casa De La Luna, 710 South La Luna. (805) 646–4528. B&B on the rural outskirts of town. Follow Ojai Avenue west; turn right on El Roblar to La Luna; turn left and follow the signs. A popular hideaway in the owner's former home, with seven large, well-decorated rooms and suites, each with modern private bath. On seven acres of large oaks and rambling gardens. Full breakfast cooked to order and served in large formal dining room. No pets, children, or smoking indoors.

Oak View

Avanti!, 710 Ventura Avenue. (805) 649–9001. Five minutes from Ojai. It's not much to look at from the road, but this popular, upscale, moderately priced restaurant has patrons lined up outside on Friday nights. Tasty Italian specialties range from lobster-stuffed ravioli to four-cheese pizza, with great sauces and desserts. Lunch and dinner daily.

The Oak Pit, 820 North Ventura Avenue, Highway 33. (805) 649–9903. This is your best pitstop on your way to or from Ojai for pork ribs and hefty hand-carved beef and ham sandwiches, barbecued beans, and chili, to eat there or take out. Help yourself to the array of fiery sauces, including "X-Rated" and "Killer." Closed Monday.

For More Information

Ojai Chamber of Commerce, 338 East Ojai Avenue, P.O. Box 1134, Ojai, CA 93023. (805) 646–8126. Open Monday through Saturday from 9:30 A.M. to 5:00 P.M. and Sunday from 10:30 A.M. to 4:00 P.M.

For further information about parks and camping, call the City of Ojai Recreation (805–646–1872) or the Ojai Ranger Station, 1190 East Ojai Avenue, Los Padres National Forest (805–646–4348).

Santa Barbara

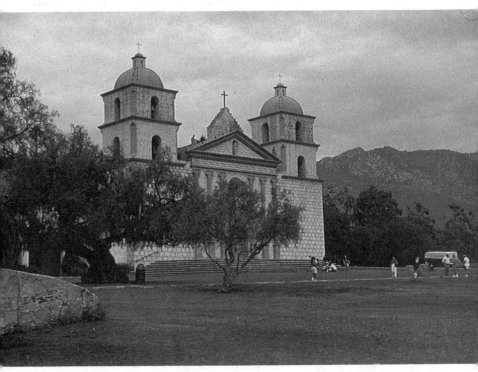

Santa Barbara's Mission of 1786

American Riviera

_____ 2 NIGHTS _____
Beaches · Fine dining · Mission · Wharf · Children's zoo
Botanical garden · Sailing · Biking · Whale-watching · Antiques shopping

Here's a three-day getaway to Santa Barbara, Southern California's own Riviera, a small, prosperous seaside resort community with a special panache tucked between the Pacific Ocean and the rugged Santa Ynez Mountains. Sleek yachts dance in its snug, flag-festooned harbor, and tall, skinny palm trees frame miles of white sandy beaches dotted with picnic tables and barbecue pits.

With its festive air, profusion of flowers, slower pace, and Old World flavor, Santa Barbara is a cultural community of style, old money, and gracious living blended with the romance and tradition of its ancient Spanish heritage.

Santa Barbara's temperate weather began luring wintering Eastern socialites back in the late 1880s. Moreover, the city has always been a retreat for celebrities (Julia Child, Michael Douglas, Jonathan Winters, Robert Mitchum, among them), who unwind in the casual life-style and anonymity of a small town. And when the Reagan administration's hilltop Rancho del Cielo was nicknamed the "Western White House," Santa Barbara became a world-renowned, glamorous Southern California destination.

Few cities can boast such a robust, historic past and different cultures, dating from 1782, when Spanish soldiers accompanied by Franciscan Father Junípero Serra founded Santa Barbara, establishing a military presidio and a mission. Remnants of the ancient fort still remain, and Mission Santa Barbara is the city's greatest treasure and most famous landmark.

The city was an important Spanish stronghold in the New World for forty years, until California became a Mexican territory. During the Mexican-American War, Santa Barbara became part of the United States, in 1845, and the sleepy pueblo began to stir and grow.

Day 1

Morning

Drive north from Los Angeles 90 miles to Santa Barbara on Freeway 101, also known as Ventura Freeway 101. As the road traverses the rural San Fernando Valley, through fringes of small towns like Calabasas, the low, rolling hillsides are studded with clusters of large oaks trees, native to the area. Approaching Camarillo, the dramatic downswing of Conejo Grade presents a panoramic sweep of the misty green valley spread out below.

After Ventura, the freeway, enlivened with a flowered divider strip of colorful oleanders, now borders the glistening ocean, and there is the graceful curve of white beaches and small coves. Oil tankers far out on the horizon are camouflaged to resemble small tropical islands, even to tall palm trees waving in the distance.

The blue ocean fades in and out of sight as you note the cutoff to Lake Casitas. Passing the small town of Carpenteria, you'll see a huge Santa Claus figure looming over **Santa Claus Lane,** a year-round enclave of Christmas gift and toy stores off Highway 101 on the ocean side. Mail posted here gets a Santa Claus postmark.

Arriving in Santa Barbara, note **Stearns Wharf,** at the foot of State Street, the town's main thoroughfare; built in 1872, it is the West Coast's oldest operating wharf, really a 3-block-long extension of State Street over the Pacific Ocean. The engaging **Dolphin Fountain** marks the beginning of State Street, as well as the entrance to the busy pier, where one can fish, shop, dine or snack, browse, and drive or stroll.

Along the pier, the **Vintner's** is fun for wine tasting on its sunny terrace, and **Madame Rosinka** can read your palm with true gypsy finesse.

In **The Sea Center,** operated by the Museum of Natural History, marine life exhibits feature awesome, life-size models of whales and dolphins. (Open Sunday, Monday, Wednesday, Friday, and Saturday from 10:00 A.M. to 5:00 P.M. and Tuesday and Thursday from noon to 5:00; admission. Public parking available on the wharf.) (805) 963–1067.

From the pier the scene inland is an enchanting Dufy painting— cushy yachts preen in the sunlit harbor along the curved waterfront and the little city spreads up into the mauve foothills and the protective embrace of the mountains.

The lively area around the wharf is a fine starting point to explore Santa Barbara's charming beachfront, where cycling and jogging paths weave through **Chase Palm Park** beneath soaring palm trees. Bikes, roller skates, and **Pedalinas** (jaunty four-wheel cycles with surry on top) are rentable across from the wharf at Beach Rentals, 8 West Cabrillo Boulevard (805–963–2524). In this same area, every Sunday from 10:00 A.M. until sunset hundreds of regional artists sell and exhibit their work in a bustling arts and crafts show held along a sunny, 1-mile oceanfront stretch.

Santa Barbara is noted for its beaches, and each has its own attractions: **East Beach** is the most popular, with bikepaths, volleyball courts, and picnic areas, plus a great cafe. **West Beach,** on the other side of the wharf, offers the best sailboarding, swimming, and sunbathing, as well as beginning sailboarding lessons and rental equipment. **Leadbetter Beach,** at the breakwater with a landscaped picnic area and the Sea Cove cafe right on the sand, is well known for some of the best surfing and sailboarding.

Lunch: **East Beach Grill,** 1118 East Cabrillo Boulevard, Santa Barbara. (805) 865–8805. An upbeat spot right on the sand, with good sandwiches and grill food, where you can watch the action on the bikepaths and the ocean.

Afternoon

The **Andree Clark Bird Refuge,** at 1400 East Cabrillo Boulevard, is near the intersection of Cabrillo Boulevard and Highway 101. At this lovely lagoon and gardens adjoining the Child's Estate Zoo you can feed and watch the many varieties of freshwater fowl. A bikeway and footpath fringe the lagoon. Park on the north side of the lagoon. (Free.)

The adjacent **Santa Barbara Zoo,** 500 Ninos Drive (805–962–6310), on a clifftop off Cabrillo Boulevard east of Milpas, was designed primarily for children in a delightful garden estate setting. The zoo features almost 500 animals, including baby elephants, big cats, giraffes, monkeys, and sea lions, as well as exotic birds. A playground, snackbar, and picnic area are here too. Kids particularly love the domestic-animal petting park and the miniature train ride. (Open daily from 10:00 A.M. to 5:00 P.M. and in summer until 6:00 P.M. Admission fees; parking fee.)

Before leaving the beach area, pick up a handy, free "Santa Barbara When and Where" map and calendar guide at Santa Barbara Visitors Information Center, 1 Santa Barbara Street (805–965–5334), at the corner of Cabrillo Boulevard. These guides are also available at the courthouse, most restaurants, and shops.

Incidentally, from the beach at Stearns Wharf you can ride the free shuttle bus east and west on Cabrillo Boulevard to Coast Village Road and back, as well as up State Street to Sola Street, just past the Museum of Art. It runs round-trip every fifteen minutes from 10:00 A.M. to 5:00 P.M. and till 8:00 P.M. on Friday and Saturday. Or you can hop on the open trolley at the wharf for a ninety-minute sightseeing tour of the city (fare). City lots in the downtown area provide free parking for the first ninety minutes.

State Street, Santa Barbara's foremost promenade, is truly one of the most attractive main streets anywhere and a favorite shopping and browsing stroll for visitors and residents alike. State begins at the ocean and leads you through the Old Town historic section and the city's important dining and shopping hub of specialty shops, galleries, and upscale department stores. You'll soon notice that traffic moves at a slower pace in sedate Santa Barbara. Along this appealing boulevard, large trees in huge planters share sidewalk space with tall eucalyptus and palm trees, decorative iron grillework, arched passageways, and lots of flowers.

It is a planned harmony and beauty. The people of Santa Barbara are determined to preserve their city's Spanish inheritance in timeless, graceful architecture of red-tiled roofs, arched facades, benches, and courtyards. The city acquired this distinctive look following a severe earthquake in 1925 that destroyed much of the downtown section. Everything was rebuilt in a unified motif still adhered to. Even sidewalk telephone booths must conform to the red-tiled-roof theme. There is a noticeable absence of glitz. No high-rise buildings intrude into Santa Barbara's clear blue skies, and billboards have long been banned.

Along State Street you'll want to browse the recently opened **Paseo Nuevo,** bordered by Chapala Street, an engaging, two-level, Spanish-style mall of restaurants, fountains, courtyards, galleries, and boutiques. Farther along in the 1100 block, the 16-foot-tall sidewalk clock with Westminster chimes and inviting shade trees enhance the entrance to **La Arcada Court,** with its specialty shops, fountains, plants, and Acapulco Mexican Restaurant, a convenient upbeat place to snack and people-watch at the outdoor tables.

Continuing up State Street, you'll arrive at the **Santa Barbara Museum of Art,** 1130 State Street (805–963–4364), whose colorful banners welcome you to one of America's foremost small museums; boasting a prestigious permanent collection of art and ancient sculpture, plus important changing exhibitions. The Museum Bookstore is a good bet for art books and distinctive jewelry made by local artisans. Free guided tours are held Wednesday at 12:30 P.M. (Open Tuesday through Saturday, 11:00 A.M. to 5:00 P.M. Admission. Free admission Thursday and the first Sunday of each month.)

Dinner: **Allegro Restaurant,** 920 De La Vina, Santa Barbara. (805) 965–6012. Don't be fooled by the modest cottage exterior. Formerly called Norbert's, with the same noted chef-owner, who features exceptional dining selections, including breast of squab and gourmet Mediterranean specialties.

Lodging. **Four Seasons Biltmore,** 1260 Channel Drive, Santa Barbara, CA 93108. (805) 969–2261. The city's most luxurious hotel, with 234 rooms, suites, and private cottages on 19 rambling garden acres. Three lighted tennis courts, two swimming pools (one beachfront), two hydrotherapy pools, private beachfront cabanas. Guest room amenities include refrigerated mini-bar, clock radio, terry robes, and hair dryer. Complimentary putting green, bikes, croquet, and shuffleboard. Concierge service, four restaurants, elegant Sunday brunch. Golf arrangements with local courses.

Day 2

Morning

Breakfast: **Montecito Cafe,** 1295 Coast Village Road. (805) 969–3392. In the Montecito Inn (see "Other Recommended Restaurants and Lodgings"), the small hotel Charlie Chaplin and Fatty Arbuckle built in the 1920s and the inspiration for the song "There's a Small Hotel." This amiable cafe with laid-back service offers good, traditional breakfast fare, plus southwestern and California cuisine touches, such as pancakes with caviar.

All visitors want to see the city's most famous landmark, **Mission**

Santa Barbara, Laguna and Los Olivos streets (805–682–4149). Take State Street to Mission Street or to Los Olivos Street. Turn right toward the mountains and continue to the mission, situated in the scenic rural foothills overlooking the city; both streets run into it. Known as the "Queen of the Missions" for its graceful symmetry and tall twin bell towers, it is the tenth of twenty-one California missions, founded in 1786 by the Spanish Franciscan Fathers and still a Catholic parish church. The annual Italian Street Festival is held on its broad terrace. A self-guided tour encompasses the gardens, museum, courtyards, chapel, and cemetery. The small giftshop features pretty fans, books, T-shirts, souvenirs, and religious objects. (Open daily from 9:00 A.M. to 5:00 P.M. Admission; children under 16, free.)

Since it's just 2 blocks north of the mission, you're within walking distance of the **Museum of Natural History, Planetarium, and Observatory,** 2559 Puesta del Sol Road. (Take Mission Canyon Road and follow the signs.) (805–682–4711.) The museum is housed in a rambling ranch-style building around a courtyard. The highlight is the knockout 72-foot skeleton of a giant blue whale, outside to the right of the entrance. Exhibit halls include the West's largest collection of Chumash Indian artifacts. Check out the full-scale model of a 33-foot giant squid, suspended from the ceiling in the Marine Hall. The Museum Store offers pottery, T-shirts, Indian and Southwest jewelry, and souvenir items. (Open daily from 9:00 A.M. to 5:00 P.M. and 10:00 A.M. on Sundays and holidays. Admission. Free admission Wednesday and the first Sunday of each month.)

In the same quiet area, about 1.5 miles north of the mission, is the spectacular **Botanic Garden,** 1212 Mission Canyon Road. (805–562–2521). Take Mission Canyon Road to Foothill Road, go right 1 block, then left on Mission Canyon Road to the garden. You'll find some sixty acres of California wildflowers and native flora, a redwood forest, and miles of nature trails. The giftshop features books, souvenirs, and native plants. Guided tours are held daily. (Open daily from 8:00 A.M. to sunset. Fee. Free admission Tuesday and Wednesday.)

Drive back to the city center for lunch.

Lunch: **Chase Grill Downtown,** 1012 State Street, Santa Barbara. (805) 965–4351. Along with its checkered tablecloths and congenial atmosphere, Chase's has been voted as having the best Caesar salad for eleven years and keeps customers happy with good pasta and other Italian specialties.

Afternoon

While you're downtown, head over to another famous landmark, the **Santa Barbara County Courthouse,** in the 1100 block of Anacapa

Street (805–681–4200). Considered one of the most striking public buildings in the United States, the handsome, impressive Spanish-Moorish building, completed in 1929, boasts a 70-foot clock tower and grand-scale archways and turrets, all surrounded by spacious lawns, palm trees, and lush tropical plants. The attractive interior is rich in its hand-painted ceilings, wrought-iron chandeliers, murals, and historical exhibits. From the observation deck the panoramic city view sweeps from the lavender Santa Ynez Mountains over the carpet of red-tiled roofs to the sparkling Pacific Ocean and occasionally to the Channel Islands floating in the mist 20 miles offshore. (Open Monday through Friday from 8:00 A.M. to 5:00 P.M. and weekends and holidays from 9:00 A.M. to 5:00 P.M. Free. Tour information: 805–962–6464.)

El Paseo ("The Street in Spain"), in the 800 block of State Street between State and Anacapa, one of the city's loveliest and oldest Spanish-style shopping and dining complexes built in and around the 1827 adobe home of the historic De la Guerra family, has undergone extensive renovation and restoration resulting in several new specialty shops and restaurants.

For those hipped on history, the compact downtown area is rich in landmarks of Santa Barbara's colorful past. Among historical highlights are: **El Cuartel—El Presidio de Santa Barbara** (State Historical Park), 122 East Cañon Presidio Street (805–963–3633). This is where the city began in 1782 and includes buildings that were part of the Presidio Real, the original fortress. In addition to a slide show, you'll find a scale model of the old fort and a giftshop. Open Monday to Friday 9:00 A.M. to noon and 1:00 P.M. to 4:00 P.M. Free.

Just south of the Presidio, the **Santa Barbara Historical Society Museum,** 136 East De La Guerra Street and East Cañon Perdido (805–966–1601), is a complex of colonial Spanish houses built in the 1800s. The museum features many exhibits as well as memorabilia of the city's four cultural eras: Indian, Spanish, Mexican, and American. Open Tuesday to Friday from noon to 5:00 P.M., Saturday and Sunday from 1:00 P.M. to 5:00 P.M. Free.

Antiques buffs will admire the string of little shops on **Brinkerhoff Avenue** at Cota, between Chapala and De La Vina. This nostalgic, charming, 1-block-long, tree-shaded street, named after Santa Barbara's first physician, Samuel Brinkerhoff, is a designated Special Historic District. Tiny Victorian-style clapboard houses line the street in an array of bright sherbet colors; white picket fences border old-fashioned gardens. They are now antiques and specialty shops, plus some galleries, to browse for memorabilia, old treasures, and gifts. Most are open Tuesday through Sunday from 11:00 A.M. to 6:00 P.M.

Dinner: **The Palace Cafe,** 8 East Cota Street, Santa Barbara. (805) 966–3133. A longtime local favorite for hot, Louisiana-style Cajun, Creole, and Caribbean cuisine. Look for jambalaya, fresh fish, *andouille* sausage, and Key Lime Pie for dessert. Closed Monday.

Lodging: **Four Seasons Biltmore.**

Day 3

Morning

Breakfast: In your hotel or at **Tutti's,** 1209 Coast Village Road, Montecito. (805) 969–5809. A bright, airy local breakfast hangout great for fresh, huge muffins, pancakes, waffles, and such. Quite busy.

You're in the heart of lively **Coast Village Road,** an intimate, tree-shaded strip of posh cafes, galleries, wine shops, designer boutiques, and long-legged blondes driving gleaming Jaguars and Ferraris. After browsing the shops, take the time to drive around the residential section of affluent **Montecito,** where the wealthy people drawn to Santa Barbara during the 1890s established their luxurious estates. The millionaire migration included Rockefeller, Carnegie, Du Pont, McCormick, Cudahy, and other barons of industry, who built palatial vacation mansions in Montecito's rolling woodlands. For the scenic hillside drive, take Olive Mill Road at the end of Coast Village Road to Alameda Padre Serra. Along "APS" the famed Riviera view is a photogenic panorama over the city that reaches to the palm trees along the beachfront. Then drive back to the ocean for lunch.

Lunch: **Citronelle,** 901 Cabrillo Boulevard (in the Santa Barbara Inn), Santa Barbara. (800) 231–0431. Opened in 1991 by Michel Richard (owner-chef of Citrus, in Los Angeles), the restaurant has become a gourmet choice for signature dishes favoring scallops with sautéed Maui onions, inspired desserts, and stunning harbor views.

Afternoon

At oceanside the **yacht harbor and breakwater,** home to around 1,200 pleasure and working craft, grab your attention with strikingly colored flags flapping high overhead. The broad, paved walkway atop the breakwater offers a scenic .5-mile walking tour around the harbor, the Yacht Club, marine stores, and restaurants, along with fine views of surfers and boats. This is the departure point for shoreline tour boats and sportfishing excursions, as well as a source of boats for rent and charter.

There's More

Farmer's Market each Tuesday and Saturday is a fun place to shop. Local growers sell fruits, vegetables, nuts, eggs, flowers, and plants at reasonable prices, with puppet shows and other entertainment enlivening the scene. The Tuesday market takes place in the 500 block of State Street from 3:00 to 5:30 P.M.; the Saturday market—larger and more crowded—is held at the corner of Santa Barbara and Cota streets from 8:30 A.M. till noon. For information, call (805) 963–0303.

Boating, sailing, and fishing opportunities are at the breakwater. The Sailing Center of Santa Barbara (800–350–9090) specializes in sailing classes, boat rentals, and coastal and whale-watching cruises.

Golf. You can hit the sticks at two 18-hole municipal courses open for daily play:

Santa Barbara Golf Club, Las Positas Road and McCaw Avenue. (805) 687–7087. Bordering the Earl Warren Showgrounds.

Sandpiper Golf Course, 7925 Hollister Avenue, Goleta. (805) 968–1541.

Tennis. Use permits are required, obtainable at the courts or at the Recreation Department, 820 Laguna Street, (805–568–5418). Lighted courts include Las Positas Municipal Courts, 1002 Las Positas Road (six courts). Nonlighted courts include Municipal Courts, 414 Park Place (twelve courts), and Pershing Park Courts, near the intersection of Cabrillo Boulevard and Costillo Street (eight courts). All in Santa Barbara.

Hang gliding. Keep a lookout for the daring hang gliders near the bluffs at Arroyo Burro Beach. The Hang Gliders Emporium, 613 Milpas Street, Santa Barbara. (805–965–3733), gives lessons.

Whale-watching. Track the big grays off the coast during their southward migration to Baja, mid-November through March, and again when they head back north, during February, March, and April. Best viewing spots are along the bluffs at Shoreline Park. Several commercial charters offer cruises, among them Sea Landing (805–963–3564). Santa Barbara.

Polo. Santa Barbara Polo and Racquet Club, 3375 Foothill Road Carpenteria. (805) 684–8667. Polo games/matches every Sunday, April through October, at 1:00 P.M.; feature match at 3:00 P.M. Admission. Phone for information and schedule.

Special Events

January 1. Hang Gliding Festival. Daring local pilots fly in precision contests off the ocean bluffs.

Mid-February. Compadres De Los Gatos All Breed Cat Show.

Early March. International Cymbidium Orchid Show. One of the world's most prestigious horticultural events. Santa Barbara International Film Festival. Premieres and screenings of international and U.S. films; citywide festivities.

March. During the entire month from the bluffs along Shoreline Park, you can watch the big whales on their migration.

Late April. Presidio Days. Three-day celebration of Santa Barbara's birthday and multiethnic heritage, held at the historical El Presidio.

End of June. Santa Barbara Writer's Conference. Summer Solstice Parade on State Street. A spectacular—with costumes, dancers, and music.

July 4. Independence Day Festivities. Parade, special arts and crafts show at the mission.

Late July–early August. Old Spanish Days (fiesta). Santa Barbara's biggest event, begun in 1926. A five-day festival, featuring a grand parade with gaily decorated horse-drawn carriages; Spanish marketplaces; and carnival, rodeo, and dancers.

Mid-August. Santa Barbara Museum of Natural History Wine Festival.

Late September. Santa Barbara Concours d'Elegance. Antique car show.

Early October. Santa Barbara International Jazz Festival.

Late November. Santa Barbara National Amateur Horse Show.

Early December. Christmas Parade.

Mid-December. Yuletide Boat Parade.

Other Recommended Restaurants and Lodgings

Santa Barbara

Oyster's, 9 West Victoria Street. (805) 962–9888. Attractive, with open kitchen and menu posted outside to scan; specializes in oysters in many variations. Other entrees include grilled chicken and pastas. Lunch and dinner Monday through Saturday; Sunday dinner only.

Four Seasons Biltmore, 1260 Channel Drive. (805) 969–2261. A hands-down winner for consistently good food, elegantly presented. Try the ocean-view Patio terrace for lunch and buffet dinner, La Sala Lounge for high tea and the famed Biltmore Brunch, and La Marina for romantic candlelight dining. (Pricey.)

Soho, 21 Victoria Street. (805) 963–5497. A comfy yuppie hangout, with a varied California cuisine menu. Live jazz. Lunch Monday through Friday; dinner nightly. Reservations recommended.

The Harbor Restaurant, 210 Stearns Wharf. (805) 963–3311. At the end of the wharf, it's just right for grilled fish, salads, steaks, and cocktails while you enjoy some of the best views of Santa Barbara. Lunch and dinner daily; Sunday champagne brunch.

Fess Parker's Red Lion Resort, 633 East Cabrillo Boulevard. (800) 879–2929. On the boulevard across from the beach and sprawled over 24 acres, each of the 360 rooms and 24 suites has a private patio and minibar. Concierge service, swimming pool, Jacuzzi, gym, sauna, three lighted tennis courts, putting green, two restaurants, and lounge.

Montecito Inn, 1295 Coast Village Road. (800) 843–2017. Charming small hotel with European ambience, two blocks from the beach, well-furnished rooms (some have refrigeration and VCR) and nice bathrooms, swimming pool, Jacuzzi, sauna, exercise room, complimentary bikes, and complimentary trolley passes. Additionally, complimentary continental breakfast is served in lobby. Good restaurant/cafe.

Hot Spot, 36 State Street. (805) 564–1637. For reservations and information about lodgings, attractions and events.

For More Information

Santa Barbara Visitors Information Center, 1 Santa Barbara Street (corner of Cabrillo Boulevard at the beach), Santa Barbara, CA 93102. (800) 927–4688. Ask for destination guide.

Solvang and Santa Ynez Valley Wine Country

Solvang's windmills are delightful Old World sights.

Windmills and Wineries

———————————— 1 NIGHT ————————————

Historic villages · Shopping · Mission · Lake boating and fishing
Horseback riding · Ethnic dining · Open-air theater

This two-day itinerary takes you north to "Little Denmark," where windmills spin lazily in blue skies in a fairytale village of curving streets lined with shops and cafes. You'll visit and tour wineries in acres of vineyards flourishing in rural Santa Ynez Valley, which has become one of California's richest grape-growing and winemaking regions, and you'll visit small, quiet pioneer villages that haven't quite marked the turn of the past century.

Day 1

Morning

Drive north from Los Angeles on Ventura Freeway 101 about 132 miles to Solvang, the delectable smorgasbord of Denmark tucked in the peaceful Santa Ynez Valley of rich farmlands and vineyards, located about an hour past Santa Barbara.

Follow 101 through dramatic Gaviota Pass, with its soaring cliffs, go through the tunnel, and continue past the turnoff for splendid Nojoqui Falls Park, named for the 164-foot waterfall and including a playground and picnic area. Take the Buellton/Solvang exit, turn right onto Highway 246, and continue for about 5 miles to Solvang.

Lunch: **Continental Inn,** 1645 Copenhagen Drive, Solvang. (805) 688–5410. Select from the varied menu of Danish, German, and American foods; go for the full smorgasbord; or try the house specialties: *aebleskiver*—the toothsome, ball-shaped waffle—and thin Danish pancakes. Open daily from 9:00 A.M. to 8:00 P.M.

Afternoon

After lunch explore Solvang's sunny streets with their brightly colored buildings and brick and cobblestone sidewalks. Danish half-timbered farm-style buildings have tall, steeply pitched roofs of simulated thatch or heavy shake shingles adorned with weather vanes, dormer windows, steeples, and hand-carved storks. Gas street lamps glow in the evening, and buildings are outlined with tiny lights.

"The Danish Capital of America" has a storybook quality, as you stroll past fairytale murals on building facades and tall, country-style windmills that creak in the soft breezes. Some windmills house gift-shops or restaurants, and all provide ideal photo opportunities.

Solvang's inviting streets are lined with more than 200 tempting shops whose open Dutch doors reveal arrays of fine imports, including crystal, pewter, porcelain, handcrafted candles, antiques, and clocks. You'll find dolls, trolls, leather fashions, music boxes, Old World bakeries, and such famous designer names as Royal Copenhagen, Dansk, Georg Jensen, Hummel, and Rosenthal.

Appealing restaurants and bubbling sidewalk cafes with colorful umbrellas offer great dining variety. You'll never have a better opportunity to enjoy authentic Danish specialties such as *gravlax,* smorgasbord, *frikadiller* (Danish meatballs), *bof med log* (chopped beef with onions), and don't overlook *smorrebrod,* the hefty Danish open-face sandwich that can feed a small battalion. Additionally, change-of-pace menus offer American, Italian, Mexican, continental, and even Chinese cuisine. Many Solvang restaurants close between lunch and dinner (usually 3:00 to 5:00 P.M.), European fashion; most have menus posted outside.

Solvang, meaning "Sunny Field," was founded in 1911 by a group of Midwest Danish educators who wanted to establish a Danish colony and folk school to preserve their culture and traditions in an area where settlers could farm the rich soil. Other pioneers included carpenters and workers who built the first buildings and school. The strong Danish heritage is evident in local customs and holidays. The lively Danish Days, held the third full weekend in September, is when the city celebrates its Old World ties: Residents dress in Danish costume; prepare, cook, and serve traditional *aebleskiver* and sausage on the streets; there's entertainment, music, dancing, and parades.

Along Copenhagen Drive, on the corner of Alisal Road, **Rasmussen's** (1697), with wide arches and a tall roof steeple—the oldest, most complete department store in town—is known for Swedish crystal, Danish porcelain, handmade sweaters, gift items, and kitchenware. **Danish Village Gifts** (1683) features gourmet cookware and Royal Copenhagen dishes. The **Blue Windmill,** at Hamlet Square, has a fine assortment of T-shirts. You don't get to shop in a windmill every day, so explore the large one on Alisal Road; it's filled with a variety of gift items, many suspended from its tall ceiling.

On Mission Drive, the **Ugly Duckling** (1557), where music announces your entrance, is filled with gnomes, dolls, and amusing items. The **Jul Hus,** at 1580 Mission Drive, is Solvang's most unusual store, selling only Christmas merchandise year-round. This festive store where you hear Christmas music is filled with a large assortment of Christmas ornaments and decorations, toys, nutcrackers, music boxes, and the Dickens Ceramic Houses surrounding a fully trimmed Christmas tree with twinkling lights.

Stop by any of the city's six **bakeries** where they use Old Country, centuries-old recipes for favorite pastries. Don't overlook the popular, large, pretzel-shaped Kringler, filled with almond paste and raisins, topped with sliced almonds and drifts of sugar, and big as a suitcase. Small, friendly **Solvang Park,** at the corner of Mission Drive and First Street, is where Solvangers picnic and relax on the grass alongside the bust of Hans Christian Andersen, Denmark's prince of fairytales, in his famous top hat. You'll also find **The Little Mermaid,** a small replica of the famous bronze sculpture in Copenhagen's harbor, perched atop a rock and fountain at the corner of Mission Drive and Alisal Road.

Cross the street to visit the **Hans Christian Andersen Museum,** in the Book Loft Building, 1680 Mission Drive (805–588–2052), which honors the noted Danish fairytale writer, Denmark's favorite son and most famous figure. The small museum upstairs in the bookstore's loft is filled with copies of Andersen's beautifully illustrated books, many photos, letters, and memorabilia, including photographs of the beautiful singer Jenny Lind, the "Swedish Nightingale" with whom Andersen was said to have been hopelessly in love. This tall, stringy, long-nosed man wrote 156 fairytales and was greatly honored during his lifetime. The museum is open daily to 5:00 P.M. and is always accessible through the **Book Loft.** Browse the bookstore's wide selection of current, used, and collector's classics.

Drive or walk to the **Old Mission Santa Ines,** 1760 Mission Drive, established in 1804, the nineteenth of the twenty-one California missions and one of the best preserved and restored. The graceful old parish church, with its beautiful gardens around a large fountain, evokes the valley's Spanish missionary beginnings. Join a guided tour or explore on your own through the Chapel of the Madonnas, which has worn tile floors, a 29-foot-high beamed ceiling, and wall murals. The museum displays extensive artifacts of the Chumash Indian mission era; the giftshop shows religious artifacts and pottery. Frequently called the "Mission of the Passes," Santa Ines is the focus of many yearly events in the Santa Ynez Valley. (Open daily, 9:30 A.M. to 4:30 P.M.; admission.)

An easy, fun way to get around town is to ride the popular **Surrey Bike**—a four-wheel cycle with a red surrey on top and all passengers pedaling together like the Radio City Rockettes down the curving streets. Other offbeat sightseeing includes a twenty-minute narrated tour around town aboard Solvang's *Honen,* replica of an authentic Danish streetcar of the 1900s that is pulled by two massive, blond Belgian horses. Board at Mission and Alisal Road, daily during the summer season and weekends during the winter (fee). Romantics can see the city in an open, horse-drawn white carriage anytime from 3:00 to 5:00 P.M.; board it off Copenhagen and First Street.

Dinner: **Danish Inn Restaurant,** 1547 Mission Drive, Solvang. (805) 688–4813. Start your own tradition. This lovely, warm restaurant, offering fine food and service, features a gourmet Danish smorgasbord feast with an extensive variety of hot and cold delectables, plus American entrees of steak and prime rib.

Lodging. **Petersen Village Inn,** 1576 Mission Drive, Solvang, CA 93463. (800) 321–8985. AAA four-diamond rating. Discover Old World flavor in each of the forty-two good-size, individually decorated suites, with canopied beds, antique and period furniture, TV, and turndown service. Cafe; complimentary buffet breakfast served in dining room; wine-and-cheese in the lounge from 6:00 to 7:00 P.M.

Day 2

Morning

Breakfast: At the inn. Beautifully presented, generous complimentary buffet in the dining room includes juice, coffee, Danish pastry, rolls, ham, and cheese.

After breakfast select foods for a picnic lunch at the wineries by stopping at the **Solvang Market and Deli,** corner of Fifth Street and Mission (805–688–6117). You'll find extensive deli items, buckets of chicken, and BBQ foods on weekends.

There's a mystique and romance about wine associated with the pleasurable and better things in life. The experience is enriched by driving along the peaceful backcountry roads of **Santa Ynez Valley,** with its natural beauty of pastures and orchards and acres of lush vineyards. As you visit the unpretentious wineries and unchanged, hundred-year-old villages, you are far removed from the daily bustle.

Pick up a "Santa Barbara County Wineries" map from your hotel or the Solvang Visitor Bureau (1571 Mission Drive) and follow the wine route. This one-night itinerary doesn't visit all the wineries, as you won't have sufficient time unless you plan to stay over another night, but you might mark the rest for a return visit to Solvang.

From Solvang take Highway 246 to Refugio Road; turn right and it's 1 mile to **Santa Ynez Winery,** 343 Refugio Road, Santa Ynez (805–688–8381). This family-owned winery was the first commercial vineyard planted in Santa Ynez, in 1974. With 100 arces planted in thirteen varietals, the most popular are Chardonnay and Riesling. Tastings and self-guided tours are available from 10:00 A.M. to 5:00 P.M. daily. There's a giftshop and picnic area.

After your wine tasting and tour, continue to the sleepy little town of **Santa Ynez,** founded in 1882. There's not much traffic in its 2-block-long business center. Drop by the **Santa Ynez Historical Museum,** on Sagunto Street and Farady (805–688–7889), where eight rooms ramble around a shady courtyard. Immerse yourself in early California history and memorabilia. The Indian Room exhibits a diorama of Chumash Indian life; the Pioneer Room displays turn-of-the-century furnishings; and the West Room shows saddles, guns, and other items. (Open Friday through Sunday, 1:00 to 4:00 P.M.)

Parks-Janeway Carriage House, part of the museum, displays about thirty-five gleaming carriages that seem right out of western movies, including the "Wells Fargo" and the "United States Mail"; silver-mounted saddles and many other items are here too, as is a giftshop. (Open Tuesday through Thursday from 8:00 A.M. to 4:00 P.M. and Sunday from 1:00 to 4:00 P.M.)

From Santa Ynez take Edison Road north, turning left at Baseline Avenue to **Ballard,** the valley's oldest and first town, founded in 1880. Turn right on Cottonwood Street to see its landmark, little two-room red schoolhouse, set back on a broad lawn shaded by two ancient trees. The school has been in continuous use since its dedication in 1883.

From Ballard continue a few miles on 154 through a soft country-side of apple orchards, farmhouses, and ranches to **Los Olivos,** which has a flagpole in the center of the main street. Once a major Butter-field stagecoach stop, the town, with its many resident artists, has evolved into a fine-arts center for the Santa Ynez Valley. Visit historic **Mattie's Tavern** on Highway 154, built in 1896 as an overnight inn and still a warm, intimate restaurant for fine dining.

After driving around Los Olivos, go back through Ballard, turning right on Edison Road to Highway 246 to the **Gainey Vineyard,** 3950 East Highway 246 (3 miles east of Solvang), Santa Ynez (805–688–0558). This family-owned winery, begun in 1984, sits atop the family's 1,800-acre ranch. Gainey is one of the most visitor-oriented and popular facilities and features the largest tasting room in the area and good-size picnic gardens. The 12,000-square-foot winery and visitor center are surrounded by 65 acres of premium varietal grapes, producing Chardonnay, Sauvignon Blanc, Pinot Noir, Merlot, Johannisberg Riesling, and Cabernet Sauvignon. Daily tastings are from 10:00 A.M. to 5:00 P.M., with a $2.50 charge to taste four major varietals; the logo glass is your souvenir. The giftshop sells T-shirts and giftpacks.

Afternoon

Lunch: Picnic at **Gainey Vineyard.** To visit more wineries, go east on Highway 246 to 154; turn left, staying on Highway 154 to 101; then turn right on Zaca Station Road and left up the hill to **Firestone Vineyard,** 5017 Zaca Station Road, Los Olivos (805–688–3940), the largest winery in the valley. The impressive building sits atop 260 acres of estate vineyards and is augmented by an attractive garden patio, a fountain, and picnic tables. The twenty-minute tours begin in the vineyard, go to the fermentation room, and then end in the large tasting room. Sampling is of Firestone's most popular varietals: Riesling, dry Riesling, Johannesberg Riesling, and a Merlot Rosé available only at the winery. The giftshop features logo T-shirts, totebags, and wine accessories.

After sampling the wines, turn left on Zaca Station Road; continue on it until the name changes to Foxen Canyon, about 3 miles, to the new **Fess Parker Winery,** 6200 Foxen Canyon Road, Los Olivos (805–688–1545). The winery sales and tasting room opened in February 1992, though the first release was in 1989. The 714-acre ranch has 31 acres planted in Chardonnay, Johannesberg Riesling, Sirah, and Merlot. Tasting is from 10:00 A.M. to 4:00 P.M. in the barrel room, with a $2.00 fee for tasting three or four wines; you keep the logo glass. No tours are offered yet, as buildings are still under construction. If celebrity owner Fess Parker is around, he'll autograph a bottle of wine for you.

Carey Cellars, 2.5 miles north of Highway 246, at 1711 Alamo Pintado Road, Solvang (805–688–8554), is framed by mountains and beautiful old trees and surrounded by twenty-three acres of estate vineyards. The winery was established by a family of doctors who refurbished an old dairy barn into a winery and had their first harvest in 1978. After Firestone Vineyards purchased the enterprise in 1987, the facilities were upgraded; Kate Firestone is now vintner. Carey's tasting room is in a small, rustic farmhouse with a homey front porch and a picnic area. The winery is open daily from 10:00 A.M. to 4:00 P.M. for visitors to sample its four varietals: Chardonnay, Sauvignon Blanc, Cabernet Blanc, and Cabernet Sauvignon.

To return to Los Angeles, get back on Highway 246 through Buellton/Solvang and pick up Highway 101 south.

There's More

Bethania Lutheran Church, 603 Atterdag Road, Solvang. Built in 1928, the Danish-style, rural church reflects tradition, with its replica of a fully rigged ship suspended symbolically from the ceiling. Regular Sunday worship; Danish services once a month.

Elverhoy Danish Heritage and Fine Arts Museum, 1624 Elverhoy Way, Solvang. (805) 686–1211. On a quiet residential street, this Danish-style farmhouse is very browsable. Gallery and period rooms depict Solvang's pioneer past with early photos, antique furnishings, and artifacts. Open Saturday and Sunday from 1:00 to 4:00 P.M.

Hans Christian Andersen Park, on Atterdag Road, 3 blocks north of Mission Drive, Solvang. The rustic setting is relaxing for fun, picnics, and barbecues. A great place to pick up a variety of picnic items—sandwiches, salads, and deli fare—is the Solvang Market & Deli at the corner of Fifth and Mission. A small creek, a children's playground, and tennis courts are here too.

Festival Theatre, Second and Oak streets. The Pacific Conservatory of the Performing Arts (PCPA) Theaterfest presents six plays in repertory under the stars July through mid-September in Solvang's 780-seat, open-air theater-in-the-round. (800) 549–7272. Inquire about hotel-theater-dinner packages.

Factory outlets. Izod/Gant Factory Store, 435 Alisal Road, Suites B1 and G2A.

Cachuma Lake, 12 miles east of Solvang. If you're a fisherman, like to camp or go boating and hiking, and enjoy other year-round outdoor recreation, this 8-mile-long lake is for you. Snackbar, general store. Admission per car.

Special Events

End of February. Storytelling Festival. (805) 688–9533. International stories in a twelve-hour period, Solvang Royal Scandinavian Inn.
Early March. Solvang/Santa Maria Century Bike Ride. (805) 943–9440. One-hundred-mile bike ride.
Mid-April. Solvang Custom Knife Show, Solvang Royal Scandinavian Inn. (805) 688–3612. Annual Easter Egg Hunt, Hans Christian Andersen Park. Easter Sunday Children's Parade.
End of April. Santa Barbara County Vintner's Festival. (805) 688–0881. Santa Ynez Valley Carriage Classic. (805) 688–4454. Exhibitors and celebrity guests.
Early May. Los Rancheros Visitadores Annual Santa Ynez Valley Trek. Riders parade through Solvang. Cinco de Mayo celebration, Mission Santa Ines. (805) 688–9533. A 10K run and day-long entertainment. Gourmet Century Bike Ride. (805) 688–6385. One hundred miles around Santa Ynez Valley.
May 16–17. Pepper Tree Art Show and Barbecue. (805) 688–6205.
Mid-June. Old Santa Ynez Days. (805) 688–5318. Celebrates the town's birthday.
July 4. Solvang's Fourth of July Parade.
Mid-August. Old Mission Santa Ines Fiesta. (805) 688–4815.
Third weekend in September. Two-Day Danish Days Festival. (805) 688–0701. Dancing, music, food, fun.
End of September. Day in the Country, Los Olivos. (805) 688–5083.
Mid-October. Vintner's Association Wine Harvest, Rancho Sisquoc. Celebration of harvest.
November. PCPA Winter Backstage Theater Season. (800) 221–9469.
Early November. Solvang Prelude. Twenty-five and 50-mile bike ride. Two-Day Pepper Tree Art Show.
Mid-November. Dixieland Jazz Festival, Solvang Royal Scandinavian Inn.
End of November to mid-December. Winterfest in Solvang.
Early December. Christmas Tree Lighting and Window Walk, Christmas Parade, Winterfest.

Other Recommended
Restaurants and Lodgings

Solvang

Mustard Seed, 1655 Mission Drive. (805) 688–1318. Home-style American cooking, featuring sandwiches, salads, soups, and daily specials. Patio dining. Closed between lunch and dinner.

Mollekroen, 435 Alisal Road. (805) 688–4555. Across from the post office; walk upstairs to the large, sunny dining room for hearty Danish smorgasbord, including meatballs, herring, red cabbage, cold cuts, and fruit; plus American menu.

Paula's Pancake House, 1531 Mission Drive. (805) 688–2867. Popular for good food. Extensive breakfast and lunch menu features thin Danish pancakes, waffles, eggs, homemade soups, salads, and burgers. Patio dining, closed from 3:00 P.M.

Alisal Guest Ranch, 1054 Alisal Road. (805) 688–6411. Three miles down the road from city center. There's a genuine western flavor to this 10,000-acre, upscale dude ranch. Sixty-six well-furnished bungalows with studio rooms and two-bedroom suites feature wood-burning fireplace, coffeemaker, wetbar, refrigerator with icemaker. No TV, radio, or telephone mars your peaceful escape. Play golf on the 18-hole championship course, where deer watch you tee off. Heated swimming pool and spa, seven tennis courts, riding stable, private lake for fishing and boating, library, recreation/TV room, dining room, lounge with evening entertainment, conference center. Full breakfast and dinner included in two-night-minimum stay. Seasonal packages.

Danish Country Inn, 1455 Mission Drive. (800) 44–RELAX; (805) 688–2018. Warmly decorated; eighty-two minisuites with refrigerator, cable TV, video player, and hair dryer. Full complimentary farm-fresh breakfast in the attractive dining room; manager's cocktail reception.

Tivoli Inn, 1564 Copenhagen Drive. (800) 776–1484; (805) 688–0559. Look for the distinctive tall clock tower. Hospitality begins with a welcome basket of fruit and wine and continues with a complimentary continental breakfast in bed. Thirty-five well-designed suites with fireplace, TV, minibar, refrigerator; Cafe and Pub.

For More Information

Solvang Conference and Visitors Bureau, 1571 Mission Drive, P.O. Box 70, Solvang, CA 93463. (800) 468–6765 (in California); (805) 688–6144.

San Luis Obispo/San Simeon Cambria/Morro Bay

Morro Bay's 576-foot-tall "Gibraltar of the Pacific"

Coastline and a Castle

_____ 2 NIGHTS _____

Mission · Wineries · Farmer's market · Artists' colony
Museum · State university · Castle/mansion · Galleries

This packed, three-day excursion takes you about 200 miles north
through California's richly scenic central coast of rolling hills and pas-

toral land to a lovely, small college town. You'll also stop at a noted winery for a taste of its bubbly product; visit a legendary, art-filled castle; have lunch in a seaside artists' colony in the pines; and see California's "Gibraltar of the Pacific."

Note: This itinerary visits Hearst Castle in San Simeon, where reservations are required. Tours (about two hours long) are always available and can be reserved anywhere from a few hours to weeks or months in advance. (At this writing, all tours are $14.) Call (800) 444–7275.

Day 1

Morning

Leave Los Angeles via Ventura Freeway 101 north, driving through rural San Fernando Valley. After the turnoff for Ojai, the freeway follows the unruffled, mist-covered ocean. You're soon past Santa Barbara with no congestion, thanks to the new freeway, which bypasses the city. Curving inland, you drive through dramatic Gaviota Pass, where the road is framed with tall, rugged mountains. Exit Buellton (on the outskirts of Solvang) on Avenue of the Flags, a landscaped parkway decorated with a tall row of American flags waving in the breeze.

Lunch: **Pea Soup Andersen's,** 376 Avenue of the Flags, Buellton. (805) 688–5581. The original 1924 home of split pea soup. This large, very busy restaurant includes pea soup or salad with all sandwiches and entrees. For those in a hurry, the coffeeshop serves the same food but has faster service than the dining room. Sunday buffet brunch is from 11:00 A.M. to 3:00 P.M.

Afternoon

For the nearly 60 miles to San Luis Obispo, continue north on 101 in a tranquil, pastoral countryside where stately old oak trees dance gracefully over the hillsides. Just past Nipomo and about 3 miles south of Arroyo Grande, look for the Maison Deutz (rhymes with "Toots") winery on the right.

The white and blue entry gates of **Maison Deutz,** at 453 Deutz Drive in Arroyo Grande (805–481–1763), are immediately past the large winery sign. Maison Deutz offers a range of fine sparkling wines produced in the *methode champenoise.* Tastings of wines in a full flute glass, accompanied by appetizers—crackers, cheeses, mustards—are about $3.75 to $5.00 for each of three wines. Tastings are offered daily except Tuesdays, from 11:00 A.M. to 5:00 P.M. Guided tours of the winery are by appointment only.

After your visit to the winery, return to Highway 101 north to San Luis Obispo.

Friendly and hospitable **San Luis Obispo** (say "Lewis," not "Looey") may well be one of the most likable small towns you've visited. Its rather old-fashioned, prosperous downtown area, distinguished by tree-shaded streets, offers a pleasant variety of shopping and dining, with good food served in generous amounts. Fortunately, local restaurants tend to bypass expensive nouvelle cuisine entrees of small portions and barely cooked cauliflower, favoring moderately priced robust, American-style fare instead. The city glows during its summer Mozart Festival; the weekly Farmer's Market is the hottest ticket on a Thursday night; and a rural creek meanders through the city.

Along Higuera Street, the main thoroughfare, stately, well-preserved old buildings add stability and harmony. Many buildings have been attractively recycled. The renovated Golden State Creamery, which closed in 1974, has a new life as a trendy complex for dining and shopping.

Home to California Polytechnic State University, or Cal Poly, this is a walking town. Stroll through the **Network's** skylit arcade, which has ceiling banners, bright shops, and a sandwich bar at the rear, where you tote your order out to the dining patio overlooking San Luis Obispo's picturesque creek. You'll have to go a long way to find a prettier, more natural setting.

To see where the city was founded in 1772, when Father Junípero Serra established **Mission San Luis Obispo de Tolosa,** drive around the corner or walk across the footbridge over the creek. The mission was the fifth in the chain of twenty-one California missions. In the chapel the statues and Stations of the Cross along the walls are all the originals. The first California olive trees still grow in the pleasant mission garden. (Open daily from 10:00 A.M. to 4:00 P.M. in winter and from 9:00 A.M. to 5:00 P.M. in summer; bookstore, giftshop, and museum open daily.)

Mission Plaza, the grassy landscaped area between the mission and San Luis Creek, is the focus of community events and a quiet park of benches and shade trees. Visit the adjacent Community Art Center (open from noon to 5:00 P.M., Tuesday through Sunday) and Children's Museum.

Dinner: **F. McLintocks Saloon and Dining House,** 686 Higuera Street, San Luis Obispo. (805) 541–0686. This western-style saloon, with red-and-white checked tablecloths, long bar, and moose-head decor, is where locals meet to eat and schmooze. Hearty, delicious nightly specials include beef ribs and BBQ chicken, as well as hamburgers and BBQ beef sandwiches—and the chili has plenty of authority. Easy prices, large portions, excellent service.

Lodging: **La Cuesta Motor Inn,** 2074 Monterey Street, San Luis

Obispo, CA 93401. (800) 543–2777 (in California); (805) 543–2777. Conveniently located, seven-year-old three-story building; seventy-two good-size rooms, bathroom with extra mirrored makeup pullman, ample storage, small balcony, clock radio, TV, dining table and chairs; heated swimming pool, Jacuzzi. Complimentary continental breakfast and afternoon tea and cookies served in the lobby. Friendly, efficient staff.

Day 2

Morning

Breakfast: At the inn. Continental breakfast served in the lobby is included in your room rate. Help yourself to orange juice, coffee, mini-muffins, and sliced bagels and cream cheese. You can also tote a tray to your room.

Leave for Hearst Castle, about a 45-mile drive. Drive down Monterey Street to Santa Rosa; turn right to the freeway, taking Highway 1 to San Simeon. Alongside the rolling hills and farms in the peaceful, open country, you become aware of California's grandeur and size. You'll pass several towns to visit on your return—Morro Bay, Harmony, and Cambria, where an array of tall pine trees are raggedy green giants marching in place on the slopes. After a WELCOME TO SAN SIMEON sign where the ocean is as blue as Paul Newman's eyes, Hearst Castle is the next right.

At the visitor center board your tour bus for the fifteen-minute, 5-mile trip to the hilltop castle; the trip is accompanied by an audiotape program. (Tours begin at 8:00 A.M. and leave every ten minutes. The last tour starts at 3:00 P.M. in winter, later in summer.)

Legendary **Hearst Castle,** with its lofty twin towers atop the four-level Spanish-Moorish mansion designed by architect Julia Morgan and built by newspaper publishing tycoon William Randolph Hearst as a summer home between 1919 and 1947, resulted in this magnificent, art-filled, 165-room estate with 127 acres of gardens, pools, and terraces.

It's certainly not your everyday owner-built home, with its thirty-eight bedrooms and thirty-one baths on a quiet hilltop with an ocean view. In a forty-year spending orgy of millions of dollars and repeated forays to Europe, Hearst gathered art objects, Renaissance tapestries, paintings, silver, and ancient carved ceilings from all over. Entire castles and monasteries were dismantled and shipped stone by stone to San Simeon.

Back in the 1930s Hollywood's star-studded guest list for lavish weekends at the castle included Clark Gable, Charlie Chaplin, John

Barrymore, and Greta Garbo, plus Hearst's mistress, actress Marion Davies. There were fabulous costume balls, deluxe barbecues, picnics, and nightly banquets. Those were the golden days of Hollywood. Today's guests take guided tours for a glimpse of the life-style of the flamboyant millionaire who, for twenty years, lived in regal splendor atop his private mountain kingdom.

The place is so vast that there are four separate tours to see all of it. Each tour includes the two pools and takes about an hour and three-quarters. Tour 1 is suggested for first-time visitors for an overall look and includes the entire main floor of Casa Grande, a guest cottage, gardens, the outdoor Neptune Pool, the indoor Roman Pool, and the Morning Room, Billiard Room, and Theater.

On tour 1 you'll begin at the serene, 104-foot-long, exquisite marble-faced Neptune Pool filled with pure spring water. Then you'll see the eighteen-room guest cottage where Hearst lived during construction of La Casa Grande (the castle), your next stop.

The baronial, 100-by-42-foot Assembly Hall, where guests gathered for evening cocktails, is the castle's largest room, with Renaissance furnishings and ancient choir stalls. In the 67-foot-long Refectory (dining room)—whose fireplace is large enough to roast a rhinoceros—silk Sienese banners flutter from the 27-foot-high wooden ceiling imported from a sixteenth-century monastery.

The indoor Roman Pool, large enough to float the *Queen Mary*, is made of tiny blue Venetian tiles sprinkled with twenty-two-karat gold leaf. And on and on you go, viewing a mind-boggling collection of priceless art and furnishings, Egyptian pottery, mirrors, statues, and bathrooms with real gold fixtures. At the one-hundred-seat movie theater, you finally get to sit down, to watch a short movie of the good life at the castle, featuring famous stars and celebrities. All in all, it's the kind of place that makes you want to go home and burn the furniture.

Tour 2 covers Casa Grande's upper floors, including the Library, the Gothic Suite and study, the Doge's Suite, the Cloister Rooms, and the Pantry and Kitchen, where all the sumptuous meals were prepared.

Tour 3 guides visitors through the north wing of Casa Grande, three floors of guest suites with marble bathrooms and gold fixtures, and the Casa del Monte guest cottage; a short video is included.

Tour 4 (offered April through October) takes in the extensive gardens, the Wine Cellar, Casa del Mar, the largest guest cottage, and the Neptune Pool dressing rooms.

New, two-hour evening tours in spring and fall include a living history program with docents dressed as guests and staff; illuminated pools and gardens; and highlights of Casa Grande and Casa del Mar.

All tours are offered at the same fee and entail considerable walking and stair climbing; better wear comfortable walking shoes. The castle is open daily, except Thanksgiving, Christmas, and New Year's Day; the busiest season is late spring and summer. Hearst Castle was given to the state of California in 1958 and is a State Historical Monument. Free parking is provided. Reservations are necessary and can be charged to your credit card. Since the castle holds more treasures than King Tut's tomb, toting along a tape recorder will help you bring it all back for future reminiscing. No photo flash or tripods are permitted, however.

Leave Hearst Castle, drive across the highway, and turn right along a narrow road to **Sebastian's General Store,** its patio Cafe, adjacent post office, and Union 76 gas station. Sebastian's, built in 1852, is a State Historical Landmark. In addition to stocking groceries and wines, the store has a small section filled with attractive souvenirs, toys, and postcards half the price of those in the Hearst Castle giftshop.

Return to the highway, turning right (south) on Highway 1, and continue to Cambria, 6 miles down the road. At the Burton Drive traffic signal, turn inland into this small, appealing artists' colony surrounded by pine trees.

Cambria is frequently compared with Carmel-by-the-Sea but seems more natural, not as cutesy or as thronged with tourists. Be sure to explore both sections of Main Street—East Village, up the hill, and West Village, more in the center of town. For lunch, drive up the hill on Main Street to East Village.

Lunch: **Linn's Main Bin,** 2277 Main Street, Cambria. (805) 927–0371. A big, sunny room with a gourmet giftshop and a bakery producing luscious berry pies. Linn's is noted for chicken and beef pot pie served with fruit or green salad. Other tempters include quiche, sandwiches, and Oriental chicken salad.

Afternoon

Cambria's reconverted Victorian buildings of the 1870s house one-of-a-kind shops, cafes, galleries, and lodgings. Besides Main Street, the side streets are worth browsing as well. On Bridge Street, **Simple Pleasures** features gifts, ornaments, and folk art for year-round holiday celebrations. **Banbury Cross,** alongside, displays old English decorative items, china, crystal, and linen.

Drive back down Main Street to Cambria's **West Village,** which resembles a faded movie set with its small stores tucked in pretty cottages of soft colors, towers, dormer windows, and Dutch doors. In this very browsable stretch, you'll find a variety of galleries; antiques, gift, flower, and basket shops; and jeweler's and clothing stores.

The **Soldier Factory,** 789 Main Street (805–927–3804), here since 1973, makes tiny toy soldiers (54-mm size). Close to 800 different tiny military figures, painstakingly modeled and costumed, represent various wars, regiments, and so on. The store is open daily from 10:00

A.M. to 5:00 P.M. You'll find the Chamber of Commerce a few doors away, should you need brochures or information.

Across the street, flanked by galleries and cafes, **Chase's Olive Barrel,** at 786 Main Street, features twenty varieties of California olives grown nearby and offers free olive and pickle tasting, gourmet foods, homemade chocolates, and giftpacks.

Return to Highway 1 south. In barely ten minutes turn left at the little town of **Harmony,** population eighteen. The former one-hundred-year-old dairy community is now a one-street artists' colony, with artisans working in the old warehouses. Watch glassblowers at work in Phoenix Studio Art Glass. Next door, Harmony Cellars, a boutique winery, features local varieties. Stop by for a taste. There's a $1.00 fee to taste seven wines, the amount applied to your purchase. Across the street, Nancy Wright Designs highlights smart, hand-painted wearable art. Follow old brick paths around to the Pottery Works, a large, airy showroom.

The Old Harmony Pasta Factory, (805) 927–5882 in the former creamery building, offers cozy fireplace dining of homemade pastas, chicken, scampi, pizza, wines. Dinner nightly; Sunday champagne brunch 9:30 A.M. to 2 P.M.

Continue south to **Morro Bay,** where the enormous, 576-foot-high **Morro Rock** (the "Gibraltar of the Pacific") juts out of the water. Take the Main Street exit to the waterfront of this small fishing village and meander along the Embarcadero, with its shops, restaurants, boat activity, and harbor cruises. Then drive back to San Luis Obispo to relax before dinner.

Dinner: **Cafe Roma,** 1819 Osos Street, San Luis Obispo. (805) 541–6800. Near the train depot. Roma is consistently praised for Italian specialties and good service in its traditional candlelit dining room. Daily homemade pastas and excellent veal dishes. Lunch Tuesday through Friday; dinner Tuesday through Saturday; closed Sunday and Monday.

Lodging: La Cuesta Motor Inn.

Day 3

Morning

Breakfast: Complimentary continental breakfast served in your hotel. Or try a town favorite: **Louisa's Place,** 964 Higuera Street (805–541–0227), where everything's made from scratch. The specialties are omelets, the hotcakes are saucer-size, and the grilled ham is as tender as a new mother's smile. (Open from 7:00 A.M. to 3:00 P.M. Monday through Saturday and from 8:00 A.M. to 2:00 P.M. Sunday.)

If there's time before leaving for Los Angeles, take a walking tour or two of San Luis Obispo's **Heritage Walks,** which begin in Mission Plaza and cover many historical buildings and areas. A brochure is available from the Chamber of Commerce, 1039 Chorro Street, or inquire at your hotel.

Afternoon

En route home on Highway 1 south, stop for a look at the **Madonna Inn,** with its own freeway exit on Madonna Road. Sprawled across 2,200 acres, each of its 109 rooms is completely different, romantically awash with cupids, hearts, stained glass, and bacchanalia bathrooms. In the lobby twinkling lights cascade over a pink marble balustrade, a rose flowered carpet, and artificial plants and trees. See the powder room, of course, but the pièce de résistance is the waterfall in the men's room.

Retrace your way south to Los Angeles.

There's More

San Luis Obispo County Historical Museum, 696 Monterey Street, San Luis Obispo. (805) 543–0638. Across from the old mission; housed in the 1904 Carnegie Library Building. The museum's photos and artifacts depict the city's development from the Chumash and Salinan Indians through the mission and rancho days and the Victorian era. Open Wednesday through Sunday, 10:00 A.M. to 4:00 P.M.; closed holidays; donations welcome.

Earthling Bookshop, 698–699 Higuera Street, San Luis Obispo. (805) 543–7951. Corner of Broad Street. Bookworms appreciate the large selection, the cozy reading area around a center fireplace, and the classical-music background—who needs TV? Open daily, 10:00 A.M. to 11:00 P.M. Earthling Annex, across Higuera Street, sells books at discount prices.

Farmer's Market, San Luis Obispo. Festive, popular open-air market is held every Thursday evening (except Thanksgiving Day or if it's raining) from 6:00 to 9:00 P.M. on Higuera Street, between Osos and Nipomo, with streets closed to traffic. Local farmers bring just-picked fruits and vegetables, as well as flowers and cider. Restaurateurs barbecue chicken, ribs, and hot dogs on massive outdoor grills; food booths offer pizza, sandwiches, and desserts. There's entertainment too: jugglers, dancers, clowns, and musicians.

Farmer's Market, Veteran's Memorial Building, parking lot on West Main Street, Cambria. Held every Friday, 2:30 to 5:30 P.M., rain or shine. Fresh produce, nuts, flowers, and fun.

Farmer's Market, Morro Bay. Every Thursday afternoon.
The San Luis Obispo Trolley offers free rides, 10:00 A.M. to 5:30
P.M. daily, as it loops through downtown from the Civic Center or
Monterey Street.
Morro Bay Aquarium and Marine Rehabilitation Center, 595
Embarcadero, Morro Bay. Exhibits include live marine specimens and
seals. Open daily, except on Thanksgiving and Christmas. Admission.
Morro Bay Natural History Museum, Morro Bay State Park,
Morro Bay. (805) 772–2694. Displays mammals, fish; offers daily video,
art gallery, museum store. Open daily except Thanksgiving, Christmas,
and New Year's Day. Admission.

Special Events

Late February. Madri Gras Street Faire, Mardi Gras Jazz Festival,
Pismo Beach.
Mid-April. Mission Plaza Easter Egg Hunt, San Luis Obispo. Easter
Egg Hunt, Cambria. Easter Egg Hunt, Del Mar Park, Morro Bay.
Late April. Italian Street Painting Festival, San Luis Obispo.
Mid-May. La Fiesta de San Luis Obispo. KGBX Central Coast Wine
Classic, San Luis Obispo.
July 4. Fourth of July in Mission Plaza, San Luis Obispo. Picnic and
fireworks display, Cambria. Fourth of July celebration, Morro Bay.
July 27–31. Annual Mozart Festival, San Luis Obispo.
August 1–9. Annual Mozart Festival, San Luis Obispo.
Early September. Central Coast Wine Festival, San Luis Obispo.
Labor Day Weekend. Pinedorado Parade and Fair. Since 1948.
Cambria.
Late September. Morro Bay Triathlon. Tallship *Californian* Annual
Visit, Morro Bay.
Early October. Harbor Festival, with wine and seafood. Morro Bay.
Early December. Christmas in the Plaza, San Luis Obispo.
Late December. Christmas Street Faire. Lighted Boat Parade, Morro
Bay.

Other Recommended
Restaurants and Lodgings

San Luis Obispo

Apple Farm Restaurant, 2015 Monterey Street. (805) 544–6100; (800)
255–2040. A breakfast winner for home-style buttermilk pancakes, Belgian waffles, fresh muffins. Lunch and dinner American-style entrees

include sandwiches, chicken and dumplings, turkey, fresh seafood, salad bar. Top it all off with hot apple dumplings and fruit cobbler. Early Bird dinners from 2:00 to 5:00 P.M. daily. Best to reserve for all meals.

Linnaeas Cafe, 1110 Garden Street. (805) 541–5888. A young hangout, with garden dining, for offbeat salads, soups, and burritos. Open daily, 7:30 A.M. to midnight.

Sebastian's, 1023 Chorro Street, Mission Plaza. (805) 544–5550. The chic dining room and creekside patio are elegant for gourmet lunch and dinner. Happy Hour Monday through Friday, 4:00 to 7:00 P.M., with complimentary hors d'oeuvres; champagne Sunday brunch.

Apple Farm Inn/Trellis Court, 2015 Monterey Street. (800) 374–3705. Victorian-style, 101-room hotel, with fireplaces and country decor. Complimentary coffee, TV, radio, terry robes, turndown service, and souvenir gift. Heated swimming pool, spa; country store, restaurant, giftshop, working Mill House. Seasonal rates.

Quality Suites, 1631 Monterey Street. (805) 541–3170; (800) 221–2222. Has 138 two-room suites, each with two TVs, VCR, microwave, stereo, honor bar, refrigerator; complimentary cooked-to-order breakfast; swimming pool, spa.

Cambria

The Brambles Dinner House, 4005 Burton Drive. (805) 927–4716. West Village. The small red cottage was built in 1874 as a family residence. Everything is homemade. Medium-priced entrees feature prime rib, grilled steaks, smoked ribs, fresh seafood, English trifle. Open Monday through Saturday from 5:00 to 10:00 P.M. and Sunday from 4:00 to 9:00 P.M.; Sunday brunch served from 9:30 A.M. to 2:00 P.M. Early Bird Specials. Reservations suggested.

Cambria Pines Lodge, 2905 Burton Drive. (800) 455–6868; (805) 927–4200. Landmark lodge of 120 rooms on twenty-five hilltop acres in a rustic pine setting, with TV and coffeemakers; includes 54 fireplace suites with microwave, wetbar, refrigerator. Indoor heated swimming pool, spa, and sauna; new Main Lodge building with restaurant, lounge, giftshop, and conference rooms, open winter 1993. Seasonal rates.

For More Information

San Luis Obispo Chamber of Commerce, 1039 Chorro Street, San Luis Obispo, CA 93401. (800) 543–1323. Open 8:00 A.M. to 5:00 P.M.
Cambria Chamber of Commerce, 767 Main Street, Cambria, CA 93428. (805) 927–3624.
San Simeon Chamber of Commerce, P.O. Box 1, San Simeon, CA 93452. (805) 927–3500.
Morro Bay Chamber of Commerce, 895 Napa #A1, Morro Bay, CA 93442. (800) 231–0592 (in California); (805) 772–4467.

Eastern Escapes

Lake Arrowhead/Big Bear Lake

The *Arrowhead Queen* paddlewheeler cruises the serene lake.

Sun and Snow at Mountain Lakes

_____ 2 NIGHTS _____

Lake cruises • Zoo • Mountain biking • Alpine slide • Pine forests
Watersports • Hearty dining • Golf • Skiing and skating • Antiques

This three-day outing in the rugged and scenic San Bernardino Mountains takes you from city noise and traffic to a pair of sparkling, mile-high resort communities. Amid clear, invigorating mountain air and quiet pine forests, you'll find year-round boating, swimming, hiking, fishing, and other outdoor recreations that make these communities so stimulating to visit. The area prides itself on distinctive shopping, hearty mountain dining, and hospitality.

Lake Arrowhead, a bustling summertime getaway, becomes a serene winter wonderland, with nearby skiing and snow fun. While Big Bear lake is Southern California's major ski and winter sports center, it is a popular, refreshing destination in all seasons. Both rural cities are easily toured in this change-of-pace itinerary.

Day 1

Morning

For the 90-mile drive up to Lake Arrowhead, your first destination, head east from Los Angeles on I–10 toward San Bernardino, a pleasing drive through rolling countryside toward the majestic mountains. You'll probably find gasoline prices at least 30 cents per gallon higher in the mountains than in Los Angeles, so it's wise to fill your gas tank before leaving the city. Exit at California 215 Junction North/San Bernardino/Barstow. Drive through San Bernardino city and take the Highland Mountain Resorts 30 exit. Follow California 30 east to the Waterman/18 exit. Turn left on California 18 to Lake Arrowhead and ascend toward the mountains as you drive through the San Bernardino National Forest.

The marvelously scenic Rim of the World Highway is aptly named, as it climbs and winds around the San Bernardino Mountains up to Lake Arrowhead, at 5,200 feet. The panoramic view over the city is unparalleled as the road climbs and curves. The scenery is stark and indomitable, with tall pines covering the mountainside. Massive sand-colored boulders tower alongside the road, and the mountain air is brilliantly clear and sparkling.

After you pass the turnoffs for the familiar small hamlets of Crestline, Lake Gregory, and Twin Peaks, framed by dense forests, the road narrows and makes a few downhill squiggles. Suddenly, there's the dramatic sight of the gleaming blue Lake Arrowhead, hidden in a dense forest of sky-touching pine trees.

Continue ahead to **Lake Arrowhead Village,** an attractive, bustling, multilevel complex of some eighty shops, galleries, and restaurants sprawling around the lakeshore.

Everything in this friendly, sunny mountain town focuses on the glittering, man-made blue lake. Lake Arrowhead, developed in the 1920s, became a glamorous, popular, year-round resort area for sailing and swimming in summer and for skiing in winter. The exclusive North Shore attracted wealthy vacationers and privacy-seeking celebrities. Almost everyone who was "somebody" had a second home in Arrowhead. The studios used the area for frequent movie locations and found the perfect setting for *Heidi,* starring Shirley Temple.

The privately owned, thriving village you see today is, like a Hollywood movie, a remake of the original 1923 community. The village was completely rebuilt in 1979, except for the eye-catching, red-roofed, former 1920s dance pavilion, which was restored as the Theme Building and now houses upscale boutiques.

The lower lakeshore level is the busiest, with its cluster of **shops** and restaurants that snuggle close to the water's edge. The Village Christmas Shop is filled with Christmas merchandise year-round. Just Browsing, the big, main store in the village, is ideal for gifts, mobiles, and postcards. The Village Sweet Shoppe and the Ice Cream Castle keep busy dispensing what you like best. Antiques lovers may find treasures in Ye Olde Tintype. Surrounding stores feature souvenirs, posters, clothing, T-shirts, and gifts.

Among the Pavilion boutiques, The Leather Shop has leather gifts, wool skirts, silk blouses, and other apparel. The Harvest offers lovely country Americana furnishings of crystal, linens, and pretty afghans. Galleries, restaurants, and stores present still more variety on the traffic-free Peninsula level.

Lake Arrowhead **Children's Museum,** (28200 Highway 189, 714–336–1332), which opened in August 1991 alongside the lake, is for ages twelve and under, who'll enjoy the hands-on exhibits, various activities, and puppet theater. (Closed Monday and holidays; admission.)

Lunch: **Tulips Cafe.** (714) 336–4302. An ever-popular lakefront favorite. The lunch bunch goes for the Chinese chicken salad, sandwiches, or pasta, either in a dining room full of tulips or on the sunny patio.

Afternoon

Cruising Lake Arrowhead is a memorable way to appreciate the beauty and serenity of the lake in its forest setting. During a one-hour narrated **cruise** aboard the sixty-passenger paddlewheeler *Arrowhead Queen,* your captain points out historical sites and landmarks. (No drink or food sold aboard; hourly departures from 10:00 A.M. to 6:00 P.M.; purchase tickets at Leroy's Sports Store.)

After your delightful cruise around the lake, take a short drive to **Blue Jay Village** to explore its many shops, restaurants, and ice-skating rink. Drive uphill from Lake Arrowhead Village; turn right past the Arrowhead Hilton Resort on Highway 189 for about 1.5 miles, along a quiet country road where chalet-style homes are sheltered among tall trees.

In Blue Jay Village, Front Street's row of stores includes Jensen's Finest Foods gourmet supermarket, the Mountain Gift Shop, and the Alpine Deli. Across the highway you'll find Thrifty Drug store and a strip of choice dining places.

On your return to Lake Arrowhead Village, stop at the **Ice Castle** skating rink, 27307 Highway 189 (714–337–SKATE), in Blue Jay. In this Olympic-size, covered outdoor skating center you're apt to find a hundred or more ice skaters gliding effortlessly across the rink to lilting music. Even if you don't skate, it's fun to watch, and visitors are welcome. (Skate rentals, snackbar, and pro shop; open year-round; admission.)

You shouldn't miss **Santa's Village** amusement park, in Skyforest (714–337–2481). It's about five minutes from the lake and appeals to the child in most of us. Head out of Lake Arrowhead Village to the Rim of the World Highway; turn left and continue east about 2 miles on Highway 18. Look for the two giant candy canes flagging the narrow highway entrance.

Santa and storybook friends welcome visitors in an enchanting outdoor forest fantasyland of little rainbow-colored picture-book houses tucked beneath tall pines. Christmas music and Disney movie songs fill the air. Besides a petting zoo, children enjoy a variety of thirteen rides, especially the giant Bumble Bee monorail that brushes lofty treetops. You'll also find toy shops, unusual Christmas ornaments, a bakery, and souvenirs. (Open daily, 10:00 A.M. to 5:00 P.M., from mid-June through mid-September and from mid-November through January 2; closed Christmas Day. Open weekends and holidays all other months, weather permitting. Admission includes unlimited rides.)

Dinner: **Candlewood Restaurant and Bar,** Lake Arrowhead Village, Lower level. (714) 336–4301. A longtime local dinner choice, with its cozy fireplace lounge and lake views. People come for the chef specialties too, of rack of lamb, prime rib, duck, chicken, and fresh seafood, plus the popular Weekend Dinner Show.

Lodging: **Lake Arrowhead Hilton Lodge,** 27984 Highway 189, Lake Arrowhead, CA 92352. (800) 800–6792. Adjacent to the village, sprawled along the lakeshore, and featuring a private swimming beach and fishing dock, plus 271 luxurious rooms, suites, and villas, this is the largest hotel on the mountain. Heated swimming pool, health and fitness spa; two restaurants; other recreational activities. Sunday buffet brunch.

Day 2

Morning

Breakfast: At your hotel. Or opt for **Belgian Waffle Works** (714–337–5222), in the village at the edge of the lake, for delectable waffles and croissant sandwiches. Try the fruit waffle with strawberries and sliced bananas topped with whipped cream.

Leave for Big Bear Lake by driving out of Lake Arrowhead Village, turn left to Rim of the World Highway 18, and continue for about 26 miles. The road zigzags to Big Bear Lake, curving down the heroic San Bernardino Mountains; past Running Springs, which has many roadside stores; and past forests and Green Valley Lake. Massive boulders loom on both sides of the highway. The road winds and curves, the air is very clear, and the forest trees march tall on buff-colored slopes. You'll spot the sign to Big Bear Lake to the right and then glimpse the placid blue lake in its travel-brochure setting beneath tall pine trees.

Big Bear Lake is considered a premier year-round recreation area because of its variety of activities for outdoor enthusiasts of all ages— sailing, fishing, hiking, lake tours, mountain biking, water sports, snow skiing, shopping, dining, and sightseeing. From mid-November through early April, its three skiing facilities, with miles of snowy slopes, have made it a major winter sports headquarters.

Friendly and unhurried, Big Bear Lake is the ultimate escape, a world removed from crowds and freeway traffic, secure in its beautiful mountain valley on the fringe of a fairytale forest. So far, the small frontier town hasn't been prettified or boutiqued. It just meanders around the glittering, 7-mile-long, man-made lake, with 27 miles of undulating shoreline.

There's a satisfying feeling of open space, similar to that of small towns in Alaska, throughout this sparsely built community, sheltered as it is beneath the tall mountains that provide the long ski runs in winter. Flashes of the cobalt lake are visible through towering pines; the quiet, rural atmosphere is relaxing; the sun is richly warm, even in October; and the air is gorgeous and clear, at a nearly 7,000-foot altitude. Restaurants with sunny dining patios abound, featuring excellent food in generous portions, and there's a large choice in lodging accommodations of all types.

The focus of the city is **The Village,** a lively area along Pine Knot Avenue, which runs at right angles away from the lake toward the mountains and is the main drag, filled with shops, dining places, and people. The Village continues as Pine Knot ends up at another Big Bear Boulevard, this one having several busy blocks of more shops and restaurants. Then you're in wide-open space at the foot of the mountains and ski areas at the edge of the forest.

Lunch: **Old Country Inn Restaurant,** 41126 Big Bear Boulevard, Big Bear Lake. (714) 866–5600. Dark walnut paneling, red leather booths, a peaked ceiling, and plants provide a just-right atmosphere for large-portioned specialties, such as Wiener schnitzel with potato pancakes, red cabbage, and sauerkraut; also served here are Italian entrees of veal, chicken, and pasta.

Afternoon

For shopping and browsing after lunch, drive back along Big Bear Boulevard to Pine Knot Avenue (The Village) and turn left toward the mountains. Among the many select shops along this vibrant stretch is **Der Weihnachts Markt** (The Christmas Mart), 652–4 Pine Knot Avenue. Here for twenty years, the shop sells only imported Christmas merchandise—year-round—and there are Christmas music and a beautifully decorated Christmas tree. Big sellers are the little village houses, beer steins, and colorful, fierce-looking nutcrackers.

A few stores away, **Ice House,** at 626 Pine Knot Avenue, displays magazine-cover home accessories and handicrafts in Americana or French country style—baskets, glassware, and lovely handmade patchwork and appliqué quilts. In **Mountain Country House,** 633 Pine Knot Avenue, you'll find lots of Raggedy Ann dolls lounging around in a feminine setting of ruffled pillows, afghans, wooden toys, and other giftware. **Teddy Bear Miniatures and Dolls** offers limited-edition dolls, such as Madame Alexander and Hildegard Guenzel, as well as other collector dolls, doll furniture, cuddly bears, and designer quilts with fine appliqués.

For a relaxing respite you can tour the calm blue lake in a one-hour narrated **cruise** on the ten-passenger *Sierra,* which leaves from Pine Knot Landing at the foot of the village (714–866–2628), or on the sixty-passenger *Big Bear Queen* paddlewheeler, which leaves from Big Bear Marina, Paine Road at Lakeview (714–866–3218). Both charge the same rate.

Dinner: **Big Bear Prospectors,** 40771 Lakeview Boulevard, Big Bear Lake. (714) 866–6696. Bring a hearty appetite along to this congenial local institution that offers top food and service. Despite the corny menu terms, try the excellent Whisker Licken Bear Trap Beef Ribs or other flavorful, mesquite-grilled specialties. Dinner nightly; Sunday Chuckwagon Champagne Buffet Brunch.

Lodging: Big Bear Inn, 42200 Moonridge Road, Big Bear Lake, CA 92315. (800) BEAR–INN; (714) 866–3471. Near the ski resorts. An upscale, small, privately owned, very European hotel, with seventy-five handsomely furnished guestrooms and three suites; Venetian chandeliers, antiques; heated swimming pool and year-round Jacuzzi; restaurant and lounge. Free shuttle to ski resorts.

Day 3

Morning

Breakfast: At the inn. Enjoy a leisurely continental breakfast of fresh fruit and assorted pastries and muffins, or sample the variety of breakfast buffet selections.

Drive up Moonridge Road to the 9-hole **Bear Mountain Golf Course** (714–585–8802) and freshen up your game. Just beyond is **Moonridge Animal Park,** a small, charming zoo in a rustic, hilly clearing at the foot of Bear Mountain Ski. Look for silvery timber wolves; bobcats; huge, black-feathered golden eagles as big as turkeys; and, of course, the big, husky black bears that gave the region its name. (Open daily, mid-May through October; free.)

In this same area shop at the Bear Mountain Trading Co., 42646 Moonridge Avenue, a big log cabin treasure chest filled with old-fashioned gifts, turquoise jewelry, bears of all sizes, Navajo rugs, and other temptations.

Lunch: **Pam's Heavenly Homemade Cooking** (in the Village), 40766 Big Bear Boulevard, Big Bear Lake. (714) 866–3229. A bright, cheery, old-time ice cream parlor serving delicious home-baked berry pies and brownies, chili, and chicken noodle soup, hefty sandwiches, and beautiful fresh salads. They're pros at packing picnic lunches for you to enjoy down at the lake, watching the boats before you leave the city. Retrace your way back to Los Angeles. Take Highway 18 south to California 30. Go west on 30 to I–215 and then south on I–215 to I–10 west. Follow I–10 west into Los Angeles.

There's More

Antiques shopping. Lake Arrowhead and tiny neighboring hamlets are a hub of antiques stores. Nearby are Addie's Attic, 318 Highway 173, for home accessories, gifts, and Attic Babies. Open Saturday to Thursday; closed Wednesday in winter.

Way Back When Antiques, 25852 Highway 189, Agua Fria. Features heritage lace, Tiffany lamps, gourmet coffees, teas, and gifts.

Pacific House West, Highway 18 and Kuffel Canyon, Skyforest. Here's a chance to pick up beautiful estate linens, china, gifts, and Victorian silver. Open Friday and Sunday, also by appointment.

Skiing. Snow Valley (Lake Arrowhead), 14 miles east toward Big Bear Lake, from mid-November through March or April. Five double chair lifts, eight triples; longest run is a mile and a half. Snowboarding with half-pipe available. Snow-making machine capability of well over 170 acres. Full facilities include cafeteria, bar, après-ski music, rentals. General information, (714) 867–2751; recorded ski and snow report, (714) 867–5151.

Big Bear Lake's three full-service ski resorts are open throughout its long season from mid-November through early April, whether there's snow or not. They all have high-tech snow-making systems for miles of snowy slopes:

Bear Mountain Ski Resort, P.O. Box 5812. (714) 588–2519. In the Moonridge area, about 1 mile east of Snow Summit, is Southern California's highest major resort with the biggest vertical rise. At an 8,805-foot elevation, Bear Peak, the highest and most challenging, has nearly 1,700 vertical feet of continuous skiing. Eleven chair lifts include one high-speed detachable quad, one quad chair, three triples, four double chairs, and two surface Pomas. Also snowmobiling, food, instruction, rentals. Ski hotline, (310) 289–0636.

Snow Forest Ski Area, P.O. Box 1711. (714) 866–8891. The smallest but the oldest is located right above the village. With five lifts and fourteen runs, it claims the lowest prices and the shortest lines; caters to skiers and snowboarders of all levels. Rentals, free shuttle transportation, restaurant. Twenty-four-hour ski report, (714) 866–5503.

Snow Summit Ski Resort, P.O. Box 77. (714) 866–5766. One mile east of the village center; well-rated by *Ski* magazine, it is one of the most popular. Eleven chair lifts and more than 18 miles of ski runs—the most of any Southern California ski area. Night skiing and snowboarding. Food, rentals, ski school, licensed day-care center. Ski hotline, (310) 613–0602.

Mountain biking. In Lake Arrowhead at Snow Valley, from Memorial Day through Labor Day.

In Big Bear Lake, mountain biking terrain covers miles of forest trails and roads. During summer, riders take their bikes on Snow Summit Ski Resort's Sky Chair to the mountaintop, enjoy the valley views, have lunch, and hit the riding trails. Rentals and information: Team Big Bear (714) 866–4565.

Boat rentals for sailing, waterskiing, fishing, and cruises. Lake Arrowhead. Call Pine Knot Landing at (714) 866–2528.

The Trolley in Big Bear Lake runs through The Village with three routes. A convenient place to board is at the visitor center on Bartlett Road in The Village. Fee.

Horse-drawn carriage rides are a romantic, leisurely way to sightsee Big Bear Lake. Contact Victoria Park Carriages, Ltd., at the carriage stand location, corner of Lakeview and Bartlett.

Hiking and gold-fever trails in Big Bear Lake offer historic insight into the 1864 Gold Rush in nearby Holcolmb Valley. Maps available at Big Bear Ranger Station on the North Shore and at the Chamber of Commerce.

Alpine Slide at Magic Mountain, on Big Bear Boulevard, .5 mile west of The Village in Big Bear Lake. (714) 866–4626. Hop on a scenic chair lift above the lake, then shoot down a thrilling toboggan-style slide with controlled speed. Also a water slide, miniature golf, and a snackbar. Open year-round, weather permitting.

Special Events

Early January. California Handicap Ski a Thon, Bear Mountain Ski Resort.

Mid-January. Playboy Winter Ski Fest, Snow Summit Ski Resort, Big Bear Lake.

Early February. First Annual Bear Mountain Corporate Cup, Bear Mountain Ski Resort.

Mid-February. U.S. Men's Pro Ski Tour, Snow Summit Ski Resort, Big Bear Lake.

End of February. Inland/Alpine Race League, Bear Mountain Ski Resort.

Early March. Ninth Annual Steve Kanaly Celebrity March of Dimes Classic, Bear Mountain Ski Resort. Jimmie Heuga Mazda Ski Express, Snow Summit Ski Resort, Big Bear Lake.

Mid-March. José Cuervo Games of Winter, Snow Summit Ski Resort, Big Bear Lake.

End of March. Los Angeles Council Race League, Bear Mountain Ski Resort. Easter in the Village. Easter egg hunt, musical entertainment, candy, Lake Arrowhead.

Mid-May. Trout Classic, Big Bear Lake. (714) 866–6260.

End of May through June. Spring Jamboree. Big Bands and Dixieland, Lake Arrowhead.

Early June. Fireman's Muster, Big Bear Lake. Lake Arrowhead Antique Classic Wooden Boat Show.

End of June. Rotary Art and Wine Festival, Tavern Bay, Lake Arrowhead. Scottish Highland Games, Bear Mountain Ski Resort.

July 4. Fireworks over the lake at dusk, if approved by the fire marshal, Lake Arrowhead. Fourth of July Celebration, Rotary BBQ, and fireworks display over Big Bear Lake.

Early July. Mountain Festival Arts and Crafts Faire, Santa's Village parking lot, Skyforest.

Mid-July to early August. Old Miners' Days. Contact the Chamber of Commerce, Big Bear Lake.

Early August. Swap meet, Santa's Village, Skyforest.

Labor Day Weekend. Forty-Ninth Annual Rodeo, Big Bear Lake.

Labor Day Weekend to the last weekend in October. Annual Oktoberfest, Big Bear Lake.

Mid-September through October 27. Fall Fling Celebration/Oktoberfest, Lake Arrowhead.

End of November through December 29. Dickens Christmas Celebration, Lake Arrowhead.

End of November. Christmas in the Village. Christmas Tree Lighting in Big Bear City.

Early December. Professional Snowboard Tour of America (PSTA), Bear Mountain Ski Resort.
Mid-December. Jeep Challenge Series, Bear Mountain Ski Resort.

Other Recommended Restaurants and Lodgings

Lake Arrowhead

Beau Rivage Cafe, in the Lake Arrowhead Hilton Lodge, 27984 Highway 189. (800) 800–6792. A winner for Sunday buffet brunch and for romantic gourmet dinners overlooking the lake.

Woody's Boat House, lakeside (714–337–BOAT), with dining booths shaped like antique wooden boats. Offers salad bar, seafood, prime ribs, and steaks. Weekend breakfasts feature Outrageous Omelettes and Awesome French Toast.

Saddleback Inn–Arrowhead, P.O. Box 1890, 300 South State Highway 173. (800) 358–5253; (714) 336–3571. Come for B&B in this totally restored, 1917 historical landmark at the entrance to the village. Thirty-four guestrooms and cottages, with stone fireplaces, double whirlpool baths, minirefrigerator. Complimentary breakfast daily and welcome cocktail. Restaurant and bar. Several guestrooms are named after previous celebrity guests, including Howard Hughes and Mae West.

Romantique Lakeview Lodge, 28051 Highway 189. (800) 358–5253. A Victorian B&B that's a nine-room hideaway offering lake views, antique furnishings, and fireplaces. Continental breakfast features huge cinnamon rolls from local bakery.

Blue Jay Village

Teacher's Restaurant, 27200 State Highway 189. (714) 336–4303. An early daytime hangout for breakfast and lunch, starring home-baked ham and chili.

Big Bear Lake

Boo Bear's Den, 572 Pine Knot Avenue. (714) 866–2932. The inviting, parosoled patio lures lots of diners for daily seafood catches, sandwiches, ribs, steaks, and chicken.

Hansel's, 40701 Big Bear Boulevard. (714) 866–9497. Resembles a Bavarian lodge, with tall beamed ceiling and large dining patio. Continental and American dishes include chicken, goulash-stuffed potato, German sausage, and New York pepper steak.

The Iron Squirrel, 646 Pine Knot Avenue. (714) 866–9151. There's select country French cuisine in this intimate dining room that serves dinner nightly. Sunday champagne brunch.

Paoli's Italian Kitchen, 40831 Big Bear Boulevard. (718) 866–2020. Enjoy family-style pasta, veal, chicken, and seafood, served in its large, sunlit patio or indoors.

Castle Wood Cottages, P.O. Box 1746, 547 Main Street. (714) 866–2720. Each of the "theme" cottages is an adventure—for instance, the European decor of Heidi's Room, with a rock-covered Jacuzzi in front of the fireplace, a kitchen, and a wetbar. Miss Kitty's Boudoir is draped in black lace and red velvet, while Davy Crockett's Cabin has a frontier theme. Midweek rates and ski packages.

For More Information

Lake Arrowhead Communities Chamber of Commerce, P.O. Box 155, Lake Arrowhead, CA 92352. (714) 336–1547; (800) 545–5784 (lodging information). At the entrance to Lake Arrowhead Village in the Vineyard Bank Building; on weekends it's in the information booth or Thrifty Drug Store in Blue Jay Village.

Big Bear Lake Visitors Authority/Big Bear Lake Chamber of Commerce, 630 Bartlett Road, P.O. Box 2860, Big Bear Lake, CA 92315. (714) 866–4608.

Forest Ranger Station 76. (714) 866–3437 (for information on camping and hiking).

Note: The (714) area code listed in the phone numbers for this escape has changed to (909).

Palm Springs/Coachella Valley

Ancient palm trees frame rocky gorge in Palm Canyon.

Desert Retreat

_____ 2 NIGHTS _____

Swimming and sunbathing · World-class shopping · Fine dining
Botanical garden · Desert wildlife center · Indian canyons · Aerial tramway
Water park · Horseback riding · Golf and tennis tournaments

The dry desert climate and radiant sunshine have lured sun-wor-
shipers since the 1930s, when Palm Springs was a small-town winter
haven for movie stars. Its natural splendor, glamour, deluxe resorts,
and lush golf courses enhance its reputation as a posh playground

and home for presidents and celebrities, who frequent local shops and restaurants and have city streets named for them.

The desert area is one of Southern California's most popular weekend getaways, boasting winters of more sunny days and less rainfall than other regions. Summer temperatures soar to 100 degrees or higher, but the drastically reduced hotel rates are irresistible and the season is getting longer. Evenings are always cool; dress is casual. But you don't have to be Elizabeth Taylor or a VIP to enjoy the seductive sunshine in this cactus paradise. There are accommodations and restaurants for all budgets.

The Palm Spring seasons begins October 1 and runs through the end of May. The busy "high season" is from mid-January through mid-April.

Favorite good-life pursuits are swimming and lounging around the pool in the lazy sun, as well as swinging a golf club or tennis racquet. You'll also visit Indian canyons, tour wildlife and garden centers, bike along sun-washed streets, shop in indoor air-conditioned malls, and enjoy people-watching in sidewalk cafes.

This three-day desert jaunt explores the mystique and romance of Palm Springs, and neighboring desert communities of the widespread Coachella Valley, where snowcapped, lavender mountains frame groves of towering date palms and emerald golf fairways.

Day 1

Morning

For the two-hour, 110-mile trip to the desert, head east from Los Angeles on San Bernardino Freeway I–10. After you've passed through Redlands and Banning, the signs for Yucaipa lead to **Oak Glen,** the unique little mountain apple community. This is a fine sidetrip, especially in fall harvest season, when apple ranches offer just-picked apples and fresh-pressed apple cider for sale and little shops offer country preserves and gifts; in addition, you can visit the charming **Edward Dean Museum of Fine Arts** on the return back to the freeway.

The tall majestic gray mountains are topped with snow. After Beaumont, roadside billboards advertise **Desert Hills Factory Stores,** 48–850 Seminole Road (714–849–6641), in Cabazon. If you're a dedicated discount shopper, go ahead and take the Cabazon Main Street exit, turning left past Hadley Fruit Orchards. The sprawling outlet center showcases fifty-two leading names in fashion and home furnishings, with prices reputed to be 30 to 60 percent below retail. The stores are open daily from 9:00 A.M. to 8:00 P.M.; Sundays are quite crowded. (Make a note to return to Hadley Fruit Orchards en route back to Los Angeles, to check out its large variety of dried fruits, nuts, and other edibles.)

Return to I–10 heading toward Palm Springs by turning left at the small road sign and left again on I–10 east. You soon feel close enough to the tall mountain ranges to almost touch them. The windy San Gorgonio Pass at the junction of Highway 111 and I–10 is the site of one of California's three large **wind farms,** where 4,000 wind turbines resembling silvery windmills spinning in the sun generate electricity for some 93,000 homes.

At the junction follow 111 into **Palm Springs,** curving around the tall mountain. Just past the city limits, **Palm Springs Aerial Tramway'**s cable cars whisk you up 8,516 feet to the cool wilderness of Mount San Jacinto State Park in a fifteen-minute ride. In the brisk mountain air, you'll have breathtaking views and opportunities for hiking, cross-country skiing, and a picnic; a restaurant and giftshop are here too. The cars run year-round every thirty minutes. (Fare.)

At **Palm Springs Visitors Information Center,** 2781 North Palm Canyon Drive (619–347–7746), you can pick up maps and brochures, make hotel reservations and purchase souvenirs. On North Palm Canyon Drive, lined with palm trees, **Loehmann's Plaza** houses the discount clothing store and other specialty discount stores.

Lunch: **Billy Reed's,** 1800 North Palm Canyon Drive, Palm Springs. (619) 325–1946 A convenient dining stop at the northern entrance to the city. You'll like the looks—and the food—of this large, rambling, popular restaurant with Victorian furnishings. The moderately priced menu features French dip and other sandwiches, salads, chicken, a kids' menu, fast service, and a full bar.

Afternoon

Palm Canyon Drive is inviting to stroll, with its many shops, cafes, and galleries. There's ample parking space, and you won't find parking meters. The city still retains its village atmosphere, even though it is quite busy Saturday nights and crowded with college students during the Easter spring break, when adjacent desert cities are quiet. Palm trees are illuminated at night, and midweek canyon strolls are highlighted by festive street fairs and sidewalk parties.

For quick insights into the city's history, stop at the **Village Green Center,** 221–223 South Palm Canyon Drive (619–823–6297), where several small museums share a garden setting and fountain. Miss Cornelia White's House, built in 1894 and made entirely of railroad ties, displays paintings, bibles, photos of memorabilia, and the town's first telephone, complete with hand crank.

The McCallum Adobe, the town's oldest building (1885) and the family home of Judge John McCallum, the city's founder, contains photographs and the collections of the Palm Springs Historical Society. Both historical sites are open Wednesday and Sunday from noon to 3:00 P.M. and Thursday, Friday, and Saturday from 10:00 A.M. to 4:00 P.M. (Nominal admission.) Ruddy's General Store Museum, a replica of an old-fashioned general store of the 1930s, displays hundreds of authentic items of that bygone era. Open Thursday through Sunday 10:00 A.M. to 4:00 P.M. (Nominal admission.)

Next door is the recently opened Agua Caliente Cultural Museum Information Center, which displays historical artifacts and photos of the Cahuilla Indians, the city's first settlers. Open Wednesday through Saturday from 10:00 A.M. to 4:00 P.M. (except Thursday from 6:00 P.M. to 9:00 P.M.), Sunday noon to 3:00 P.M. (Free.) **Palm Springs Desert Museum Annex Gift Shop,** recently opened, offers books, cards, posters, and toys. Tuesday, Wednesday, and Friday from 10:00 A.M. to 4:00 P.M.; till 9:00 on Thursday; Saturday and Sunday from 10:00 A.M. to 5:00 P.M.

Up the street you'll find **Desert Fashion Plaza,** an elegant indoor shopping mall of more than one hundred shops. With its striking marble floor and a huge fountain, the mall is anchored by Saks Fifth Avenue, I. Magnin, and Gucci. Around the corner and just behind the mall, the stunning **Palm Springs Desert Museum,** 101 Museum Drive (619–323–6297), with its sunken sculpture garden and Annenberg Theater, presents changing exhibitions, along with its permanent collection of Western and contemporary California art. (Open October through June; closed Monday. Admission.)

To visit **Moorten's Botanical Garden,** 1701 South Palm Canyon Drive (619–327–6555), follow South Palm Canyon Drive about 2½ blocks past Lyon's Restaurant; it's on the right-hand side of the road. Wander through more than two private acres of 3,000 varieties of desert plants, including giant cacti, and birds. All plants are labeled; the dirt paths are cool and shady under the tall plants. Pick up a map showing different trails and plant locations. The old red-roofed adobe house with the sunny green lawn is the owner's residence. (Admission.)

Afterward, check in at your hotel (see Lodging below). Since this is Palm Springs, you'll probably want to enjoy some swimming and sunbathing before going on to dinner.

Dinner: **Boo Bear's,** 777 South Palm Canyon Drive, Palm Springs. (619) 327–8840. Dine inside or on the surrounding flower-filled patios under colorful umbrellas. You'll find good menu variety and good service for steak or prime rib sandwiches, hamburgers, and other entrees and a delightful salad bar with dinner.

Lodging: **L'Horizon,** 1050 East Palm Canyon Drive, Palm Springs, CA 92264. (619) 323–1858. Quiet luxury in a newly refurbished, handsomely decorated hotel. Twenty-two rooms/suites (some with kitchens), with minirefrigerator, TV, and other amenities, situated around a large swimming pool on two beautifully landscaped, grassy acres of orange trees and flowers, all framed by Mount San Jacinto. You can't beat the location or the warm hospitality, which includes complimentary continental breakfast, plus daily *Los Angeles Times* and complimentary use of bicycles, library, horseshoes, and croquet.

Day 2

Morning

Breakfast: At L'Horizon. Relax over a beautifully served, complimentary continental breakfast (included in your room rate) of fresh fruit juice, a thermos of coffee, tea, or hot chocolate, plus fresh pastry, brought to your lovely room or the private poolside patio in the desert's bright morning sun.

To see the unusual **Oasis Waterpark,** 1500 Gene Autry Trail (619–325–7863), drive east on East Palm Canyon Drive to Gene Autry Trail, then turn left for about 1 mile, till you see the tall slide. The twenty-one-acre family water playground features water slides, innertube rides, food, private cabanas, and a health club. (Open daily mid-March to Labor Day; weekends only September 12 to October 25.) Admission.

Follow South Palm Canyon Drive to its end for a visit to the magnificent **Indian Canyons,** settled centuries ago by ancestors of the native Agua Caliente Indians, the city's largest landowners. Palm Canyon, the most accessible, is remarkably beautiful, with its thousands of native *Washingtonia filifera* fan palm trees. A fifteen-minute scenic drive through the quiet foothills leads you up to a small Trading Post, crowded on Sundays, which sells jewelry, T-shirts, artifacts, and Indian souvenirs. Follow the pathway down to the canyon floor and a dramatic, 15-mile-long rocky gorge of waterfalls and mountain streams alongside a towering grove of palm trees said to be more than 1,500 years old. (Open daily September to June; admission.)

Lunch: **Cedar Creek Inn,** 1555 South Palm Canyon Drive, Palm Springs. (619) 325–7300. Lots of greenery and airy French country decor. It's noted for innovative specialties of seafood, pasta, a large salad bar, and handsome sandwiches. Bread made on the premises, and desserts are dazzling.

After lunch why not return to your hotel for a refreshing, leisurely swim and a bit of relaxation in the warm sunshine.

Afternoon

Neighboring desert resort communities cut a a distinctive swath east and south across the Coachella Valley. To get to the **Living Desert**

Reserve, 47900 Portola Avenue, Palm Desert (619–346–5694), drive east on Highway 111 through Rancho Mirage, where Eisenhower played golf, Gerald Ford tees off, and you can stand on the corner of Bob Hope Drive and Frank Sinatra Drive.

Turn right at Portola Avenue and continue for about 1.5 miles to the 1,200-acre wildlife center and botanical park. Maps guide you to the exotic Arabian oryx, slender gazelles, bighorn sheep clambering the hillsides, and other animals, as well as to the aviary, picnic areas, and hiking trails. If you're lucky, you'll meet docents displaying live animals and birds. The Tortoise Shelf bookstore/giftshop additionally sells cool, refreshing ice cream. (Open daily September through June; admission.)

Take Portola Avenue back to Highway 111 to explore **Palm Desert,** another celebrity haunt of designer golf courses, deluxe resorts, and El Paseo Drive, the long stretch of carriage trade shops, galleries, and cafes.

The Coachella Valley's palm groves have flourished since the 1800s. Considered the "Date Capital of the World," the area produces about ninety-nine percent of America's dates; harvested from 250,000 date-producing palms which thrive in the brilliant desert sun, intense heat, and natural underground water supply.

Continue easterly, where, at Indian Wells city limits, a dramatic grove of tall date palms looms on the right side of the highway beneath the massive mountain range. Another grove is farther along. At harvest time you can watch the agile date pickers high up in the trees. Across the highway the deluxe high-rise Hyatt Grand Champions Hotel and Stouffer Esmeralda Hotel share two well-manicured golf courses.

Among the many date ranches open to the public, **Shield's Date Gardens** roadside store, at 80–255 Highway 111, Indio (619–347–0996), has been growing, packing, shipping, and selling many varieties of dates since 1924. Here you can also purchase local grapefruit and oranges; enjoy the house drink specialty, a refreshing date milk shake, and watch a movie, *The Romance and Sex Life of the Date.* Shield's is open daily, except on Christmas.

To get to the **Indio Bingo Palace and Gaming Center,** 84–245 Indio Springs Drive (619–342–5000), on Indian reservation land (about 30 miles southeast of Palm Springs), continue toward Indio on Highway 111 to Auto Center Drive; turn left, drive over the bridge to I–10, and then turn right at the sign for the Indio Bingo Palace. The vast, twenty-four-hour casino, which opened in January 1992, is crowded with casually dressed patrons and features off-track-betting horse racing, bingo, poker, pan card casino, a restaurant, and a bar. To return to Palm Springs, go back to the first stop sign and turn left onto I–10; go past another stop sign, then turn right at the first traffic signal on

Highway 111 Palm Springs. You're soon back at your hotel in time for some exhilarating swimming and relaxing before going out to dinner.

Dinner: **Le Vallauris,** 385 West Tahquitz Canyon Way, Palm Springs. (619) 325–5059. Better wear your Guccis to this fine French restaurant, with its romantic courtyard and flower-filled dining room. Pasta, fish, lamb, seafood, and other specialties are prepared French country style. (It's also a great place to see celebrities.)

Lodging: L'Horizon.

Day 3

Morning

Breakfast. At your hotel. After breakfast there's time for more swimming and sunning on your last morning in the desert.

Lunch: **Las Caseulas Terrazza,** 222 South Palm Canyon Drive, Palm Springs. (619) 326–2794. Have your last lunch in Palm Springs at everybody's favorite spot for tasty Mexican cuisine, people-watching, and Haagen-Daz mudpie dessert.

Afternoon

Try not to leave town too late in the day, particularly on Sunday, when traffic heading out of the city gets very heavy.

To return to Los Angeles, drive north on Indian Canyon Drive, following it around to North Palm Canyon Drive and the wind turbines as it becomes divided Highway 111, then I–10 west. On the way home you can stop and shop at **Hadley Fruit Orchards** (714–849–5255), about 20 miles from Palm Springs in Cabazon. Take the Apache Trail exit and park in front. Besides a wine-tasting salesroom, Hadley offers a wide selection of California dates, dried fruits, nuts and bakery items, plus a small snack area; it's open daily from 7:00 A.M. to 9:00 P.M. To get back on I–10 west to Los Angeles, drive down the frontage road past the discount factory stores, turn left at the second stop sign, and turn right on I–10 west. Stay on it all the way to Los Angeles.

There's More

Golf is the leading desert sport, with more than eighty courses to play. Deluxe resorts feature their own; other hotels can generally provide tee-time for their guests at nearby private links. These golf courses are open to the public:

Palm Springs Golf Course, 1885 Golf Club Drive. (619) 328–1005. Eighteen holes.

Canyon South Golf Course, 1097 Murray Canyon Drive. (619) 327–2019. Eighteen holes.

Mesquite Country Club, 2700 East Mesquite Avenue. (619) 323–1502. Eighteen holes.

Fairchild's Bel Air Garden Greens, 1001 South El Cielo Road. (619) 327–0332. Nine-hole executive course.

Tennis enthusiasts can try 600 courts. Besides hotel facilities, you'll find free court time at the following:

Demuth Park, 4375 Mesquite Avenue. Four courts.

Palm Springs High School, 2248 East Ramon Road. Six courts; free weekends, holidays, and summer.

Ruth Hardy Park, Tamarisk and Caballeros. Eight courts.

Bicycling was part of the Palm Springs life-style long before it became a national sport. Miles of bike trails are well marked. Maps are available in the Leisure Center, 401 South Pavilion Way, and at rental shops. Some hotels offer complimentary bike use to guests. To rent a bike, try these:

Burnett's Bicycle Barn, 429 South Sunrise Way at Ramon Road. (619) 325–7844. Year-round; closed Wednesday.

Canyon Bicycle Rentals and Tours, 305 East Arenas Road. (619) 327–7688. Seasonal.

Mac's Bike Rentals, 70–155 Highway 111, Rancho Mirage. (619) 327–5721.

Horseback riding. Smoke Tree Stables, 2500 Toledo Avenue. (619) 327–1372.

Vanderburg Equestrian Center, 69+380 Converse Road, Cathedral City. (619) 328–4560.

Tours. Desert Adventures Jeep Tours (619–324–3378) takes you for guided, narrated tours of the Coachella Valley, including Indian Canyons.

Celebrity Tours (619–325–2682) offers guided one- and two-hour sightseeing tours to movie stars' homes, country clubs, and other attractions.

Gray Line Tours, 455 East Tahquitz Way (619–325–0974; 800–635–1859), has daily celebrity tours.

Covered Wagon Tours, P.O. Box 1106, La Quinta (800–367–2161), requires reservations for its two-hour narrated tour through the Coachella Valley Preserve aboard mule-drawn covered wagons. Tour only or with dinner. Fee.

Village shuttle. Open-sided buses provide low-cost transportation to tourist attractions, restaurants, and shopping. Daily round-trip departures from the Spa Hotel. Quick and cheap.

Ice Capades Chalet 72–840 Highway 111, inside the Palm Desert Town Center mall. (619) 340–4412. Large ice rink is a neat way to cool your heels; boutique and rental skates here too.

Special Events

Early January. California Gold Cup, Eldorado Polo Club, 50–950 Madison Street, Indio.
Don Drysdale's Hall of Fame Annual Golf Classic.
Palm Springs Annual International Film Festival. Call Visitor Center for dates.
Mid-January. Annual National Collegiate Tennis Classic.
Annual Bob Hope Chrysler Golf Classic.
Mid-February. Annual Date Festival, Indio. Agricultural exhibits, junior fair, entertainment.
End of February to beginning of March. Palm Springs Annual Invitational Senior Olympics. For all sports.
Annual Palm Springs Mounted Police Rodeo. Parade, cowboy dance.
Annual Frank Sinatra Celebrity Invitational Golf Tournament. Fashion show and luncheon as well.
Early March. *Newsweek* Champions Cup Tennis Tournament.
End of March. La Quinta Annual Art Festival. Juried show.
Annual Nabisco Dinah Shore LPGA Major Tournament, Mission Hills, Country Club, Rancho Mirage.
Mid-April to August. Palm Springs Angels baseball season. Home games at Angels Stadium, Sunrise Way and Baristo Road.
Early July. Independence Day fireworks displays, Angels Stadium.
Mid-November. Palm Springs Annual Vintage Car Racing.
End of November. Annual Christmas Tree Lighting Ceremony, Desert Fashion Plaza.
Early December. Annual Christmas Tree Lighting Ceremony, at the top of the Palm Springs Aerial Tramway. Celebrity guest and entertainment, 6:00 P.M.

Other Recommended Restaurants and Lodgings

Palm Springs

Eveleen's, 664 North Palm Canyon Drive. (619) 325–4766. A dressy, romantic place for intimate dinners of excellent traditional French cuisine and service. Specialties include roast duck with Grand Marnier plum sauce and steak Eveleen.
Paul D'Amico's Steak House, 500 East Palm Canyon Drive. (619) 325–9191. Besides good steaks and salads, popular entrees feature Lake Superior white fish and other fish and seafood.
Elmer's Pancake & Steak House, 1260 South Palm Canyon Drive.

(619) 325–2537. Friendly place, with prompt service, for pancakes, sandwiches, steaks, salads, and burgers. Crowded Sunday morning.

Palm Springs Hyatt Regency Suites Palm Springs, 285 North Palm Canyon Drive. (619) 322–9000; (800) 233–1234. Luxury hotel in the heart of downtown, with 192 one- and two-bedroom suites; swimming pool, whirlpool; two restaurants, lounge; golf and tennis arranged at country club.

The Riviera Palm Springs, 1600 North Indian Avenue. (619) 327–8311. Expensively refurbished, with 462 rooms and 36 suites on seventeen acres. Large swimming pool; Sonny Bono's restaurant; 18-hole putting green, volleyball and boccie courts.

Palm Desert

Doug Arango's Fine Foods, 73695 Highway 111. (619) 341–4120. Diners enjoy the imaginative California cuisine and home-baked breads, Matzobrie and eggs, pasta, and specialty chicken.

Marriott's Desert Springs Resort & Spa, 74855 Country Club Drive. (619) 341–2211. The area's largest resort, with 892 deluxe rooms on 400 acres of lush grounds and lakes. Spectacular lobby waterfall; lagoon with gondolas. Two 18-hole golf courses, 18-hole putting course, sixteen tennis courts, two swimming pools, health spa, ten restaurants.

Rancho Mirage

Westin Mission Hills Resort, Dinah Shore and Bob Hope drives. (619) 328–5955. Has 512 deluxe rooms amid 360 acres; two 18-hole golf courses, seven lighted tennis courts, three swimming pools, whirlpools, fitness center, two restaurants, lounge, pool bar.

Indian Wells

Hyatt Grand Champions Resort, 44–600 Indian Wells Lane. (619) 341–1000. Featuring 336 deluxe guestrooms and suites on thirty-four acres; two 18-hole golf courses, twelve tennis courts and stadium, four swimming pools, two spas, health/fitness center; three restaurants.

For More Information

Palm Springs Visitor Information Center, 2781 North Palm Canyon Drive, Palm Springs, CA 92262. (800) 347–7746. Provides maps, brochures, hotel reservations. Open daily.

Palm Springs Desert Resorts Convention and Visitors Bureau, 69–930 Highway 111, Suite 201, Rancho Mirage, CA 92270. (617) 770–9000.

Las Vegas

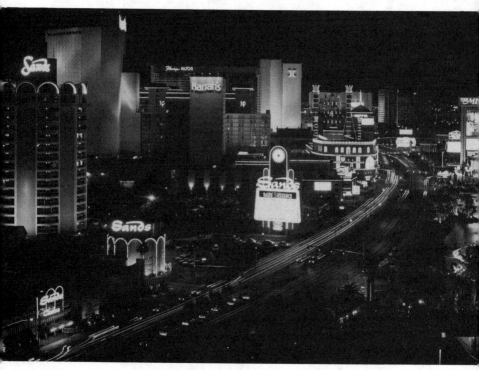

Las Vegas's famed neon-lit hotel casino strip

Gambling and Glitter

_____ 3 NIGHTS _____

Gambling casinos · Shopping · Golf and tennis · Antique car collection
Factory outlet stores · Museums · Resort hotels · Musical shows

This jaunt takes you 300 miles northeast of Los Angeles to the internationally famous "Gambling Capital of the World," the "City That Never Sleeps." This twenty-four-hour party town is neon-lit glitzy, crowded, and noisy, with fast-paced casinos offering plenty of action, mega-resorts vying for fantasy themes, showgirls in lavish musical productions, inexpensive food buffets, and magicians who make little white birds appear from red silk scarves. Bugsy Siegel, the playboy mobster who built the Flamingo Hotel in 1946, as a 105-room "carpet joint" where all employees wore tuxedos, said, "Come as you are—enjoy yourself!"

Day 1

Morning

From Los Angeles take San Bernardino Freeway 10 east past Ontario/Upland to 15 north to Las Vegas via Barstow. Look for I-15 about a half-hour from downtown Los Angeles; at the I-15 TWO MILES sign, stay to the right for Barstow–Las Vegas/215 north, follow the curve, and you're on I-15 north toward the smoky lavender mountain range. The freeway curves to the left for Barstow and climbs as you enter San Bernardino National Forest. The road travels through curving, barren landscape and lots of boulders, and it climbs again as you reach Cajon Summit, an elevation of 4,900 feet.

Just south of Barstow, the midway point between Los Angeles and Las Vegas, take the Lenwood exit for lunch; gas, if you need it; and **discount shopping.** Factory Merchants Outlet Plaza (2837 Lenwood Road, Barstow; (619) 253-7342 in a large cluster of white buildings houses fifty manufacturer-owned outlet stores, which claim savings from 20 to 70 percent off retail prices and include such well-known names as Bugle Boy, Evan Picone/Gant, Toys Unlimited, Bass Shoes, Johnston & Murphy, Levi's, Lenox, and Adolfo II. Turn left on Mercantile Avenue into the parking lot. Stores are set among grassy courtyards, red-brick paths with planters, and covered walkways in an attractive complex. (Open daily from 9:00 A.M. to 8:00 P.M.)

Lunch: **In-N-Out Burger,** 1561 Lenwood Road, Barstow. (800) 786-1000. Large, busy fast-food eatery with long lines that move quickly for hamburgers, fries, coffee, or soft drinks. With many pleasant young people in the kitchen and behind the counter, service is pretty fast.

Afternoon

Many drivers prefer to fill their gas tank here at the halfway point, even though gas is more expensive than in Los Angeles or Las Vegas, as 150 miles of long, deserted road lie ahead. After lunch return to I-15 north; it curves left for Las Vegas, and you drive through magnificent scenery, enjoying the grandeur and peace of the desert, which is ringed with mauve mountains and filled with perky Joshua trees amid the scrub. You climb to 4,000 feet again at Halloran Summit Road for quite a distance. When you cross the Nevada state line, where gambling is legal, the first thing you see is Whiskey Pete's Casino, along with other gambling halls.

The Las Vegas city high-rise skyline is visible beyond the mountains as you arrive, after a five-hour drive. Take exit 34 to the Las Vegas Strip, beneath low-flying planes from nearby McCarran International Airfield. Drive down Las Vegas Boulevard, also known as The Strip, past many hotels with familiar names: Excalibur Hotel, the largest resort hotel in the world, with 4,000 rooms, different colored towers, and a medieval Disneyland look; the Tropicana Resort, with lush landscaping, waterfalls, and massive Easter Island–type sculptures; and the Alladin Hotel, Bally's, and Caesars Palace.

Las Vegas hotels are different from others because you enter through areas of labyrinthine, bustling casinos filled with people playing slot machines, blackjack, roulette, craps, poker, keno, bingo, pan, and sports book wagering. You may find it difficult to have a drink at the bars, since those counters too are covered with card slots, whereby players feed the machines and have a drink. Bars are open twenty-four hours. Though hotels have their special features and glamorous window dressing, the casinos are the focal point. Better bring a sweater along, as many of the casinos have their air conditioning set to freezing.

The tables at different casinos have different betting minimums. Slots are from 5 cents to $5.00 to a special $100 and $500 slot machine. All over the casinos you hear the steady sounds of slots whirring and beeping and the winning clatter of coins dropping, murmurs of dealers, conversation, people walking, talking, cocktail waitresses offering drinks to players—there's constant movement, noise, color, and people. Day and night run together. It's a great place for insomniacs; there are no clocks in the casinos and hardly any water fountains.

Dinner: **Crown Room,** Flamingo Hilton, Las Vegas. 3555 Las Vegas Boulevard, (702) 733–3111. Las Vegas hotels are noted for lavish buffet dining at inexpensive prices. You pay as you enter, before dining, but be sure to retain your receipt, as the hostess asks for it. The Crown Room has two large, separate restaurants, with two different extensive buffets, one American and the other following an international ethnic menu that is changed monthly. The American buffet includes salad bar, cold cuts, fried chicken, hand-carved roast beef, beef bourguignon, mashed potatoes, vegetables, and many other items. The second buffet offers similar foods but adds tasty ethnic specialties. For dessert you can make your own sundae with ice cream, chocolate syrup, whipped cream, pineapple, and nut bits, plus elaborate pastries.

Lodging: **Flamingo Hilton,** 3555 Las Vegas Boulevard South, Las Vegas, NV (800) 732–2111; (702) 733–3111. Centrally located on the Las Vegas Strip, this is the second largest resort in the world, with 3,530 luxe rooms and suites, eight restaurants, two heated swimming pools, Jacuzzi, health spa, four lighted tennis courts, game arcade, conference facilities, and tour lobby for group travel. Aside from slot machines and video poker, fast-paced casino games of chance including craps, blackjack, Pai Gow Poker, Sic Bo, Big Six Wheel, keno, and mini-Baccarat; free lessons in all its table games. Bugsy Siegel's suite is still in the original Garden Building, with its escape routes and tunnels. Although Siegel was gunned down in 1947 in Los Angeles, his dream is now five towers tall.

Day 2

Morning

Breakfast: **Food Fantasy,** Flamingo Hilton. (702) 733–3333. A pretty room with cafeteria-style service, where short-order cooks will prepare your eggs and bacon, waffles, and other specialties while you wait. Coffee is served at your table.

Since most visitors come to Las Vegas to try their luck, they soon join the throngs in the busy, lively casinos. Others may prefer to relax in and around the large swimming pools. Still others like to see more of the town and drive along The Strip, to visit the different shops and hotels. Hotels are widely spaced, with many entrances through acres of convention-hall-size casino rooms—you'll find yourself doing as much walking as driving. Caesars Palace, across from the Flamingo Hilton, is acknowledged as the city's finest and, with its fountains and sidewalk people-movers, most flamboyant hotel. Self-park in the covered structure and take the people-mover into the casinos, or park in the lot near valet parking. Valet parking is free at most hotels, and you usually tip $1.00 when the attendant delivers your car. But chances are good that there'll be a considerable wait, so you're better off parking your car yourself. At some hotels you may try to park in the fifteen-minute Registration Zone, if there's a space for just a quick look-around.

The **Forum Shops** in Caesars Palace attract many visitors with an hourly spectacle. About seventy upscale specialty shops and restaurants, including Gucci and Louis Vuitton, encircle an elaborate fantasy rotunda of an ancient Roman piazza with tall marble columns and marble floors. In the center of an ornate, massive fountain reminiscent of Trevi fountain in Rome, realistic, robotic, animated figures of Bacchus (god of merriment), Apollo, and Venus perform on the hour in an entertaining ten-minute show.

Alongside Caesars Palace is the **Mirage Resort,** another showpiece offering many diversions, including its magnificent 100-foot waterfalls cascading into rocky lagoons; its lobby atrium filled with tall, exotic trees to a glass dome; and the tropical fish aquarium behind the front desk. Additionally, in a special pool you can watch five bottlenose dolphins dive and play, but there's an admission. The Tiger Habitat is home to five beautiful royal white tigers featured in the nightly shows of magicians Siegfried and Roy, and are on view twenty-four hours. The Three-Minute Volcano, at the Mirage's front entrance 100 feet above the rocky lagoon, erupts on the hour from dusk to 1:00 A.M.— the earth rumbles, there's thunder, eerie red coals glow, and the water roils in the lagoon.

Hotels in Las Vegas are lit up with electric and neon lights that move, go on and off, up and down, and sideways in different, gaudy colors and shapes, and you see kitsch you never thought possible on such a large scale.

Driving toward downtown, you pass many wedding chapels in little white cottages of fanciful design and whimsy. Las Vegas is considered the "Marriage Capital of America," with no red tape or blood test or waiting period required.

Continue to Fremont Street, known as Glitter Gulch, where every inch of every building is ablaze to the max with lights of every color— all moving, blinking, rotating, and just glittering.The light is so bright that you can take photos without a flash. The lowest-price gas station in town is just below Fremont Street on the corner of Ogden and Las Vegas Boulevard—cheaper than Los Angeles and far less than Barstow. Many fine lower-priced restaurants are in this vital area.

Lunch: **The Flamingo Room,** Flamingo Hilton. (702) 733–3333. Pretty, airy room in pink and blue decor, popular for its attractive seafood salad bar with many choice dishes and for its views of the gardens and swimming pool.

Afternoon

Las Vegas was discovered in 1829 by a party of traders who found abundant waters in its artesian springs. Later, in 1844, John C. Frémont led his first overland expedition west and stopped here. His visit is commemorated with his name on many hotels and businesses. In 1855 Mormon settlers arrived and built a fort, now preserved as a historic site. Las Vegas (Spanish for "The Meadows") became a city in 1905, when the railroad made it a definite stop on its route east from California.

Gambling was forbidden by law in Nevada until it was legalized in 1931, during the Great Depression. The first hotel built was the El

Rancho Vegas, in 1940. Several others followed, and the Las Vegas Strip was on its way.

After World War II, resort building in Las Vegas began to flourish. The Desert Inn, opened in 1950; The Sahara and The Sands, in 1952. The nine-story Riviera, built in 1954, was the first high-rise. The Dunes, Hacienda, Tropicana, and Stardust were built between 1955 and 1957. In 1989 the 3,034-room Mirage mega-resort opened; the 4,000-room Excalibur opened in 1990. More and bigger hotels are on the boards and under construction.

Las Vegas also calls itself the "Entertainment Capital of the World," with such regular superstar headline entertainers as Frank Sinatra, Dean Martin, and Liza Minnelli. Many hotels have their own musical production shows in which lissome, long-legged singing and dancing Las Vegas showgirls are lavishly costumed or half-costumed. Some visitors see two musical shows in different hotels each night and additionally watch the lounge entertainment.

If you're an antique car buff, the **Imperial Palace Hotel & Casino,** 3535 Las Vegas Boulevard South (800–634–6441), has more than 200 antique classic automobiles on display. It's worth the long hike through two casinos, then up the elevator to the fifth floor. The stunning collection of splendid, gleaming cars includes a 1922 Renault, a 1931 burgundy Pierce Arrow, a 1920 Minerva, a 1929 Cord with front-wheel drive, a separate room of Model J Deusenbergs, and a 1932 Stutz Rollsten convertible. Also here, among the many gorgeous gleaming cars, are Adolf Hitler's bulletproof armored Mercedes Benz, and Benito Mussolini's 1939 Alfa Romeo. (Open daily, 9:30 A.M. to 11:30 P.M.; pick up a free admission ticket as you enter the hotel.)

Across from The Desert Inn, the **Fashion Show Mall** encompasses Neiman Marcus, Saks Fifth Avenue, Bullock's, Dillards, and more than one hundred specialty shops and a food court. Stores on the rest of The Strip offer pretty tacky, overpriced souvenirs, though there's the occasional bargain. Besides, most hotels have their own giftshop and exclusive boutiques. In another area about 1 mile east, **The Boulevard Mall,** 3538 Maryland Parkway, at Desert Inn Road, is a major shopping hub, with Sears, Marshall's, The Broadway, and other department stores; specialty shops and restaurants; and lower prices than The Strip.

Dinner: **Alta Villa,** Flamingo Hilton. (702) 733–3333. It's much easier to dine in your hotel than to drive elsewhere, especially since hotels have many dining choices. This small, intimate room, tucked in a corner on the lower level, features Italian cuisine, including stuffed scampi, pizza, and pasta specialties served with soup or salad in a quiet, relaxed atmosphere. Reservations required.

Lodging: Flamingo Hilton.

Day 3

Morning

Breakfast: **Bally's Big Kitchen** buffet, Bally's Casino Resort, 3645 Las Vegas Boulevard South, Las Vegas. (800) 534–3434; (702) 739–4111. You need to thread your way through one of the largest and busiest casinos in Las Vegas, then take the mirrored escalator up to the second floor to a pleasant, cheery dining room with windows offering views of The Strip. Pay as you enter and save your receipt. The Big Kitchen buffet, set in a smallish, rather plain, cafeterialike kitchen, offers scrambled eggs, bacon, ham, pancakes and French toast. There's also hand-carved roast beef and ham, and you serve yourself bagels, croissants, muffins, and pastries.

See more of Las Vegas or spend time in your favorite fashion before you leave for the five-hour trip back to Los Angeles.

There's More

Circus Circus, 2880 Las Vegas Boulevard South. (800) 634–3450; (702) 734–0410. Walk up the ramp to the arcade/midway to see the high-wire and trapeze artists, unicyclists, and other circus acts and to play carnival games.

Ethel M Chocolate Factory & Cactus Garden, 1 Sunset Way, Henderson. (702) 458–8864. Free self-tour in which you watch them make caramels, nut clusters, and liqueur-filled chocolates and receive a free sample. Afterward visit the large cacti garden. Open daily, 9:00 A.M. to 5:30 P.M.

Guinness World of Records Museum, 2780 Las Vegas Boulevard. (702) 792–3766. This new museum houses photographs, plaster creations, and records of the world's fastest-talking, tallest, and fattest man; bizarre figures; and some musical records of Michael Jackson. Open daily, 9:00 A.M. to midnight.

Hoover Dam and Lake Mead are 30 miles from The Strip; bus tours leave daily. Dedicated in 1935, Hoover Dam is the highest dam in the country. Guided thirty-five-minute tours ($1.00) take visitors deep within the awesome, 726-foot (seventy-story-high) dam to the banks of generators and provide information on the history and inner workings of the dam. Be prepared for long lines, though the tours leave every few minutes. Lake Mead, the largest man-made lake in the United States, offers 550 miles of recreation, with boating, fishing, waterskiing, and camping.

Liberace Museum, 1775 East Tropicana Avenue (corner of

Spencer). (702) 798–5595. Take Las Vegas Boulevard to Tropicana Avenue; turn left (east) for about 2.5 miles. The small, popular museum exhibits personal items of the flamboyant entertainment personality who wore elaborate sequinned jackets and fur-trimmed capes and made the candelabra famous. Features include fifteen miniature pianos, one covered completely with rhinestones. In the Car Gallery, ornate, customized cars are covered with gold glitz and rhinestones, and a Rolls-Royce Phantom V is covered with thousands of mirror tiles. The Costume Gallery displays jewelry and furs. Open Monday through Saturday from 10:00 A.M. to 5:00 P.M. Admission.

Ripley's Believe It or Not, in the Four Queens Hotel & Casino, 202 Fremont Street. (800) 634–6045; (702) 385–4011. Ten rooms of 1,000 exhibits from Ripley's world travels include displays of torture and horror equipment, bizarre eating habits, and unusual inventions. Open daily, 9:00 A.M. to midnight. Admission.

Wet 'n Wild Water Park, 2601 Las Vegas Boulevard. (702) 737–8819. Water-oriented family recreation in flumes, wave pool, slides, water roller coaster, fountain, and lagoons. Open daily May through October, 10:00 A.M. to 8:00 P.M. Admission.

Golf. Las Vegas boasts many fine golf courses, and, with a lot of sunny days, it's best to reserve a tee time.

Desert Inn Country Club, 3145 Las Vegas Boulevard South. (702) 733–4444. Directly behind the hotel and casino; eighteen holes. Open only to Desert Hotel Inn guests and their guests. Green fee includes cart.

Desert Rose Golf Course, 5483 Club House Drive. (702) 431–4653. Eighteen-hole championship course.

Dunes Emerald Green Country Club, 3650 Las Vegas Boulevard South, Dunes Hotel. (702) 737–4749. Frequent site of PGA tour events; one of the longest courses in the city.

Las Vegas Municipal Golf Course, 4349 Vegas Drive. (702) 646–3003. Eighteen holes, with night driving range, pro shop, lounge, and coffeeshop.

Sahara Country Club, 1911 East Desert Inn Road. (702) 796–0016. Eighteen-hole championship course, driving range, pro shop, snackbar, lounge.

Tennis. Most large hotels feature courts for guest use.

Special Events

Late January. Triple Mini Slot Tournament, Riviera Hotel.

February 6–27. Las Vegas International Marathon, Vacation Village Hotel.

February 28–March 2. $200,000.00 Slot Tournament, Imperial Palace Hotel.

Late March. Eighth annual Angel Planes Airfest, Boulder City Airport. Great American Train Show, Cashman Center.

Mid-April. Clark County Fair, Logandale. Henderson Industrial Days, Henderson.

April 20–May 13. World Poker Championship Series, Binion's Horseshoe Hotel.

End of April to May 2. Spring Jamboree & Crafts Show, Boulder City.

Mid-June. $100,000.00 Slot Tournament, Imperial Palace Hotel.

End of October. Henderson Expo, Henderson Convention Center.

December 3–11. National Finals Rodeo Cowboy Christmas Gift Show, Cashman Field Center.

December 3–12. World Championship National Finals Rodeo, Thomas and Mac Center.

Other Recommended Restaurants and Lodgings

Las Vegas

Dining is inexpensive in Las Vegas, and the operative word is *buffet,* featured throughout the day at most hotels. The largest buffet is at Circus Circus; the longest line is the one you're standing in. Prices vary, as do the specialties offered. Brunches are also appealing, especially Sunday champagne brunch. Because of price and enjoyability, you'll usually find long buffet lines. At most buffets you pay before you enter the dining room. One way to avoid standing in line is to prepay your meal. Walk around the line to the cashier and tell him or her that you want to return in a half-hour or an hour (whatever time you desire) and that you'd like to prepay your meal to avoid waiting. Get a receipt. Play the slots, watch TV, and return later—present your receipt to the cashier and you'll be seated immediately, without standing in line. Worth a try.

If you don't enjoy standing in buffet lines, try the coffeeshops. The wait for your order may be interminable, but you'll be sitting down. Other alternatives for breakfast include McDonald's, in the basement of the Barbary Coast Hotel, across from Caesars Palace. Pancakes, scrambled eggs, biscuits, bacon, and sausage are reasonably priced and served hot, which is more than you can say for many breakfast buffets. Plus no line, no wait.

Celebrity Deli, 4055 South Maryland Parkway at Flamingo Road, in the Boulevard Mall. (702) 733–7827. Deli lovers rate it tops for corned beef and pastrami sandwiches.

Circus Circus Steak House, 2880 Las Vegas Boulevard South. (800) 643–3450. Residents favor this handsome, walnut-paneled room for great steaks grilled in an open hearth.

Gold Coast Hotel & Casino, 4000 West Flamingo Road. (702) 367–7111. Across I–15; the Monterey Room is noted for excellent Chinese specialties at lunch.

Hugo's Cellar, Four Queens Hotel, 202 East Fremont Street. (702) 385–4011. Look for the large yellow neon sign. In this upscale spot for gourmet dinners, Caesar salad is prepared tableside, specialties include tender rack of lamb, and women guests receive a rose.

Palace Station Hotel & Casino, 2411 West Sahara Avenue. (702) 367–2411. Where the Amtrak station is right in the hotel. Frequent visitors recommend The Feast as one of the best buffets in town.

Union Plaza Hotel, 1 Main Street. (702) 386–2110. Second-story Centerstage Restaurant, with glass-domed ceiling, offers first-rate steaks and chicken, plus a great view of Glitter Gulch.

Caesars Palace, 3570 Las Vegas Boulevard South. (800) 634–6661. Ranked number one in town, with 1,500 elaborately appointed rooms and suites, cable TV, two heated swimming pools, spa, four tennis courts, Omnimax theater, three casinos, six gourmet dining rooms, deli, buffet restaurant, lounges, and food court. Forum Shops, conference facilities, Roman gardens, $100 slot machines.

Sahara Las Vegas Hotel & Casino, 2535 Las Vegas Boulevard South. (800) 634–6666; (702) 737–2111. Has 2,100 guestrooms with garden or Strip views, two heated swimming pools, health club, large casino and Pan game room, five restaurants, lounges, convention center, special rates.

Note: Experienced visitors recommend joining the free Slots Clubs in the casinos; get your name on the hotel mailing list of members eligible for discounts on rooms and food, special rates, and other perks not available to nonmembers. Sign up at the Slot Club booths in your hotel's casino. Additionally, check out your hotel *Fun Books*—they contain coupons for free cocktails, discounts, and other goodies.

For More Information

Las Vegas News Bureau, Convention Center, Las Vegas, NV 89109–9095. (702) 735–3611.

Las Vegas Chamber of Commerce, 711 East Desert Inn Road, Las Vegas, NV 89109. (702) 735–1616.

Laughlin

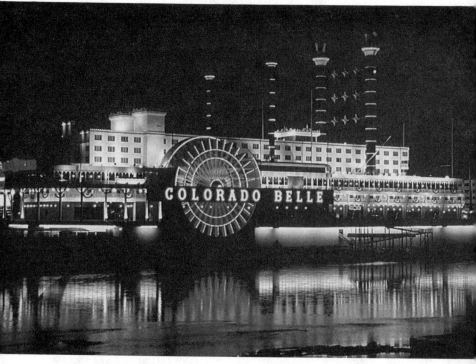

Laughlin's hotel-casinos are on the Colorado River.

Gambling on the Riverfront

_____ 2 NIGHTS _____

Gambling casinos • Resort hotels • Davis Dam • Tennis
Museum • Entertainment • River Walk • Swimming

This three-day excursion is to a small, friendly riverside gaming resort city tucked in a hot, dry, desert area in the southwest corner of Nevada at the edge of Arizona. Scenically located on the sunny banks of the Colorado River, Laughlin offers casinos and high-rise resort hotels that are geared to those who like to gamble on a less expensive scale than is found in Las Vegas and who prefer a slower-paced, more relaxed, and uncrowded small-town atmosphere.

There are ferryboat cruises, strolls along the River Walk, a small historic museum to visit, and the clear, dry desert air.

Don Laughlin, who founded the burgeoning town, and owner of the Riverside Resort Hotel and Casino, wants everybody to feel welcome and "have a good time."

Day 1

Morning

Leave Los Angeles via San Bernardino Freeway 10 to Laughlin, Nevada, about 286 miles, via Barstow. (The route to Barstow is the same as to Las Vegas.) Past the Ontario/Upland signs look for I–15 north, about a half-hour from downtown Los Angeles; I–15 goes past Rancho Cucamonga and curves left as you enter the San Bernardino National Forest toward Barstow. In the barren desertscape of sand and scrub, armies of skinny Joshua trees march in the sun.

You pass the cutoff to Arrowhead as I–15 curves to the left for Barstow, and the road goes up and down as you travel through lonely miles of boulders and sand, climbing steadily and easily to Cajun Summit, at 4,900 feet.

Just before reaching Barstow, which is about midway between Los Angeles and Laughlin, exit at Lenwood to have lunch (there are many fast-food places), fill the gas tank, and browse the discount outlet stores. Fast-food places include Arby's, Del Taco, Carl's, Jr., Quigley's Restaurant, Kentucky Fried, In-N-Out Burger, and Denny's.

Lunch: **In-N-Out Burger.** 1561 Lenwood Road, Barstow. (800) 786–1000. Similar to McDonald's but on a very large scale. Crowded and busy; however, with many fast-moving young people in the big open kitchen, the long lines move about as quickly as they can for hamburgers, fries, coffee, and soft drinks.

Afternoon

After lunch explore the Factory Merchants Outlet Plaza (2837 Lenwood Road, Barstow 619–253–7340), where fifty manufacturer-owned outlets stores, offering reported savings of from 20 to 70 percent of retail prices. You'll find such familiar names as Levi's, London Fog, Bass Shoes, Toys Unlimited, Evan Picone/Gant, Anne Klein, and Bugle Boy. The stores, grouped attractively along covered walkways and grassy courtyards, are open daily from 9:00 A.M. to 8:00 P.M.

Lenwood also provides an opportunity to tank up for the nearly

150-mile drive in to Laughlin, even though gas is higher-priced here than in Los Angeles.

From Barstow, follow I–40 east past Daggett, Newberry Springs, and Ludlow through barren hilly desert to Needles/Park Avenue exit (about 144 miles and two-and-a-quarter hours). Take the Park Avenue exit, turn left, and follow Park Avenue to River Road, about .5 mile. Turn left on River Road to Laughlin (about 20 miles). You come into Laughlin from the south past the new high-rise developments and little Laughlin city snuggled in the desert hills and curve down Casino Drive past Harrah's to the strip of neon-lit hotels.

All of the city's brightly lighted casino hotels are located on aptly named Casino Drive, and most of them back up to the Colorado River, with scenic views and promenades along the water. **Laughlin** is likened to an Old West boomtown and claims to be the fastest-growing resort destination in the country, visited by more than four million tourists in 1991.

The city has grown rapidly from the small, river-town fishing village where in 1966 enterprising Don Laughlin bought a bankrupt eight-room motel on six acres of the Colorado River. He used four rooms for the family and rented out the other four, charged 98 cents for all-you-can-eat chicken dinners, and added twelve slot machines and two gaming tables. The residents named the town after him, and other casino hotels are still coming in.

Laughlin is now a flourishing city of about 7,200, with ten casino hotels and is rapidly becoming a popular destination for those who like fast-action gambling but at low-minimum tables, as well as less expensive dining and accommodations and plenty of slots. It's less crowded than Las Vegas, has less glitz, and offers the romance of the mighty Colorado River.

The slots are the most popular **gambling** attraction as they accommodate all budgets and are convenient to play at any hour. All the casinos also offer video poker, keno, 21 machines, blackjack, poker, bingo, roulette, and sportsbetting.

The large casinos are bright and airy. Picture windows frame the sunlit river and the Arizona mountains just across the water—in contrast to Las Vegas, where casino windows are definite no-nos. Some casinos permit guests to take photographs. All the hotels feature top-name entertainment or production shows.

Dinner: **Bountiful Buffet,** Edgewater Hotel Casino, 2020 South Casino Drive, Laughlin. (800) 67–RIVER. Walk through the casino to the windows along the river side; then take the escalator or elevator downstairs to the large buffet and dining room, where you pay as you enter. This is a well priced, well-run buffet, where the food is good and the hot entrees are kept hot, as they should be. The appealing variety includes tasty fried chicken (fried in pure canola oil), mashed potatoes, fresh vegetables, a meatless entree, stewed fruits, cole slaw, beef stew, hand-carved ham and roast beef, and rolls and muffins. Make your own sundae for dessert, adding to your ice cream toppings of pineapple, chocolate syrup, nuts, and whipped cream, and snaffle some luscious pastries as you pass them. Like Las Vegas, Laughlin is a cash-and-carry town: No credit cards are used in restaurants or casinos, nothing is charged to your room, everything is cash. Well, perhaps if you're a big shot or high roller or VIP.

Lodging: **Edgewater Hotel Casino,** 2020 South Casino Drive, Laughlin, NV 89028. (800) 67–RIVER; (702) 298–2453. At twenty-six floors high, this is the tallest hotel in town; 1,450 fair-size guestrooms and large bathrooms, including nonsmoking rooms on request, all with color TV (no remote). Many rooms overlook the scenic Colorado River, tucked below the mountain ranges. Heated swimming pool; free gaming lessons offered daily in the twenty-four-hour casino. Senior discounts.

Day 2

Morning

Breakfast: **Bountiful Buffet,** Edgewater Hotel Casino. Extensive array of breakfast foods includes scrambled eggs, French toast, bacon, potatoes, sausage, corned beef hash, ham, oatmeal, and other power foods, such as fresh fruits. But like searching for the Holy Grail, you just can't find hot scrambled eggs in breakfast steamers. Unless you get lucky.

After breakfast take a pleasurable walk along the narrow ribbon of the Colorado on the **River Walk,** a promenade that follows the water and connects the hotels. You can watch the pretty paddlewheeler ferries going past and jet-skiers racing by. Across the river in Arizona, the jagged edges of the charcoal mountains glint in the morning sun. The river is clean and clear, with many large fish visible swimming close to the shoreline, and offers numerous recreational activities, including fishing and waterskiing, scenic tours, and dinner cruises.

Take a **cruise on the river** aboard the 120-passenger USS *Riverside,* which leaves from the Riverside Resort & Casino dock, for a ninety-minute narrated cruise in a 65-by-18-foot luxury cruiser specially designed to sail under the Laughlin Bridge to the Davis Dam and back.

The observation deck offers more sun and better viewing on this smooth, pleasant ride. The Laughlin Bridge, which opened to traffic in 1987 cost Don Laughlin $3.5 million to build. "It took four years and thirty-eight different city, state, county, and national agencies to get the bridge approved," says Laughlin. "And it took less than three months to build it!"

The cruise narrator advises that the mighty, 1,400-mile-long Colorado River runs from the Rockies through the Mohave Valley and almost to the Sea of Cortez in Mexico, providing hydroelectric power, public water, and irrigation to parts of California, Nevada, and Arizona. The 200-foot-high **Davis Dam** was completed in 1953 to control flash flooding of the area and to generate hydroelectric power; free self-guided tours are available weekdays from 9:00 A.M. to 5:00 P.M. The boat sails close to the dam and turns about, continuing past the hotels as you learn a bit about each one—the Flamingo Hilton, the Edgewater, the Colorado Belle, and Harrah's, with its private beach. As the boat turns about again, your attention is directed to the opposite riverbank and **Bullhead County Park,** where many trees mark the old Bullhead City boundary line.

Lunch: **Colorado Cafe,** Harrah's Del Rio Hotel & Casino, 2900 South Casino Drive. Laughlin. (800) 447–8700; (702) 298–4600. Enjoy sit-down lunch in the pretty cafe with patio umbrellas and a make-believe grape arbor. In the airy and bright room, you feel far away from the noise and bustle of the casinos. The lunch menu offers cocktails, sandwiches, and salads; hamburgers with fries are a good choice.

Afternoon

Most visitors prefer to return to the casinos for their favorite game. Others can drive around along Casino Drive to see the different hotels. You might want to drive across the Laughlin bridge to the Arizona side to visit the **Colorado River Historical Society Museum,** on Highway 95 (702–754–3399). Drive across the bridge and turn left at the first signal (Locust Avenue) for the museum, .5 mile north of the bridge at Davis Camp. The small museum, which opened in February 1992, exhibits a model display of the 1871 Fort Mohave, early trapper equipment, a square Steinway grand piano shipped around the Horn to San Francisco and then to Colorado before the turn of the century, and other historical artifacts and memorabilia of Laughlin, Bullhead City, and the surrounding area. (Open Wednesday through Sunday, 10:00 A.M. to 3:00 P.M.)

Dinner: **(**As in Las Vegas, guests tend to dine in their hotels for convenience.) **Bountiful Buffet,** Edgewater Hotel Casino. This extensive, hearty, inexpensive buffet features the same basic nightly foods, with a few changes. Help yourself to fruits, salad, good fried chicken, vegetarian entrees, fish, hand-carved roast beef, chicken-fried steak, and hand-carved ham. You get to splurge on desserts—ice cream sundaes with lots of toppings and fancy pastries and cakes.

Lodging: Edgewater Hotel Casino.

Day 3

Morning

Breakfast: **The Garden Room,** Edgewater Hotel Casino. (800) 677–4837. If you tire of breakfast buffets, the coffeeshop is a good alternative, particularly for waffles and pancakes. This is a pleasant room, though service is rather slow.

After breakfast enjoy a last look at the Colorado River as you walk along the sunny River Walk and watch the boats go back and forth. Or play the casino games till it's time to leave for Los Angeles. Checkout time is an early 11:00 A.M., but you can turn in your room key and linger a bit.

Afternoon

Retrace your way back to Los Angeles heading south on Casino Drive to Needles Highway; turn left, continue until Park Road, and turn right to I–40 into Barstow.

There's More

Katherine Landing, 9 miles north of Laughlin at Lake Mohave. The former mine district is an RV recreation facility with full hookups, boat rentals, marina, launch ramp, fishing, swimming, and sandy beaches, restaurant. Motel accommodations.

Laughlin River Tours, Inc. (800) 228–9825; (702) 298–1047. *Little Belle* river cruises. Authentic-looking, nostalgic, 150-passenger double-decker sidewheeler riverboat offers one-and-a-quarter-hour narrated cruise daily; leaves from the Edgewater Casino dock. Enclosed lower deck features a full-service bar; upper deck is canopy-covered. Cruise goes back and forth to the casinos, from Riverside Resort to Harrah's, and includes narration about the area, the river, and the casinos. Fare; purchase tickets at *Little Belle* ticket booth at the Edgewater Casino dock.

Special Events

January. Annual Bed Races, Oatman, Arizona.
Mid-April. Harley Davidson Annual Run.
End of April. Laughlin-Bullhead City Chili Cook-Off.
Mid-May. Laughlin River Days.
Mid-December. Annual Parade of Lights, Lake Mohave Resort.

Other Recommended
Restaurants and Lodgings

Laughlin

Colorado Belle, 2100 South Casino Drive. (800) 458–9500; (702) 298–4000. On the banks of the Colorado River; 1,237 rooms and suites, some with scenic river views, on this 608-foot-long authentic replica of a three-deck Mississippi paddlewheeler with an adjacent six-story hotel. Very attractive facade, with red and white trim; it looks as though it's floating on the water. Enclosed courtyards, two swimming pools and spa, casino, six restaurants, lounge. Free ferryboat rides across the Colorado River.

Harrah's Del Rio Hotel & Casino, 2900 South Casino Drive. (800) 447–8700; (702) 298–4600. In a widespread, rambling, Spanish-style complex; 958 rooms and suites, with heated swimming pool, secluded riverfront beach, five restaurants, lounge, main casino, nonsmoking area, RV area, and shuttle to casino.

Note: Experienced visitors join the free Slot Clubs in the casino to get on any of the hotel's mailing lists for special rates, room and food discounts, and other perks unavailable to nonmembers. Sign up at the Slot Club booths in your hotel's casino. Additionally, scan your hotel's *Fun Books* for coupons for free cocktails and other goodies.

For More Information

Laughlin Visitor Bureau, along South Casino Drive and also at 3650 South Point Circle, Suite 104B, Laughlin, NV 89029. (702) 298–3321.

Index

Acknowledgments

Many thanks to the kind people in various visitors bureaus and chambers of commerce, the patient staff at my local National Automobile Club, public relations personnel, and others who graciously shared local lore and helped me with the research and development of this book.

About the Author

Eleanor Harris, a knowledgeable traveler and photojournalist, is an expert on Southern California and has written about its vacation attractions for such publications as *Los Angeles* magazine, *Travel & Leisure*, *National Motorist*, *Cruise Travel*, and *Westways*. She is a self-syndicated columnist and former dining editor as well as a painter, expert cook, architectural consultant, and sometime golfer. She lives with her husband, Ben, in Beverly Hills, where they raised two daughters.